Rewriting the Self

Rewriting the Self explores the process by which individuals reconstruct the meaning and significance of past experience. Drawing on the lives of such notable figures as St Augustine, Helen Keller and Philip Roth as well as on the combined insights of psychology, philosophy and literary theory, the book sheds light on the intricacies and dilemmas of self interpretation in particular and interpretive psychological enquiry more generally.

Mark Freeman draws upon selected, mainly autobiographical, literary texts in order to examine concretely the process of rewriting the self. Among the issues addressed are the relationship of rewriting the self to the concept of development, the place of language in the construction of selfhood, the difference between living and telling about it, the problem of facts in life history narrative, the significance of the unconscious in interpreting the personal past, and the freedom of the narrative imagination.

Rewriting the Self deals with important but difficult ideas in an accessible and engaging way. It will be of interest to undergraduate and graduate students in psychology and related disciplines, as well as to readers, academic and otherwise, interested in the dynamics of self-understanding.

Mark Freeman is Associate Professor of Psychology at the College of the Holy Cross, Worcester, Massachusetts, where he serves as Assistant Academic Dean. He has written extensively on the relationship of hermeneutic philosophy to psychological theory and method, on the development of the self, and on the psychology of art.

Critical Psychology

Series editors

John Broughton
Columbia University

David Ingleby
Vakgroep Ontwikkeling en Socialisatie, Utrecht

Valerie Walkerdine
University of Central England at Birmingham

Since the 1960s there has been widespread disaffection with traditional approaches in psychology, and talk of a 'crisis' has been endemic. At the same time, psychology has encountered influential contemporary movements such as feminism, neo-marxism, post-structuralism, and post-modernism. In this climate, various forms of 'critical psychology' have developed vigorously.

Unfortunately, such work – drawing as it does on unfamiliar intellectual traditions – is often difficult to assimilate. The aim of the Critical Psychology series is to make this exciting new body of work readily accessible to students and teachers of psychology, as well as presenting the more psychological aspects of this work to a wider social scientific audience. Specially commissioned works from leading critical writers will demonstrate the relevance of their new approaches to a wide range of current social issues.

Titles in the series include

The crisis in modern social psychology
And how to end it
Ian Parker

The psychology of the female body
Jane M. Ussher

Significant differences
Feminism in psychology
Corinne Squire

The mastery of reason
Cognitive development and the production of rationality
Valerie Walkerdine

Child care and the psychology of development
Elly Singer

Rewriting the self

History, memory, narrative

Mark Freeman

London and New York

First published in 1993
by Routledge
11 New Fetter Lane, London EC4P 4EE

Simultaneously published in the USA and Canada
by Routledge
29 West 35th Street, New York, NY 10001

Reprinted 1995

© 1993 Mark Freeman

Typeset in Bembo by Michael Mepham, Frome, Somerset
Printed and bound in Great Britain by
Mackays of Chatham PLC, Chatham, Kent

All rights reserved. No part of this book may be reprinted or
reproduced or utilized in any form or by any electronic, mechanical,
or other means, now known or hereafter invented, including
photocopying and recording, or in any information storage or
retrieval system, without permission in writing from the publishers.

British Library Cataloguing in Publication Data
A catalogue record for this book is available from the British Library.

Library of Congress Cataloguing in Publication Data
A catalogue record for this book is available from the Library of Congress.

ISBN 0–415–04197–X (hbk)
ISBN 0–415–04198–8 (pbk)

Sometimes when you look back at certain events, the reason things happened the way they did seems pretty obvious. Yet when something is actually happening and you're right in the middle of it, you can't seem to get a handle on what's going on.

(Larry Bird 1989:128)

[I]n general people experience their present naively, as it were, without being able to form an estimate of its contents; they have first to put themselves at a distance from it – the present, that is to say, must have become past – before it can yield points of vantage from which to judge the future.

(Sigmund Freud 1927:1)

Contents

	Acknowledgments	ix
1	**Rewriting the self**	1
	To be mindful of life	1
	Interpretation and selfhood	3
	Questions	6
	The skeptical challenge	10
	Thinking beyond skepticism	13
	The cast of characters	18
2	**The story of a life**	25
	History, memory, narrative	25
	'Origins'	33
	To cast out one's demons	36
	Living in the material world	38
	Knowledge and action	41
	Retrospects and prospects	43
	Recollection and development	46
3	**In the name of the self**	50
	The danger of writing	50
	Language, thought, and reality	53
	Whose words do we speak and write?	58
	Origin/ality	63
	Authorship and selfhood	67
	To build a world	70
	Looking toward the future, in anticipation	78
4	**Living to tell about it**	81
	Pure imagination	81
	Face to face	85

	The start of something big	90
	Narrative delusion and the (meta)historical imagination	94
	The banality of existence	96
	Accidents will happen	98
	Narrative desire	103
5	**Fact and fiction**	112
	What are the facts of history?	112
	Presence and absence	120
	The manifest text	122
	In the aftermath	130
	The problem of the text	137
	To know thyself	145
6	**The primal scenes of selfhood**	149
	Secrecy and secrets	149
	Double trouble	153
	Lingering despair, appearances notwithstanding	155
	The dead end of rationality	158
	On narrative plausibility	161
	Reconstruction, restoration, and the dialectic of development	165
	Primal scenes	177
7	**Who to become**	185
	In the wilderness of the self	185
	The seeds of new life	191
	Meaning, morality, and the social construction of narrative	196
	Apostasy and authority	202
	A tale of two worlds	210
	The vertigo of development	214
	Epilogue: Toward a poetics of life history	222
	Notes	233
	References	237
	Name index	245
	Subject index	248

Acknowledgments

This book has taken a good long while to write and is the product of many influences. At the University of Chicago, where I began to reflect on the issues at hand, I wish to thank especially Bert Cohler, Mihaly Csikszentmihalyi, Jacob Getzels, Peter Homans, Paul Ricoeur, Rick Shweder, David Tracy, and Marvin Zonis, each of whom, either as mentors or as exemplary teachers, served to catalyze my own intellectual desires. I also want to thank my friends at Chicago, especially Reed Larson, Pat Lorek, Jeanne Nakamura, Rick Robinson, and Daniel Schouela. At Holy Cross, where I presently teach, I wish to thank the members of the psychology department, particularly for their willingness to hire and indeed to welcome a hybrid psychologist like myself; Deanna, the department secretary; the college, for having generously given me the time to write; the members of the Philosophy Reading Group, each of whom has stimulated my own intellectual life immensely; and finally, the many friends who have been subjected to my latest musings and who offered that sort of affirmation which gives one the conviction to continue. Special thanks are also to be given to Bernard Kaplan, whose wisdom has helped my work immeasurably. As concerns those without whom this project literally would not have been undertaken, I wish to extend my heartfelt appreciation to John Broughton, my editor and friend; to the people at Routledge, particularly David Stonestreet, who found the project worthwhile; and, last but certainly not least, to my family – my wife Deborah, and my two daughters, Brenna and Justine. It is easy to become caught up in the world of ideas. It's fun too. But it makes for strange dinner conversation and, occasionally, some self-indulgence. My family often brought me back to myself; through their very presence and care, they helped remind me about what is most real. There is no greater gift than the one they have given me.

Grateful acknowledgement is made to the following for permission to reprint copyrighted material. Jean-Paul Sartre: *Nausea*, copyright © 1964 by New Directions Publishing Corporation. Reprinted by permission of New Directions Publishing Corporation. Philip Roth: *The Facts*, copyright © 1988 by Philip Roth. Reprinted by permission of Farrar, Straus, & Giroux, Inc. Jill Ker Conway: *The Road to Coorain*, copyright © 1989 by Jill Conway. Reprinted by permission of Alfred A. Knopf, Inc. Saint Augustine: *Confessions*, translated by R.S. Pine-Coffin (Penguin Classics, 1961), copyright © R.S. Pine-Coffin, 1961.

Chapter 1

Rewriting the self

TO BE MINDFUL OF LIFE

I begin this introductory chapter, along with each of the chapters to follow, with a life. My reasons for doing so are straightforward. First and foremost, it seems to me to make good sense to ground what are ultimately some very difficult issues concerning human life in life itself. But this is not how things are most often done in contemporary academic psychology.

I learned this early on. Like so many others, then and now, I entered college in pursuit of deep truths about the human condition. For a variety of reasons, I had found myself prone to self-reflection, to trying to make sense of the world and my own possible place in it. At the time, largely as a function of my own naiveté, I'm afraid, I couldn't imagine a better way to further this project than to become a psychology major. I didn't really know anything about psychology, I should mention, other than what I had heard about it informally over the years, but as far as I could tell it was the place for me. Like so many others again, I had proceeded essentially by way of elimination: I liked reading books well enough, but the study of literature, as I had come to know it anyway, with its belabored attempt to pick apart perfectly good stories, struck me as tedious. As for philosophy, which I had only encountered in snippets, it seemed too dry and too serious for my liking. I wanted to learn about people, everyday people like you and me, and I couldn't quite manage to find them there. And so, to make a long story short, psychology it was.

It wasn't long after experiencing some of the standard fare – introductory psychology, learning, statistics, and so on – that it started becoming painfully clear that psychology wasn't quite what I thought it was. It was interesting sometimes, and even enjoyable every now and then (in much the same way that tinkering with machines can be), but my spirit was left hungry for something more. I began to gain a glimpse of what this something was in two courses taken during my junior year, one in 'visual thinking', given in the psychology department, and another in 'phenomenological psychology', given in philosophy. Heady stuff. But I felt that I had finally found some semblance of a niche for myself. It was a bit marginal, I realized, and it was still unclear how much Husserl and Heidegger I would want to hack through in the years to come, but it was no small relief to learn that psychology did indeed have a place for human beings. I was determined to make a go of it.

Little did I know at the time how few universities would permit me to do so. By most indications, this is still the case. It is a remarkable – and remarkably ironic – situation, and my only hope is that some day in the future an historian of the discipline will be able to gaze back in shock at the utter silliness of so much of it. The situation is of course a tragic one as well, both for those students who remain thoroughly dumbfounded by the discipline and, more importantly, for those 'research subjects' whose lives, whether exemplary of the heights to which we sometimes ascend or the depths to which we sink, remain uncharted and untouched.

As a graduate student at the University of Chicago, eager to make a dent in the monolith of academic psychology, with its frightening numbers and its cold anonymity, I commenced my work in the spirit of negation, my primary aim being to battle theory with theory. Perhaps for the sake of redeeming those lost souls who had stumbled through mainstream psychology as I had, I wanted to help change the face of the discipline, to make it fit for human habitation. It was terrifically exciting. Not only was I diving headlong into the dense thickets of psychological theory, but I was lucky enough to study with the philosopher Paul Ricoeur; his courses, 'The phenomenology of time consciousness', 'Historicity, history, and narrative', and several others, sent my intellectual spirit soaring. They were formative years, to say the least.

There was an odd irony to some of what I was doing, however. In the midst of this all-out assault on the mainstream, this desperate, heartfelt attempt to inject a measure of life into what I saw to be an all too lifeless discipline, I became complicitous in its profound tendency toward abstraction, my work serving as little more in some instances than a sort of inverted mirror image of the problems I wished to correct. The work was acceptable – thoughtful, meticulous, and so on – and even now I can only presume that this is what had to be done at the time (there often being little reason to chastise oneself through hindsight), but I came to feel there was something missing.

What was telling was that except for those who were immersed in similar projects, particularly those who found in 'hermeneutics' – which, for now, we can think of simply as theory of interpretation[1] – a new vision of psychology, it was hard for people to get a handle on what this work was all about. Members of my family, for instance, who were interested in learning just what exactly I had been doing all these years, read my earliest essays, which I had proudly sent their way, only to be largely befuddled by all of the lengthy, unfamiliar words. Now I am not so much of a populist as to suppose that everyone should immediately become enthralled with every last word I write, but something was wrong here, particularly in light of the fact that my stated goal was one of humanizing the discipline. So, where were the humans?

What follows is no less philosophically-oriented than any of my previous work. Nor am I about to tell you that there is something here for everyone; it would be sheer delusion on my part to assume so. The fact of the matter is, this book is irrevocably about certain fundamental intellectual issues, issues that are part and parcel of 'the life of the mind'. But what I have come to believe in recent years, even amidst the welter of theories and metatheories and methodologies that have sought to set psychology along with its allied disciplines aright, is that the life of the mind in no way excludes being mindful of life. Indeed, the one is not possible without the other. In what follows, therefore, I will indeed try to be mindful of life, precisely by inquiring into the lives of a number of people (five of whom either were or are quite real, one of whom is fictional) who will help us to understand that particular issue which is at the forefront of this work, namely, *rewriting the self*: the process by which one's past and indeed oneself is figured anew through interpretation.

INTERPRETATION AND SELFHOOD

Why this emphasis on interpretation? The reason is actually quite simple in some ways. When we deal with phenomena in the physical world – bolts of lightning, rock formations, the movement of clouds across the sky – we do not ordinarily seek to *interpret* them, in the sense of trying to understand their possible meaning. We can certainly attempt to explain these phenomena and we can also explore them for their beauty and their wonder, but as a general rule we refrain from 'reading' them for their meaning or their significance. Now 'we', it should be noted, by no means includes the whole of humanity. There are in fact people who do interpret these phenomena, who see them animated with either human or godly intention or with the very pulse of life itself. Perhaps there is some wisdom in this too: rather than looking out at a fundamentally separate, inert, and accidental world, they may see instead an extension of their own being, alive and purposeful. Be that as it may, my best guess is that most of those who are reading this book don't think of the non-human world in quite this way.

The human world, however, seems to be a bit different. This is not to say that there aren't aspects of this world that are rather like bolts of lightning in their own right, calling more for explanation than interpretation; we ourselves, as parts of nature, have things going on inside us that are indeed essentially meaning-less. There is hardly any reason, for instance, to interpret the daily churning of our digestive systems or the firing of our synapses. If we were to assume the role of scientist, of course, we would certainly have to interpret our findings about these phenomena – nothing explains itself – but we would no doubt still refrain from reading them for their existential meaning and import. Once we move beyond these sorts of phenomena, though, once we commence the task of trying to make sense of what people are saying, of how they are acting, of how they are living their very lives, it becomes patently clear that dealing with these phenomena as if they were digestive systems or synapses won't quite do. What is required instead is a process, an interpretive process, wherein we aim toward understanding what is said, acted, or lived.

I do not wish to erect too firm a line between explanation and understanding. The latter is sometimes in the service of the former, our initial attempts to make sense of things being geared toward answering why: Why did she say that? Why did he do that? Why have they chosen to live that way? Moreover, the former is sometimes in the service of the latter: upon determining why, we may find ourselves in the position to achieve a renewed understanding of the phenomena before us. In this respect, therefore, explanation and understanding, rather than being seen as opposed to one another, are perhaps better seen as different aspects, different 'moments', of the process of making sense of the human world.

Nor do I wish to erect too firm a line between what has been called the *Naturwissenschaften*, the natural sciences, and the *Geisteswissenschaften*, the 'spirit' or human sciences, as embodied especially in the humanities. If there is anything that has served to compromise and diminish the discipline of psychology over the course of the last century or so, it is its persistent difficulty in accommodating adequately nature *and* spirit – broadly taken – into its scope. Once it was decided that the discipline would do best to emulate the so-called hard sciences and to relegate the 'softer' aspects either to its unscientific margins or to the humanities, the stage was set for the future. Ne'er, therefore, the twain shall meet: either psychology is this or it is that. Human beings, meanwhile, are either reduced to objects like any other (which is to say dehumanized) or elevated into the status of the very gods they dethroned. For the sake of both the discipline and these human beings, we need to see if there are other ways to think about all this.

Integrative desires aside for the moment, it is difficult to escape the conclusion that there is no set of formulas or laws or axioms that can neatly and exhaustively account for the things that make us tick; much of human experience seems best characterized by a kind of essential secrecy and, strictly speaking, indeterminacy. Far from implying that interpretation is ultimately a grope in the dark, however, or that the knowledge it yields cannot help but be subjective or spurious, all this means is that given the beings we are – housed in language, in culture, in history – there is much about us that requires interpretation for sense to be made. To omit this glaringly obvious fact is thus to do a great disservice to the discipline and, more importantly, to who we are. Armed with this conviction, therefore, my foremost aim was to help clear a space in psychology for hermeneutic inquiry and to show that its 'findings', different though they may be from those to be found in research articles and the like, are nonetheless perfectly well-suited to contribute to our knowledge about human beings.

As for why I have elected to address the process of rewriting the self, the reason is actually quite simple here as well. For what I have come to believe is that there is no more appropriate or exciting arena for understanding what hermeneutic inquiry is – as concerns both its possibilities and its problems – than the exploration of that most unusual and elusive being we call the 'self'. In certain important respects, in fact, self-interpretation is a kind of limit case of the more general process of interpretation of which we have already spoken and may thus serve as a testing ground of sorts to determine its value and validity. Why is this so? When we try to interpret something outside of ourselves, be it a text or a painting or a person, there is something *there* before us: words or splashes of paint or actions. But what really is *there* when the object of our interpretive endeavors is ourselves? Our pasts, you might answer, the history of our words and deeds. But are these pasts, these histories, suitably compared to that which exists outside ourselves? They are *our* pasts, *our* histories, and are in that sense inseparable from who is doing the interpreting, namely ourselves: subject and object are one. We are thus interpreting precisely that which, in some sense, we ourselves have fashioned through our own reflective imagination.

Interpreting what exists outside ourselves is difficult enough. It involves a going-beyond what is, an effortful act of creating a context, a meaningful context, within which what is may be placed. What this means, of course, is that interpretation involves an inescapably subjective dimension as well as a dimension of essential contestability: strictly speaking, interpretations are neither true nor false, but better or worse, more or less valid. This, again, is one of the reasons why psychology has been so reluctant to include interpretation in its scope; for many, it reeks entirely too much of the subjective and the arbitrary, the unscientific. Aren't these problems compounded still further, therefore, when the subject and the object of interpretation are one? Indeed they are. But this should not lead us to retreat from the task at hand. In fact, what I am suggesting here is that if we can make our way through this most thorny of hermeneutic inquiries, perhaps we will be in a better position to assess the worth of this mode of comprehending human lives and to defend it against the charges of its detractors.

There is another, more fundamental reason why I have elected to address the process of rewriting the self as well. For this very process, in addition to being an interpretive one through and through, is also a *recollective* one, in which we survey and explore our own histories, toward the end of making and remaking sense of who and what we are. What this means is that we will be doing significantly more in this book than inquiring into a discrete phenomenon that happens to be interesting in a 'mindful of life' way and potentially instructive for addressing certain fundamental concepts and problems in hermeneutics. We will in fact be inquiring into some of the very conditions of self-understanding – and indeed selfhood – that are woven into the fabric of contemporary life itself. More to the point still, my own conviction is that there is no better inroad into the phenomena of self-understanding and selfhood than this process we will be exploring here. We do, however, need to pursue in greater detail some of the risks that are involved.

QUESTIONS

Let me continue for a moment with my own narrative. I have already disclosed some of the reasons why I have chosen to pursue this project and why I have found it to be a particularly challenging and exciting one. From the very start of my thinking about it, I was firmly convinced that there was something unusually 'real' and important about it, that it might serve to break some new ground in the discipline. 'You really seem to have a tiger by the tail', one of my graduate school professors had told me. He too was convinced that the project was well worth pursuing. Not too long after I began in earnest to follow through on my plans, however, it became painfully clear that there were a great many questions that I would have to wrestle with to make the whole thing work. Now questions themselves, of course, are hardly something to fret over; they are what make intellectual life interesting. But what wound up happening, early on, was that these questions often assumed the form of challenges, serious challenges, to the very position I was interested in taking, which, again, had to do with carving out a valid space in psychology for hermeneutic inquiry in general and the process of rewriting the self in particular.

One of the main challenges I encountered is already implied in the project I have outlined above. Although I have said that I will be inquiring into *lives*, in a certain sense this is not quite right. For what we will have before us are not lives themselves, but rather *texts* of lives, literary artifacts that generally seek to recount in some fashion what these lives were like. In this respect, we will be – we must be – at least one step removed from the lives that we will be exploring: we can only proceed with our interpretive efforts on the basis of what has been written, by those whose lives they are.

This basic situation, I hasten to emphasize, obtains not only in the case of literary texts of the sort we will be examining here, but in the case of interviews and the like along with the observation of human action more generally. Interviews, of the sort that social scientists often gather, are themselves texts, and while they may not have quite as much literary flourish as those we buy in bookstores, they are in their own right literary artifacts, taking the form of words, designed to give shape to some feature of experience. As for the observation of human action, the story is actually much the same: human action, which occurs in time and yields consequences the significance of which frequently extend beyond the immediate situation in which it takes place, is itself a kind of text; it is a constellation of meanings which, not unlike literary texts or interviews, calls forth the process of interpretation (see especially Ricoeur 1981). In any case, the long and short of this brief excursion into 'textuality' is that our primary interpretive takeoff point will not be lives as such but the words used to speak them.

Now for some, particularly those of a skeptical bent, this situation may be extremely troubling. For if the ultimate interest is in fact in an enhanced understanding of human lives and not only in the words that are used to speak them, how exactly are we to move from the latter to the former? How, that is, are we to say anything cogent at all about lives themselves when all we have before us are texts? This is no minor problem, however academic it may seem on the face of it. Indeed, as Steiner (1989) has written, this 'break of the covenant between word and world', in addition to being 'one of the very few revolutions of spirit in Western history', 'defines modernity itself' (93).

No longer, therefore, can we complacently assume that texts provide windows on the world, that they refer to obdurate realities – 'real presences', Steiner calls them – 'out there'. If texts refer to anything at all, it might be held, it is only to other texts, this chain of 'intertextuality' being endless, infinite; and what this implies, in turn, is that there may really *be* no 'lives' apart from this infinite play of language itself. If in fact, with the exception of our preverbal years, everything we do, everything we are, is bathed in language to begin with, isn't 'life' itself another link in the chain of texts?

But let us assume, for argument's sake, that there still remains some wisdom in the common parlance and that we can, cautiously, speak of human lives themselves. Right away, there is a further problem to be addressed. We noted that we would be dealing with texts that generally seek to *recount* the lives of their authors. Doesn't this mean that the situation at hand is complicated still further? Texts of immediate experience may be troubling enough. But doesn't the fact that we will be dealing for the most part with *recollections* of experience place us yet another step removed from the lives we wish to understand? Consider the countless distortions and falsifications to which recollections are subject. Consider as well that even in the absence of these, one is inevitably remembering selectively, and perhaps conferring meanings on experience that did not possess these meanings at the time of their occurrence. Consider finally that one will no doubt be weaving these meanings into a whole pattern, a *narrative*, perhaps with a plot, designed to make sense of the fabric of the past. How are we to escape the conclusion that these narratives, however much they might aspire to depict the lives of real people, are anything more than fictions – 'mere' fictions, as some might have it – that may be interesting and fun to read but ultimately suspect in regard to understanding human lives?

Moreover, if indeed the process of rewriting the self cannot help but culminate in fictions, in selective and imaginative literary constructions of who we have been and are, how are we to escape the conclusion that *we ourselves* are ultimately fictions? The self, after all, is not a *thing*; it is not a substance, a material entity that we can somehow grab hold of and place before our very eyes. Again, unlike actual texts (like those we buy in bookstores) or paintings or what have you, it doesn't even exist outside of – well, ourselves. Is it therefore no-thing, save what we ourselves conjure up in those moments of reverie when we wish to make sense of experience? For many years the self has been seen by many to be a part of the furniture of the world: I think, therefore I am. But if the covenant between word and world has been broken, what am 'I', what are 'we', besides the very act of enunciating these words? '*I*', writes Barthes (1977), 'is nothing other than the instance saying *I*' (145). What else could it be?

One last barrage of questions seems only fitting. It is probably not surprising that a number of the narratives we will be exploring are attempts to recount the *development* of their authors. Many autobiographical texts, particularly those that document 'coming of age' in one form or another, are tales of progress and growth or of 'seeing the light' or, more generally, of coming to understand who and what the writer might conceivably be. From the present moment of writing, in other words, one often gazes back upon the past and charts that 'upward' trajectory whereby one has managed, despite the trials and travails that have come one's way, to prevail, to come into being.

There are of course exceptions to this scenario, but no matter; we are concerned for the time being with those narratives that adhere to it. Doesn't this mean that the concept of development, despite its customary connotations of moving *forward* in time, can only be predicated *backward*, in retrospect, after one is in the position to chart the trajectory of the past? Indeed, isn't the implication here that the concept of development is itself fundamentally inseparable from the process of narrating the past, which, as we have already learned, has a markedly fictive dimension to it? The conclusion may once again appear to be inescapable: if narratives are ultimately to be regarded as fictions, and if the selves who write them are as well, then the concept of development itself must be too. It may be a somewhat defensive one at that. Rather than living with the existential dizziness of the fact that our lives are headed essentially nowhere but simply keep on, now this way, now that, perhaps we delude ourselves into supposing that there is indeed some rhyme and reason to what's been happening.

Our bodies grow and maybe our minds do too, at least when we are children; we get bigger and smarter. But beyond this, what can development possibly mean? By most indications, there is no great and wondrous absolute endpoint to which human lives lead. We're not acorns that grow inexorably into trees of a specific sort. We're people, living in history, affecting and being affected by all the things that happen around us. Some of us will be happy, others sad; some fulfilled, others not; some will go on to do things that are conventionally regarded as good and worthwhile (thereby earning them the status, perhaps, of being highly developed), others will seem more stagnant or even retarded. Aren't these just value judgments, though? And again, when we're talking about ourselves, don't these value judgments crop up mainly in retrospect, when we pause to assure ourselves that we have indeed been heading somewhere good? Consider what we often want out of books. We want the episodes to be related to one another in some way, we want to see a plot develop, and in the end we want to be able to see the point of it all. Now in books there usually *is* a point, and the author probably tried to put it there, which is why, if it's a good book, we read on. But is there really a comparable kind of point to be found when the text is us? Or do we create one, precisely so that we can *live* on?

THE SKEPTICAL CHALLENGE

Perhaps, some might argue, it is time to move beyond these securities. If there are in the end not lives but only texts, then perhaps we should abandon the attempt to consider what exists outside of texts. If there is anything at all 'prior' to what is said or written – which, for some, there is not – it is inaccessible anyway. With this in mind, rather than struggling to determine the relationship between word and world, we might do better to immerse ourselves, more freely and playfully than is ordinarily done, into words themselves, into discourse, and leave well enough alone; the research projects can keep on coming, and even though they won't aspire to generate quite the same sort of theoretical knowledge as that which is usually subsumed under the rubric of 'science', there will be plenty to talk about.

Perhaps the foremost advocate of this basic perspective is Jacques Derrida, a leading 'deconstructionist' philosopher.[2] Among other things, what Derrida has pointed out is that the human world, owing especially to its being bathed in language, is so ambiguous, complex, and heterogeneous that any attempt to capture it and hold it steady, as if it were an object, a physical thing, is simply not possible. There are two ways of understanding this situation, Derrida notes. This idea of capturing the world, which he refers to as 'totalization', may be judged 'impossible in the classical style: one then refers to the empirical endeavor of either a subject or a finite richness which it can never master. There is too much, more than one can say' (1978: 289). Along these lines, in other words, the world is just too big and dense, too meaningful, to be represented exhaustively. Even in the most painstakingly heartfelt attempts at disclosure, therefore, in romantic poetry for instance, one must always fall short of the mark of 'getting it', saying it all. Not surprisingly, there may be some sorrow and angst accompanying this perspective: if we can never really find the words to say it, if all we can do is speak and write, in the hope of merely moving in the direction of that promised but unattainable land of the truth, then we will more than likely suffer every now and then over our own finitude, our own scarce resources.

But there is another way to approach these matters, Derrida suggests.

The idea is basically that if indeed the world we have before is always and inevitably bathed in language, if indeed there really *is* no world (to speak of) apart from language, then there really isn't much reason to become distraught over the alleged fact that we can never get it quite right. From this perspective, in other words, there *is* nothing to 'get'; there is only language itself, discourse, texts, 'social constructions' of the world, nothing more. The absence of the possibility of getting it right is thus understood not so much as *im*possibility – a failure, a stopping short – as *non*-possibility: language, rather than referring to the world 'in itself', refers only to language (which refers only to language, which refers only to language, and so on, ad infinitum). Again, except for preverbal children and a few other unfortunates, has anyone ever beheld an 'unlanguaged' world, a pure and pristine presence, untouched by words, untouched by social constructions, issuing from the specific surrounds in which we live? The answer, many would say, is surely 'No'. So why be angst-ridden? Why mourn the absence of what isn't there? Why not just speak and write and try to make things interesting?

As concerns the issue of recollection and the consequent fictionalization of the past that is seen to follow from it, this is only a problem, it might be held, if one presumes that there are truths beneath the fictions. Along these lines, notions such as falsification and distortion, since they tend to rely on the positing of some form or other of 'presence', some realm of the 'really real', may be essentially beside the point. If there *is* no presence, no really real – in this case, no true past – then there is little reason to worry about these notions; they are themselves products of just that epistemology that many are seeking to cast into question.

Even the notion of self-deception may be deemed spurious from this point of view, in that it presumes that something like 'un-deception' is possible; and even if this hypothetical state of un-deception is taken to refer not to the absolute truth but only to a region of truth, a region of undistorted self-communication, it may still be deemed complicitous in that basic conception of truth which posits a correspondence, however rough, between word and world. From this perspective, then, we might simply avow and embrace the fictional dimension of both recollection and those narratives based upon it, leaving truth claims behind. This would spare us the burden of seeking those presences which are not to be found anyway.

That the elusive phenomenon we call the 'self' may be a fiction is not an especially new idea. As we will see in detail later on, Hume wrote about this, as did Nietzsche, Skinner, and a variety of others besides. More recently, there has been the work of such prominent 'poststructuralist' thinkers as Barthes, from whom we have already heard, and Foucault, each of whom, in his own way, has sought both to 'de-substantialize' the self – that is, to show why it is not to be regarded as a thing, a bounded entity – and to situate it within the texture of discourse itself, which is where it is most often thought to belong.[3] Rather than the self being seen as a primary *origin of* meaning, therefore, which is how most forms of humanism have tended to conceive it, it is seen instead as being already *enmeshed in* meaning, in language, and is thus more of a product or a destination, we might say, than an origin. In any case, the fictionality of the self, from this perspective, is hardly something to lament: the death of the substantialized humanist self, not unlike the (alleged) death of God, can only serve to free us further from the illusory comforts of those modes of thought that repress and bury our own essential heterogeneity and otherness.

Finally, in regard to the concept of development – which requires as its very condition of possibility something akin to that vision of the self that many wish to dismantle – there has been talk not only about exposing it for the value-laden fiction it ostensibly is, but about jettisoning it altogether. Now for old time's sake perhaps, the word itself may continue to be used by many; given that there is an entire portion of a discipline built around it, and given as well that many earn their livelihood by participating in it, it isn't one that is easy to shake. In principle, however, this is exactly what may need to be done. Following what was said earlier, the reasoning here is quite basic. For one, if in fact the self is much more heterogeneous and 'other' than it has been made out to be, then it is difficult to posit that sort of 'central subject' for whom development would occur; again, heterogeneous selves are more likely to simply go on, in largely random fashion. For another, if in fact the concept of development is bound up with the narratives people tell about the trajectory of the past, and if these narratives are essentially fictional in nature, then development may be little more than that familiar story of progress and self-realization that many wish to tell.

As an aside, it might be noted that this situation may be seen to hold not only in the case of autobiographical reflection, but in that of developmental research more generally. As I have noted elsewhere (Freeman 1984), even in the case of 'prospective' developmental research, such as longitudinal studies, one can only speak about development per se *after* the findings are in – after, that is, one is in a position to narrate what has been going over the course of time in question. In a certain sense, then, the project of revealing developmental trends is itself a form of historical inquiry, requiring a backward gaze for sense to be made. Might it not be the case, therefore, that the concept of development itself ultimately represents an attempt to smuggle into the psychological picture exactly those evolutionist myths of progress and growth that have outlived their day?

Finally, on a somewhat more philosophical plane – and here I think we find the most serious challenge of them all – it is indeed the case that it is extremely difficult to talk about development without positing an endpoint, a telos, in which the process culminates. To the extent that the concept retains its traditional forward-moving connotations, it is, and must be, *toward* something: a goal, a place on high. But the question, of course, is, *Whose* goal? *Whose* place on high? In addition to modernity being noted for the aforementioned break of the covenant between word and world, it is also noted for its distinct reticence to embrace absolutes, binding for all; we live in a post-absolute world, where one person's telos may be another's worst dream. But this too may be nothing to lament. For once we are able to move beyond the tyranny of the absolute, once we are able to live with the fact that perhaps there *is* no discrete end to human development, at least not of the sort that can command universal assent, we will perhaps have freed ourselves in still another way from that 'metaphysics of presence', as Derrida (1976) has called it, that serves to obstruct the infinite play of meaning.

What exactly was to be done about all these questions? I had hoped, again, to situate my project in the discipline of psychology and to suggest, moreover, that the findings of hermeneutic inquiry could make a bona fide contribution to psychological knowledge. But how, in the face of these challenges, was this possible?

THINKING BEYOND SKEPTICISM

These challenges are serious ones. Moreover, I want to acknowledge from the very start that I am sympathetic to a good many of them; some, as I noted earlier, I have raised myself in previous work. What I have found in recent years, however – and I realize that this may sound entirely too 'personal' for some – is that many of the claims we have been considering, whatever their logical validity and whatever their resistance to firm refutation, simply do not do justice to the life I live: even if the furniture of the world doesn't really exist apart from the words I use to speak it, which on some level I am fully prepared to avow, I still bump into it all the time. More to the point, even if my 'self', fleeting as it is, doesn't exist apart from my own consciousness of it, from my own narrative imagination, indeed from my own *belief* in its very existence, it is nonetheless eminently real and – within limits – eminently knowable.

Consider this: I believe, wholeheartedly, that I am writing this book, in part, because of an interest that was sparked in graduate school. Now it could be argued in this context that there are, in principle, an infinite number of ways to account for the event of my writing. If, for instance, I lived in some far off land – in a world 'languaged' in an entirely different way from this one – I might conclude that I was possessed by an ancient spirit ancestor or that something I ate long ago planted a seed in me, a seed that turned into a spark. It is true enough, then, that had I been thrown into a completely different world from the present one, my account may well be other than it is. It is also true, of course, that my account of this event ten years from now could be quite different from the one being offered today; maybe through analysis, I could learn more about my secret desires and hidden reasons, thereby rendering this largely intellectual account obsolete. More troubling still – and this gets us to the heart of some of the problems with which we will be dealing in this book – this spark of which I am speaking has only come to be understood as such in virtue of its outcome. Had I not moved on to do this very work, I would not have spoken of a spark at all, only a few interesting courses perhaps, existing as fond memories. The significance of that earlier experience, therefore, is being predicated in retrospect, in narrative, as I gaze back and try to understand how I have gotten to be here, doing what I am. Strictly speaking, therefore, we're not talking about a cause, propelling its inexorable effects in the future, but a reason, a motive, an *episode*, that is only able to be designated *as* an episode owing to the part it seems to have played in this story I am interested in telling.

But do I 'merely' believe that the experience I have been referring to sparked my interest or that it is only a yarn that I have spun in order to stem the tide of meaninglessness? I am fully prepared to say that the answer to this question is a firm and unequivocal 'No'. Why? Because I *know* that there is something to this connection: my own way of understanding things, as local and as transient as it may be, tells me so. Can I prove it? Is there some kind of material chain in me that I could pull out and show you: 'See, I told you there was a connection'? Hardly. But this is no reason to suspend belief.

It is exactly this suspension of belief, however, that has come to characterize much of the contemporary intellectual landscape. Indeed, what seems to have happened, particularly in those quarters of psychology where the natural science approach to the discipline has been cast into question, is that there has emerged a kind of intellectual 'reaction-formation' to the traditional ways, such that the 'old' project of attaining valid knowledge – bound as it ostensibly is to the calculative machinations of the dreaded Science – effectively gets left in the dust. As for the result, it is twofold. First, there emerges a seemingly irrevocable split between those who are understood to be doing science and those who are understood to be doing a more humanities-oriented 'something else', more literary and artful and humane. Second, and more important, the discipline itself is left essentially intact: its critics, frequently by their own choice, are either relegated to the margins of the discipline or leave it entirely, and its mainstream advocates can continue doing their own scientific thing, perhaps even heaving a sigh of relief that their upstart foes have finally left the premises. The traditional ways thus come out on top, alive and well, the same as ever, the transformation of the discipline having been obviated by a rather crude and pointless opposition of terms. Hermeneutics, moreover, all too often becomes little more than the inverted image of exactly that reified vision of science that many seem eager to explode; it becomes a parasite, living in the shadow of what is apparently an all too formidable host.

I do not intend to offer one of the usual 'neo-conservative' knee-jerk responses to the putative nihilism of the present day; there is more going on in the challenges we have been considering than reckless Dionysian abandon. Nor do I intend to sneak some kind of positivism in through the back door, as often happens; there is too much about the positivist program, especially in the social sciences, that I loathe. What I am about to do instead is offer a reasoned response to these claims, precisely by taking up the serious challenges they present.

Now I say 'reasoned' here mainly because I will be presenting a series of interconnected arguments in the pages to follow. These arguments will partly and admittedly be based on 'the life I live', but they will also extend well beyond this singular place, assuming a more scholarly format. Let me be quick to add, however, that I am more than willing to avow the limits of reasoned, especially 'theoretical', argument. I need to be clear about this. I am no fundamentalist, nor am I a theologian. Formally speaking, in fact, I am not even a particularly religious person. I do believe, however, that when one takes up issues of the sort to be taken up here, there is no getting around the fact that ultimate questions do, and I think must, come to the fore: 'the final stakes', writes Steiner (1989), 'are theological' (87). What this means, more concretely, is that while I will indeed be going the usual argumentative route in significant part, I will not shy away from offering certain claims that are, in the end, based on a kind of faith, on modes of intuition that cannot be reduced, without remainder, to the logic of theoretical postulates. Indeed, one argument to be made here is that this logic of theoretical postulates, whether it assumes the form of positivism or those more au courant forms associated with poststructuralism, serves ultimately to remove us, defensively perhaps, from those questions and concerns that are at the heart of our embodied existence in the world.

I didn't really become fully aware of it until the past couple of years, but the shadow of Paul Ricoeur seems to loom large in the way I have come to think about things. There are of course certain obvious connections, tied to the ideas of narrative, history, and so on. Without all those courses that I took with him it would be hard to say where exactly I would be on the academic map. More than this, however, Ricoeur was a remarkable mediator, whose primary aim was to work patiently through some of the numerous intellectual dilemmas and crises that have emerged throughout the course of modernity. In the eyes of some, I realize, he was perhaps too much the mediator; in his adamant refusal to embrace extreme – or, more appropriately, extremist – positions, perhaps he landed himself too much in the middle, thereby betraying his own ambivalent relation to the different currents of intellectual life that were clamoring for attention.

This may in fact be characteristic of hermeneutic thinking more generally, for in the case of the more prominent hermeneutic philosophers, Ricoeur and Gadamer especially, there does always seem to be this attempt to have it both ways. On the one hand, there is the attempt to wave the banner of interpretation, to show its unsurpassability in making sense of the world, to show that there does not and cannot exist an unprejudiced, neutral, wholly objective way of doing so. On the other hand, however, there is also the attempt to maintain that the very interpretive prejudices we have, far from obviating the possibility of knowing and understanding, are exactly the prerequisites for our making any sense of things at all. 'Word' does indeed achieve a certain primacy from this perspective; interpretation, of texts at any rate, begins in and with language. The task, however, as I understand it, is to maintain and embrace this primacy of word *without losing world in the process*. Stated more simply, the task is at once to avow the importance of interpretation in understanding human life and to show that this process, rather than being antithetical to the project of generating valid knowledge, is in fact perfectly compatible with it.

What I am suggesting, therefore, is that hermeneutics ought not to be considered the unscientific, relativistic, skepticism-ridden fantasy land it is sometimes assumed to be, by supporters and detractors alike. There will no doubt be some who will reject this attempt at mediation. Mainstream psychologists, for instance, may continue to find the perspective being offered too 'subjective' and imprecise. Others, perhaps, may find the perspective too 'objective', too ensnared in what they see to be the old ways. Finally, if Ricoeur's and Gadamer's critics are any indication, there will also be those who just don't like mediating philosophical positions of the sort being advanced here. But mediating philosophical positions, I will suggest, are only a problem for those who are given to extremes, perhaps out of their own ideological commitments, or given to facile either–or thinking. Some issues, it is true, you can't have both ways; intellectual life is, for better or worse, full of either–or situations. The trick, however, is not to reduce 'both-and' situations to either–or for the sake of scoring points. Again, it isn't easy. But if one has any interest at all in positing both the unsurpassability of interpretation and the possibility still of generating what we colloquially call 'knowledge', then there is little choice but to inhabit this region.

My own perspective, in short, is that there is indeed a place *in* psychology for interpretive endeavors of the sort being undertaken here. What's more, the fundamental aim of these endeavors, I believe, ought not to be to supplant or explode the notion of psychological science, but critically to transform and expand it, precisely by demonstrating as compellingly as possible that knowledge can be had in many more ways than the reigning notion would suggest. In asserting this, of course, it should be clear that a further aim in this book is to think beyond skepticism, to find other philosophical places to inhabit than some of the strange abysses which we presently witness, and to determine how some of the most salient lines of contemporary inquiry into the self may be recast.

Without meaning to seem overly grand about all this, I believe that these matters are in fact of some urgency. For it may very well be that the skepticism and uncertainty and suspicion which we now witness, rather than being a mere outgrowth of certain intellectual trends, are themselves symptomatic of precisely those abysses in which many of us dwell. Those who suffer oppression, of course, know this all too well. According to Brodski and Schenck, for instance, whose edited volume *Life/Lines* (1988) explores women's autobiography, the 'essential problem in feminist theory and practice' has to do with 'the imperative situating of the female subject', and this, they are quick to note, despite the 'campaign against the sovereign self' (14). The implication here is an interesting one. Perhaps this 'campaign', they suggest, is something of an intellectual luxury, designed by those whose selves are sovereign enough for them to afford to fritter them away philosophically as they wish. More generally, I would argue, unless we, as critical psychologists, pay some serious attention to both the development of the self and the de-formation of the self – however sketchy and ambiguous these ideas may be – we will only have succeeded in performing those academic exercises in which no moment of critique is even possible.

Now it is exactly in this context, the moment of critique, that reason finds its limits. Some may find the situation at hand disheartening, even disabling: not only is there no way of showing conclusively that 'reality' or 'mind' or 'self' truly exist, but there really is no reason why we should love the people and things we do or why we should experience horror in the face of atrocities or, for that matter, why we should care about the fate of ourselves and others. Moreover, it doesn't really require much intellectual effort to hold all of these ideas in the most profound suspicion. It is rather easy, in fact, to show that there is much about the world that is a great deal more insubstantial and unreasonable than many have assumed. It is thus all the more curious and noteworthy that so many of these insubstantial and unreasonable things have such a remarkable hold over us. Indeed, isn't it the case that the things we care about most – ourselves, others, music, art, nature – are precisely the things for which there is the least reason to do so?

As St Augustine, among others, well knew, skepticism itself was inseparable from materialism. Earlier on in his life, he couldn't quite shake the conviction, reasonable as it seemed, that only those phenomena of the world that had substance, that had concrete dimensions, were truly real; all else was hopelessly shadowy and amorphous, intangible and ungraspable. Positivism held to much the same point of view, and, ironically enough, so too does much of post-positivist thought, including some of the more 'radical' philosophies currently in vogue: it's not for nothing that those phenomena of which we are least positive, such as the self, are often the first to go when the time comes to clean the house of idols. What Augustine also learned, however, was that materialism and positivism could become dead ends, which placed at an unbridgeable distance exactly those concerns that were innermost in his being.

Let me now talk a bit more about Augustine, who will be the focus of Chapter 2, as well as the others who have found their way into this book. In addition to providing a preview of the chapters, this will also serve to make clearer still what my main lines of argument will be.

THE CAST OF CHARACTERS

I have already alluded to one of the reasons why I have chosen to begin the body of this book with an inquiry into Augustine's life, as told in his *Confessions* (1980): the story of his life shows in an unusually compelling way not only the limits of materialism and positivism but indeed of reason itself. Or, framed another way, his story shows why *faith*, broadly taken – for him, it was faith in God; for some of us, no doubt, it will be faith in something else – is integral to human existence, why, indeed, we literally cannot live without it. Now, atheists need not be frightened or put off by this. This isn't going to be a tract in the psychology of religion, and nor will I try to offer proof of the existence of God or some such thing. But if in fact there is any truth at all to the notion that the contemporary intellectual landscape can be characterized by something akin to a crisis of faith, then it may be worthwhile to think about it a bit and to see whether there exist any restorative measures. Augustine will be of considerable help in this.

There are several other reasons for my beginning with *Confessions* as well. First, and to risk one further bit of autobiographical self-indulgence, I consider it a text through which I really began to cut my intellectual teeth. As a second-year graduate student attending the aforementioned seminar, 'The phenomenology of time consciousness', in which an oral presentation was required, I reasoned it would be wisest for me to deal with the one book we were reading which was about a life. I didn't know much about this particular book, I should note, but, it seemed like the most appropriate one on which to offer some comments. The rest of the readings, which included works by Plato, Aristotle, Plotinus, and Kant, represented even more threatening territory than Augustine, particularly since nearly all of my classmates were studying philosophy or theology. I had read some philosophy in college, but for me to hold forth in front of all these people, among whom was Paul Ricoeur, about the meaning of time in Plato seemed most unwise.

So I chose Augustine, focusing mainly on the issue of memory, and found some interesting things to say. More importantly, though, what I experienced in reading this book was an amazing rush of intellectual excitement that was to catalyze much of my own subsequent work. For what Augustine's work showed, in addition to the centrality of faith, was that the idea of rewriting the self, along with the interconnected conceptual triad of history, memory, and narrative, might serve as a kind of central figure or pivot around which to think about human lives and human development. The book proved, in short, to be a master text, a point of reference and departure for the issues I was most interested in thinking about. At a very general level, therefore, what I will be doing in this chapter is laying out some of the conceptual terrain to be dealt with in greater detail in the chapters to follow.

The chapter will focus on a fundamental and rather curious dimension of autobiographical reflection often manifested in confessional texts of this sort. What happens in the book is basically this: Augustine, having seen the light, has sat himself down to recount the story of how it came to be. In a very basic sense, therefore, his story might be seen as a kind of extended historical account of how he come to be the pious fellow he now was: and then this happened, and then that, and so on, until he reached the desired destination, which culminated in the act of writing. But it is exactly this perspective that we will seek to problematize, in order to begin our inquiry into the process of rewriting the self. For is it not the case that this story is itself a function of writing, and that the outcome of what has happened over the course of all these years – namely, his conversion – has largely determined what will and will not be recounted? While on the one hand, in other words, beginning leads to end, there is also a sense in which end leads to beginning, the outcome in question serving as the organizing principle around which the story is told. One might think of it as a kind of chicken-and-egg paradox, the ultimate issue being which comes first: the events or the story. How exactly are we to resolve this paradox, if at all? We shall see.

Augustine's text, by virtue of it being a seeing-the-light story, is also very much about development, colloquially understood; he is revealing his own transformation from what he considered an inferior state of being to a better one. In this sense, again, the arrow of time seems to be moving forward, into the future. In line with what we briefly discussed earlier, though, doesn't he also show us that the very concept of development can only be predicated retrospectively, after all is said and done? What kind of story might he have told, if any, if he *hadn't* seen the light, if all of his fits and starts had led to his being the same old troubled unbeliever he had been before? There would have been a sinner rather than a saint and, by and large, sinners don't write stories of development. Can there even be development without narratives being told, narratives leading to good and valuable states of knowing and being? Do these narratives ultimately constitute a kind of apologia for who and what one has been, providing in addition a message of hope for those fellow travellers in comparable straits? Is the concept of development ultimately a modern twist on conversion narratives themselves? We shall see about this too. What we will also see in this first chapter, finally, is how we might employ the idea of rewriting the self as a vehicle for rethinking the concept of development itself (see Freeman 1985a, Freeman and Robinson 1990).

In Chapter 3, which explores Helen Keller's remarkably provocative autobiography *The Story of My Life* (1988), I will take up a number of issues pertaining to the interrelationship of language, thought, and selfhood. As we will see, Helen has something of a problem, in that she can't quite distinguish her own words (and thoughts) from those in the texts she reads; since nearly everything she comes to know about the world is acquired 'indirectly', through the eyes and ears of others, she is unsure what is 'her own' and what is 'theirs'. She — whoever 'she' may be, which is precisely what is at issue here — even feels this way about herself; she feels that she is a heterogeneous patchwork, a compilation of texts, lacking a truly coherent and unified identity. But what, we will ask, might it mean to think one's 'own' thoughts or be one's 'own' self? Is her situation ultimately any more 'secondhand' and derivative than ours? In addition, if indeed what Helen tells us about the otherness of her own thoughts is true, is this story really an *auto*biography? Is autobiography, the telling of *my* story, even possible? If 'mine' is to be understood as that which issues from me alone, then surely not; every word I speak and write and think was on the scene well before I was. It is nevertheless the case, I will argue, that rewriting the self involves significantly more than the mere reshuffling of words. Indeed, it is rather more like the resurrection of the dead, a process of breathing new life into language, of imaginatively transforming it into something different from anything before.

In Chapter 4, which takes as its point of departure a fictional text, Jean-Paul Sartre's *Nausea* (1964), we will be inquiring further into the idea of narrative, focusing specifically on the relationship between 'living' and 'telling' — that is, between life as we experience it moment to moment and day to day and the stories we subsequently tell about it. The problem here is an interesting one. For some (e.g. White 1978), since it is patently clear that we do not *live* stories, it can only be inferred that there is indeed something markedly fictional about the yarns we ultimately spin; as suggested earlier, they are a a large step away from life itself and perhaps ought not to be conflated with it. For others, however (e.g. MacIntyre 1981), the disjunction between living and telling is not nearly so great. Indeed, to the extent that living in time itself partakes of narrative, it follows that the stories we tell and write about ourselves may not be quite as fictional — in the sense of being untrue to life itself — as is sometimes supposed. The basic question to be addressed, in any case, is: Do narratives, by virtue of being told or written at a significant remove from the flux of immediate experience, inevitably falsify 'life itself'? Or is the disjunction between living and telling less severe than these falsification critics contend? Even if we do not live narratives of the same nature and scope as those we tell when we pause to reflect comprehensively on the past, the very act of existing meaningfully in time, I will argue, the very act of making sense of ourselves and others, is only possible in and through the fabric of narrative itself.

Having by this point in the book argued that life history narratives, while fictive on some level, are not to be assimilated to the epistemological status of being 'merely' so, we will move on in Chapter 5 to discuss in greater detail problems related to historical interpretation and understanding. Our takeoff point will be Philip Roth's 'autobiography', entitled *The Facts* (1988), in which, by his own account, he has temporarily set aside his vocation as fiction-writer and elected instead to tell the putatively factual story of his life without the embellishments and adornments of art. There will be no more disguises, he tells us, no more clothing the real with the fictional imagination. Roth's life had seemed to lose direction recently, and in order to determine how this had happened he had to tell it 'like it was' and thereby 'recover' what might have been lost. But can one in fact reconstruct the facts of one's life *without* the aforementioned embellishments and adornments? How, after all, does one even decide which facts are pertinent unless one already has a story in mind? And if this is so, what might it mean – if anything – to speak or write something like the *truth* of one's own history? It is a tall order to work through this particular problem, for what is involved, among other things, is rethinking the idea of historical truth itself. But this is exactly what we will have to do.

In case we may be led to the conclusion that the ideas of historical 'facts', historical 'truth', and so on are ultimately untenable, it will be useful to consider a story where these notions assume a more than academic urgency. We will already have spoken a great deal about how one's present interpretive perspective conditions and colors the story of one's past. Here, however, we will move more fully in the opposite direction, by considering the way in which one's past may condition and color one's present. We will try to work through this issue by looking in Chapter 6 at Sylvia Fraser's *My Father's House* (1987), subtitled *A Memoir of Incest and of Healing*, a text which discusses how, during her mid-forties, Fraser arrived at the startling realization that she had been sexually abused by her father as a child and throughout a portion of her youth. Interestingly enough, her life had been something of a mystery until that time, sometimes appearing as if she was being carried along by forces that could never quite be named, as indeed she was; she was in effect being determined by a past – or, more appropriately, by a 'past present' – that she didn't even know, consciously, existed.

But doesn't this commit us to a model of causation that we have already seen to be problematic? If the historical past can only be told from the vantage point of the present, if earlier events only gain their meaning and significance as a function of later outcomes, what does it mean to say that Fraser was 'determined' by this past of which she knew not? It will be suggested in this context that even though Freud's 'archeological' model of life history (e.g. 1901–5a, 1913, 1937) is surely subject to criticism in that it embodied his tendency to reify the historical past, to consider it a conglomeration of discrete artifacts, there are times when it seems quite appropriate: when, for instance, the force of repression has been powerful enough to banish certain experiences into the nether reaches of the unconscious, where they will henceforth shape the contours of a life silently and unseen. What, though, are the implications of this perspective? Is life historical knowledge essentially retrospective? Or is it more appropriately formulated 'prospectively', with what happens earlier determining, with the inexorability of fate itself, what later will be? Could it be both? It could indeed; and while this particular instance of what I earlier called 'both–and' thinking will no doubt bewilder us for a bit, as best as I can tell there is no other way.

In Chapter 7, the final chapter of the book (bar the epilogue), we will explore Jill Ker Conway's *The Road From Coorain* (1989) in order both to round out and articulate further the view of development being set forth in this book and to show why the process of development itself is frequently concomitant with social critique. Having been raised in the Australian bush, with the expectation that she would eventually step into some form or other of the customary female script operative in her homeland, Conway experienced a painful dilemma when it came to decide what sort of life she wanted to lead. While cultural expectations, along with her great love of both family and homeland, pointed in the direction of her staying put, there was also a desire to move on, to live a different narrative, more fully in line with her own unique talents and interests. It was thus only through her own coming-to-consciousness as a social subject – specifically, as a woman who had unwittingly taken on the prevailing sociopolitical ethos only to discover that it was decidedly more oppressive than she had ever realized – that there could emerge a suitable developmental resolution.

In certain respects, we will be returning here to several issues taken up earlier, especially in the chapter on Helen Keller. If in fact both lives and the stories people tell about them are 'socially constructed' and if more generally one cannot ever really step beyond the discursive order inherent in one's own culture, how does one ever manage to go on to do something new and different? How does one ever manage to become conscious enough of the discursive order of one's culture to make transgression and critique possible? How, in short, does one undergo the transformation from a kind of object, prey to the constrictive forces of society and culture, to a willful subject, able both to put into question those narratives assumed to be given and to transform in turn the sociocultural surround itself? Even if we cannot step out of history, which of course we cannot, there is reason to believe that we can sometimes move toward — develop toward — a greater consciousness of it.

Why might this be important? As Bakhtin (1986) has written, 'The better a person understands the degree to which he is externally determined, the closer he comes to understanding and exercising his real freedom' (139). As for the specific nature of the task at hand, he continues, it 'consists in forcing the *thinglike* environment, which mechanically influences the personality, to begin to speak, that is, to reveal in it the potential word and tone, to transform it into a semantic context for the thinking, speaking, and acting (as well as creating) personality' (164). When does this sort of thing happen? Among other occasions, it happens, Bakhtin goes on note, whenever there is any 'serious and probing' attempt at self-understanding — whenever, that is, one seeks to rewrite the self. Let us begin to explore in greater detail some of the different ways this can be done.

Chapter 2
The story of a life

HISTORY, MEMORY, NARRATIVE

Before moving into the details of St Augustine's *Confessions* (1980), it may be useful first to set the stage for our inquiry. In addition to rewriting the self on the plane of personal experience, it has been suggested that Augustine is partly responsible for rewriting the very meaning of selfhood itself. 'At the edge of modern times', Gusdorf (1980) has written, 'the physical and material appeal of the reflection in the mirror bolsters and strengthens the tradition of self-examination of Christian asceticism'. More to the point, Gusdorf continues,

> Augustine's *Confessions* answer to this new spiritual orientation by contrast to the great philosophical systems of classical antiquity – Epicurean, for example, or Stoic – that contented themselves with a disciplinary notion of individual being and argued that one should seek salvation in adhering to a universal and transcendent law without any regard for the mysteries (which anyway were unsuspected) of interior life.
>
> (33)

With Augustine, in other words, we see exemplified an essentially new orientation to the meaning of human existence, a new method for charting the world of the self, a 'new fascination with the secret springs of personal life. The rule requiring the confession of sins', therefore, 'gives to self-examination a character at once systematic and necessary' (33).

Notice that according to Gusdorf, Augustine has done much more in this work than merely pay greater attention to an already mysterious self. The mysteries of interior life, Gusdorf argues, had been largely 'unsuspected' prior to Augustine; they were simply not an integral part of personal existence as it had been understood up until that time. What Augustine has begun to do in this work, therefore, is reconstitute the very meaning of selfhood: with the mysteries of interior life having now become an appropriate and indeed necessary object of self-examination, the self in turn comes to be understood as an elusive, capricious, and in some cases opaque being, which requires painstaking and deep attention to psychological detail for its secrets to be revealed.

Needless to say, this basic vision of the self remains very much with us to this day. As Weintraub has suggested in *The Value of the Individual* (1978), which traces through 'autobiography' (as it has only more recently been called) the history of self-conception from classical antiquity on up through Goethe, there is in fact a distinct sense in which *Confessions* marks the beginning of autobiographical reflection as we have come to know it. 'Augustine', he writes, 'works out the presentation of a life course as no one prior to him had done' (25); no other work had the 'scope, fullness, intensity, and life-like quality' (26) that this one had. Perhaps this is yet another reason why in Weintraub's estimation, along with Gusdorf's, Augustine's work changed the very course of civilization, ushering in an entirely new picture of selfhood and what it meant to understand it.

This is not to say that the self of Augustine's concern is strictly equivalent to our own 'modern' conception of the self. Whereas in his case it is none other than God who is ultimately responsible both for bringing individuality into being and for determining its specific shape, in our own case the responsibility is most often seen to devolve upon ourselves, the self who we become emerging in significant part as a function of the irrevocably individualized life projects we set before us. Along the lines being drawn here, then, it might be suggested that although Augustine's *Confessions* surely marks an important turn in the meaning of selfhood, one that is very much concerned with *historicizing* human reality – with seeing the recounting of one's life as an appropriate and necessary vehicle for the development of self-understanding – it remains a far cry from our own present-day conception, with its profound emphasis on self-determination, 'individuality', and so on.[1]

Be that as it may, Augustine will present for us an extraordinarily important occasion to reflect on the meaning of selfhood. For however different his specific vision of the self may be from our own, there is enough in common between the two to warrant their being compared. We might therefore ask in this context: What sort of being is it who pauses long enough to engage in inner dialogue, who wishes to make sense of the personal past, and who traces its trajectory as a means of discovering the origins of the self? What sort of being is it who finds himself or herself *important* enough to write about? More simply, what sort of being is it who engages in autobiographical self-reflection?

You may well be tempted to answer 'any' to these questions, your presumption being that virtually any normal, healthy adult would do much the same thing in trying to account for his or her self. But this is most certainly not the case. Indeed, despite the fact that a *sense* of self – qua psychophysical entity, set apart from the outer world – may plausibly be considered a universal phenomenon (at least for those who have developed beyond the sensorimotor stage, primary narcissism, symbiosis, whatever we wish to call it), there is ample evidence to suggest that the *concept* of the self is very much relative to time and place.[2] As Geertz (1979) eloquently puts the matter,

> The Western conception of person as a bounded, unique, more or less integrated motivational and cognitive universe, a dynamic center of awareness, emotion, judgment, and action organized into a distinctive whole and set contrastively both against other such wholes and against a social and natural background is, however incorrigible it may seem to us, a rather peculiar idea within the context of the world's cultures.
>
> (229)

There are of course some challenging philosophical questions that might be addressed in this context (concerning, for instance, whether these variations are commensurable or incommensurable, whether they reflect different sociocultural emphases, whether they are 'variations on a theme', and so on), but for the sake of proceeding, let us assume that Geertz is correct to claim that the concept of the self we ourselves hold is, to some extent, culturally-bound.

What are the implications of this point? Among other things, what Geertz is telling us here is that the sort of project Augustine has set for himself – indeed the sort of project that is at the very heart of his book, concerned as it is to articulate certain notable features of selfhood – might be wholly unthinkable elsewhere. Thus, even while recognizing the great historical distance that separates Augustine from ourselves, there is again the need to recognize that we share certain assumptions – about this 'bounded, unique, more or less integrated motivational and cognitive universe' – that would be alien to certain other peoples. This in no way invalidates our endeavor or renders it unimportant; it simply means that the particular entity under consideration is a (somewhat) 'local' one. I can therefore state, quite unequivocally, that by and large the present book is not about 'human nature' per se; it is rather about human culture and the forms its expressions assume.

A word of clarification is in order here. To frame the issue of selfhood in the manner I just have is emphatically not to claim that we 'merely' believe that we are these beings of whom Geertz speaks – as if we could just as easily adopt another system of beliefs altogether. The fact is, we *are* these beings: they are implicated in virtually everything we think and everything we do. Most of us, therefore, have faith in the existence of our selves, and we carry this faith along with us wherever we go. Concomitant with this abiding faith in our selves, moreover, is the faith we also place in our own histories, seeing them, once more, as perhaps the most suitable means of accounting for these selves: when asked who and what we are and how we might have gotten that way, we ordinarily turn to our personal pasts for possible answers. Far from being a merely arbitrary choice, this is precisely how it must be, at least for now. The idea of the self, as we have come to know it, and the idea of history are in fact mutually constitutive.

To take but one example of a quite different brand of faith, for the Trobriand Islanders, as Lee (1959) has written, there apparently is no firm boundary between past and present. Whereas we tend to arrange events and objects 'in a sequence which is climactic, in size and intensity, in emotional meaning, or according to some other principle', for the Trobriander 'there is no developmental arrangement, no building up of emotional tone . . . stories have no plot, no lineal development, no climax' (116). As strange as it may seem, by all indications there simply is no 'history' or 'development' for the Trobriander; they are not meaningful categories of understanding. Thus, whatever selves they believe themselves to be are accounted for in ways that are entirely different from our own. Numerous other examples illustrating these sorts of ideas could be brought forth,[3] but the point is probably clear enough. One of the conditions of possibility for Augustine's life historical endeavor, along with our own, is a concept of self that necessitates it.

Let me bring some of these ideas together by suggesting that a life history, rather than being a 'natural' way of accounting for the self, is one that is thoroughly enmeshed within a specific and unique form of discourse and understanding. As such, it is but one among numerous possible modes of conceiving of and accounting for the self. By way of offering a disclaimer of sorts here, I am not suggesting that 'nature' is completely irrelevant to our concerns. Nor am I suggesting that there are no common denominators whatsoever between these different possible modes. It may well be, for instance, that people all the world over will seek to place their experience within a narrative order of *some* sort – even if this narrative order is seen, perhaps, in terms of what is timeless and eternal rather than time-bound and finite[4] – for the sake of 'containing' their experience in a meaningful way. What I am suggesting instead, quite simply, is that the self with which Augustine as well as we ourselves are concerned is constituted, defined, and articulated through its *history*. Hence the first dimension of the history–memory–narrative triad we are now considering.

What we also see in Augustine's account, along with any and all other autobiographical reflections, is the primacy of *memory*. Indeed, we might even go so far as to say that the process of self-understanding is itself fundamentally recollective, taken here in the sense of gathering together again those dimensions of selfhood that had heretofore gone unarticulated or had been scattered, dispersed, or lost. Referring once more to Gusdorf (1980), 'An examination of consciousness limited to the present moment will give me only a fragmentary cutting from my personal being without guarantee that it will continue. In recounting my history', however, 'I take the longest path, but this path that goes round my life leads me the more surely from me to myself. The recapitulation of ages of existence, of landscapes and encounters, obliges me to situate what I am in the perspective of what I have been', while my sense of unity as a self – 'this is the law of gathering and of understanding in all the acts that have been mine, all the faces and all the places where I have recognized signs and witness of my destiny'. In the immediacy of the present, Gusdorf continues, 'the agitation of things ordinarily surrounds me too much for me to be able to see it in its entirety': I am living episodes, it might be said, but I do not yet know the plot of the story to which they belong.[5] 'Memory', however, 'gives me a certain remove and allows me to take into consideration all the ins and outs of the matter, its context in time and space', just as 'an aerial view sometimes reveals to an archeologist the direction of a road or a fortification or the map of a city invisible to someone on the ground' (38). Memory, therefore, which often has to do not merely with recounting the past but with making sense of it – from 'above', as it were – is an interpretive act the end of which is an enlarged understanding of the self.[6]

Consider what Augustine aims to do in writing his confessions: More than merely documenting in an objective and disinterested manner what happened when (a task for which the word 'chronicle' might be more suitable than the word 'history'), his aim is to provide us with an interpretive account of the movement of his life, precisely for the sake of trying to understand, through this very process of writing, who and what he is all about. Two corollaries follow from this point. The first is that had he merely written a chronicle of past experiences rather than a history, these experiences themselves would need to have been 're-presented' in all of the openness and uncertainty that had initially surrounded them; all that would have been said is 'and then', 'and then', 'and then' (and so on), as if he had no idea at all of the whole of which these episodes were a part. The second corollary is that if his aim was at all to try to *understand* the past, this merely re-presentative or re-productive task could not possibly have helped him to do so. For what possible understanding, what possible knowledge, could emerge in this disinterested process of documenting what was?

There is one further interesting – and, for some, perhaps troubling – implication to be drawn from the ideas we are discussing. To the extent that one's aim is in fact an enlarged understanding of self, it is ipso facto the case that this cannot possibly be accomplished by recounting one's previous experience 'as it was'. What this means, of course, is that life historical knowledge, in so far as it is predicated on understanding rather than the retrieval of isolated facts, should never – indeed can never – be judged according to its 'correspondence' with what was; as a matter of course, it is a going-beyond what was, an attempt to situate the experiences of the past in a comprehensive interpretive context, such that their interrelationship is made evident. But if in fact the telling of a life history is, by definition, *not* a recounting of experience as it was, then what exactly is it? Is it ultimately to be seen, as was suggested in Chapter 1, as a fiction, an imaginative – even imaginary – story we weave out of those tangled threads we believe to be responsible for the texture of our lives?

On a very broad level, I suppose the answer to this question could be 'Yes', if only in the sense – the rather simplistic sense – that virtually *all* interpretations are fictions: to make sense of a text, whether it is the text of one's past or some other one, is precisely a process of creating a framework, an interpretive context, within which the relevant information may be placed; it is, again, a going-beyond this information, an attempt to confer a measure of order and coherence upon it. Furthermore, when considering autobiographical texts, texts for which the interpreter is at once reader and writer, subject and object, it becomes even more clear that the meanings one arrives at are in some sense as much *made* as *found*, the process of autobiographical reflection being a fundamentally metaphorical one: a new relationship is being created between the past and present, a new poetic configuration, designed to give greater form to one's previous – and present – experience.[7] The text of the self is thus being rewritten.[8]

Now implicit in what has been said above is the idea that this new relationship being created between the past and present occurs *in* the present, in the moment of writing: the 'ending' we are, therefore, determines both the beginning and indeed the essential nature of how we came to be.[9] Doesn't this further testify to the fictionality of the resultant account? According to Gusdorf (1980), the 'difficulty' we are now considering is insurmountable: no trick of presentation even when assisted by genius can prevent the narrator from always knowing the outcome of the story he tells – he commences, in a manner of speaking, with the problem already solved. Moreover the illusion begins from the moment that the narrative *confers a meaning* on the event which, when it actually occurred, no doubt had several meanings or perhaps none. This postulating of a meaning dictates the choice of the facts to be retained and of the details to bring out or dismiss according to the demands of the preconceived intelligibility. It is here that the failures, the gaps, and the deformations of memory find their origin.

(42)

Far from being due to 'purely physical cause' or chance, 'they are the result of the option of the writer who remembers and wants to gain acceptance for this or that revised and corrected version of his past, his private reality' (42). The implication? We must, Gusdorf suggests, 'give up the pretence of objectivity, abandoning a sort of false scientific attitude that would judge a work by the precision of its detail' (42).

In certain respects, I couldn't agree more with what Gusdorf has to say here; as we have already noted, autobiographical texts, in so far as they aim toward an enlarged understanding of the past by 'revising' and 'correcting' it, cannot be judged by either the precision of their detail or, again, by their correspondence to what was. Gusdorf, however, who has spoken of 'difficulty', 'illusion', and so forth, and who urges us to 'give up the pretence of objectivity' in our consideration of these texts, seems somewhat reconciled to the idea of treating them as fictions, as imaginative and often artful personal creations that cannot adequately be understood with 'that false scientific attitude' which is so characteristic of contemporary thinking.[10]

But there seems to be a contradiction here. Doesn't the language of difficulty and illusion issue from exactly that attitude of which Gusdorf speaks? And doesn't the idea of fiction, taken in the sense of 'imaginary' or even 'false', as it often is, rely through and through on a reified and 'substantialistic' (see Costa-Lima 1984) conception of reality itself – in this case, of that which autobiographical texts cannot pretend to disclose? While it is unquestionably true that autobiographical texts do not and cannot reveal the past 'as it was', and while it is also true that some people may indeed weave fictions about themselves that clearly deserve the name of 'illusions', my own perspective on these issues is that these texts, far from *necessarily* falling prey to illusion, may in fact be quite real and (dare I say?) true. Indeed, didn't Gusdorf himself suggest that in virtue of the 'aerial view' from which these texts are written, they may in some sense be even *truer* than immediate experience? Why call a 'revised and corrected version of the past' an illusion or a fiction?

Let us consider a most basic phenomenological fact in this context. Nearly every moment of which I am consciously aware is followed by another one, and if I reflect back on what I was just experiencing but a few seconds ago I find that it has acquired a different edge, a different sense about it: what had once been present has now become past. I may even be fashioning a kind of mini-narrative here, such that I am drawing connections between that earlier experience and the present one, a connection that is only made possible by this present experience itself. But is there anything 'illusory' about this? Am I engaging in a deceptive trick by reading the past in light of the present? Or am I simply existing in time, thinking about what was in the only way I possibly can, which is from the standpoint of now?

The point I am trying to make is simply this: if we think of 'truth' in this context only in terms of its faithful correspondence to what was, then autobiographical texts must indeed be deemed illusory and fictional; in relying on the vantage point of the present for their very sense, it could be held that truth is, of necessity, out of the question. But there is little reason, I will suggest, to think of truth in this limited and simplistic way. Can we not say, in fact, that the reality of living in time requires narrative reflection and that narrative reflection, in turn, opens the way toward a more comprehensive and expansive conception of truth itself?

Perhaps if we knew that the immediate moments we were living could never be surpassed and rewritten we would live a bit more freely and easily. We would no longer have to be humble about the tentativeness of present meanings and, more generally, we would no longer have to concern ourselves with our condition as finite, historical beings. We would know, in short, that each one of these moments was perfectly adequate to itself, and that no matter what came along later, there would never exist the need to revise and correct. Narration would thus be essentially unnecessary; it would be a luxury or a hobby perhaps, a game to play when upon growing tired of our securities we toyed with what it might conceivably mean to look backward over the terrain of the past and experience the illusion of recollective understanding. But there is, of course, something decidedly illusory about the very picture that is being drawn here. In relegating autobiographical texts to the status of mere fictions, we not only cut ourselves off from the possibility of attaining those insights that can accrue from the process of rewriting the self; we cut ourselves off from the possibility of thinking about historical truth itself in a deeper and more comprehensive way than is often allowed.

What we have seen in these last several pages, in any case, is that the *history* one tells, via *memory*, assumes the form of a *narrative* of the past that charts the trajectory of how one's self came to be. It is time now to make these ideas specific by exploring in some detail the story of a life.

'ORIGINS'

Confessions begins by addressing God, with a declaration of faith as well as a proclamation of thanks for having provided a world in which the infant Augustine might thrive. Back in those days, 'all I knew was how to suck, and how to lie still when my body sensed comfort or cry when it felt pain' (25). Beyond these most basic dimensions of his early life, he notes, there is not much more that can be said; much about those years is beyond memory's reach. Yet even then – as Augustine knows now – he was living in the glory of care and love: 'All this I have learned since then', he says, 'because all the gifts you have given to me, both spiritual and material, proclaim the truth of it' (25). Notice right away that Augustine, from the very beginning of his text, has in mind the 'ending' he has become: a man who has seen the light of God and who, consequently, could look back on his life and see how it had been orchestrated by forces unseen and unknown at the time. The child of God whom he sees, therefore, as he gazes backward under the spell of revelation, is none other than his rewritten self.

As for Augustine's boyhood, it seemed to be a quite normal one, filled with the various and sundry 'noxious pleasures' to which we are all exposed. He nonetheless fared well in his studies, in mastering the art of rhetoric, and in besting his peers in contests demanding intellectual expertise. In all of these affairs, however, he was merely swimming with the tide, succumbing to the lure of others' earthly commands, for he believed that 'the right way to live was to do as they wished' (39). To foreshadow an issue we will be taking up later on, particularly in the final chapter of this book, Augustine is here admitting that he had been 'constructed' back then strictly in accordance with the expectations of others, as if there was no other possible mode of existence than that which They (as in Heidegger's *das Man* (1962)) were advocating; he was living a narrative that others wrote. What we can also see is that this situation would in fact change at some point in the future. For how could Augustine identify his former mindlessness unless he had moved beyond it? Or, put another way, how could he identify his former psychological stasis and spiritual immobility unless he had subsequently *developed* in some way?

The fact of the matter is, Augustine continues, 'I was blind to the whirlpool of debasement in which I had been plunged away from the sight of your eyes. For in your eyes nothing could be more debased than I was then, since I was troublesome even to the people whom I set out to please' (39). What did this child of God do to be so troublesome? He lied to people so he could go out and play, he stole things, he even cheated when he played games with his friends, and for no other reason than his vain desire to win. When *they* cheated, of course, he was furious; but when they accused him of the same, he lost control completely. 'Can this be the innocence of childhood?' (40). No wonder he's confessing!

Even back then, however, there were some hints (would that he had seen them more clearly) of the divine. 'For even as a child', he writes, 'I existed, I was alive, I had the power of feeling; I had an instinct to keep myself safe and sound, to preserve my own being, which was a trace of the single unseen Being from whom it was derived' (40). Moreover, he could find 'pleasure in the truth', even in the little things that occupied his thoughts. But it was all too easy to bury these things, to lose sight of them, whatever intimations of the truth they might provide.

Augustine was avowedly another lost soul, 'inflamed with desire for a surfeit of hell's pleasures' (43). As he moved toward adolescence a crude admixture of love and lust began to 'seethe' within him. God, meanwhile, was letting all of these indulgences, carnal and otherwise, slide: 'I was tossed and spilled, floundering in the broiling sea of my fornication, and you said no word . . . You were silent then, and I went on my way, farther and farther from you, proud in my distress and restless in fatigue, sowing more and more seeds whose only crop was grief' (44). As for what his parents were thinking during all of this, their main concern was that he become still better at rhetoric, the world they all inhabited being 'drunk with the invisible wine of its own perverted, earthbound will' (45). The one exception to this drunken debauchery was Augustine's mother, who was apparently beginning to think that her reckless teenage son was getting a bit carried away with his depravity, as he was. For when did he feel most ashamed of himself? Only when he was being less depraved than his friends.

Being the normal teenager he was, his tendency was to ignore her admonitions; they struck him as silly and 'womanish'. Little did he know that she was the very voice of God, showing him that he was straying, far, from the true way. The clincher was when he and his fellow 'ruffians' stole pears from a neighbor's tree, not even to eat but to throw to the local pigs. Given the man he has become – and we will soon see what sort of man this is – it is hard to believe he could once have been so careless and dissolute. His recollections are thus suffused with humility and shame, and although he would rather not have had to tell this tawdry story, he knows he must, if only as an example to the countless others who may be inclined to stray from the fold. 'Can anyone unravel this twisted tangle of knots? I shudder to look at it or think of such abomination' (52).

Augustine's 'cauldron of lust' continued to hiss unabated. He began to be attracted by the theater too, his aim being to see his own pathetic misery mirrored, even if illusorily, by actors on a stage. It was still premature, apparently, to feel real sorrow; it was preferable instead to immerse himself in the imaginary, to witness suffering that he himself would not have to endure. He was fortunate enough to behave a bit more 'quietly' than an infamous group of hoodlums that went by the sonorous name of the 'Wreckers', but he knows full well that he wasn't far behind. 'How infinite is your mercy, my God!' (58). It was remarkable that he had been permitted to continue moving through this mockery of a life.

His rescue seems to have begun with the reading of Cicero's *Hortensius*, a philosophy book that was the first to impress him not for its form but its substance. 'All my empty dreams suddenly lost their charm and my heart began to throb with a bewildering passion for the wisdom of eternal truth' (58). He had somehow been exposed by reading this book, the fullness of its words revealing to him for the very first time the illusory and superficial void he had been living; he was jarred awake. Augustine therefore began to gain a glimpse of the world beyond appearance and to develop a love of wisdom itself, 'whatever it might be', and 'to search for it, pursue it, hold it, and embrace it firmly' (59). Nevertheless, this glimpse did not quite suffice to take Augustine where he needed to go; it was too easy, he found, to bury himself in the deepest of philosophers' words and still miss the Truth. His mother still had some serious praying to do. Indeed, it was all she could do; her entreaties had thus far come to naught.

There were a few minor consolations during this time. Yes, he was teaching rhetoric, but at least he did it honestly. Yes, he lived with a woman who was not his lawful wedded wife, but at least he was faithful to her. There were some intimations, therefore, that although Augustine was rather rotten, it wasn't quite to the core. But it would nonetheless take no small amount of time for him to see the errors of his ways. He even studied astrology for a while, thinking that perhaps there was something to it; he was desperately reaching for anything at all that might serve to deliver him from his burgeoning sense of unease in the world, an unease that was compounded by the sudden death of his closest friend. The profound emptiness he had been living through for virtually his entire life had at least become palpable enough to incite him to do something about it. Augustine thus managed to take what might be considered the first moment of the process of development, namely that of recognizing that there exists an experiential rift that must be addressed in some fashion, a disjunction between what is and what might be (see Freeman and Robinson 1990). But this was only the most rudimentary beginning of what proved to be an extraordinarily painful, harrowing ordeal.

TO CAST OUT ONE'S DEMONS

The task still remained to identify just what the nature of this disjunction was. Something was amiss, that much was clear enough, but it was unclear what. Augustine was alternately noble and base, sincere and insincere, good and bad, happy and sad: 'How can one soul contain within itself feelings so much at variance, in such conflict with each other? How does it balance them in the scale?' Why couldn't he put his life in order? 'Man is a great mystery, Lord' (84). Even those books he read with pleasure, books that appeared to shed light on the various phenomena of the world, managed to lead him further and further astray. 'I had my back to the light and my face was turned towards the things which it illumined, so that my eyes, by which I saw the things which stood in the light, were themselves in darkness' (88). It was inconceivable that God could be the source of this light: ensnared in the conviction that the world was composed fundamentally of matter, God emerged as little more than a seemingly 'bright, unbounded body', an amorphous *thing* suspended in earthly space.

At the age of 29, and still hungry for that dose of existential comfort that would serve to quell his anxious soul, Augustine came under the spell of Manichean religion, swayed especially by the reputation of a bishop Faustus, who was thought to be among the wisest in the land. Augustine, however, who had already gotten a taste of wisdom, however small and ephemeral, knew soon enough that although Faustus was to be commended for his candor and his modesty, he was a far cry from the real thing. Here again there is evidence that while he did not yet know what specific direction his life *should* take, Augustine was nonetheless becoming more and more aware of the direction it shouldn't take. As he looks back on the past from the standpoint of the present, therefore – the present in which he is writing these confessions, giving form and shape to what had no doubt seemed at the time to be a restless vagrancy, tempered by sporadic but short-lived convictions in this or that system of belief – it is plainly clear that God's providence was responsible for preventing his following those potential life paths that would culminate in dead ends. God was thus using Augustine's stubborn perversity and dissoluteness at this time in order to clear a space for the possibility of his finding a path that would finally get him somewhere real.

How did Augustine understand this perversity and dissoluteness after all these years? 'I preferred to excuse myself', he admits, 'and blame this unknown thing which was in me but was not a part of me'. He proceeded to engage, in other words, in a kind of projection process, disavowing his own propensity toward evil by considering it as an alien intruder over whom he was powerless; he divided himself into two, me and not-me, in order to cushion the blow of the possibility that he himself was a less than wonderful fellow. 'The truth, of course', he eventually realized, 'was that it was all my own self, and my own impiety had divided me against myself' (103). In psychoanalytic terms, Augustine had managed to acquire certain psychic defenses along the road of his sorry life, which served to provide that pernicious blanket of security that often keeps us hopelessly in the dark about who and what we are. Notice here as well that he is only able to identify these defenses in retrospect, after they have become stripped away. Needless to say perhaps, this is how it must be; for to be able to identify defenses as they are being employed would be precisely to rob them of their power.

Augustine's first truly 'fatal mistake', in any case, was this lingering belief that God was to be understood as a body, 'limited within the dimension of limbs like our own' (104), for his wrongheaded conception of evil, which he also saw as a kind of substance – 'a shapeless, hideous mass, which might be solid' – followed in tow. The conflict between good and evil was therefore construed as one between 'two antagonistic masses', a battle of the giants in which good (God) would, it was hoped, prove to be the stronger of the two. This conflict suffocated Augustine, bringing him to just that state of spiritual anoxia that would continue to send him reeling dizzily through his divided existence: 'Under the weight of these two masses, I gasped for the pure, clear air of your truth', but, sorry to say, he could as yet 'draw no breath of it' (106). In fact, he was beginning to lose hope, his assumption being that perhaps this path that he so wished to find was destined, like all the others, to lead nowhere.

If there was any ray of light at all during this period of his life, it was that Catholicism was turning out to be not so bad after all, especially as compared to such 'rigmarole' as the Manichees were spouting. A bit more positively, he went so far at this time as to consider the Catholic side 'unbeaten'; it couldn't easily be falsified by the other doctrines he had encountered and thus it was still very much in the running as far as being the most suitable 'system' for him to adopt. At the same time, however, he also felt that the status of being unbeaten was by no means equivalent to that of being 'victorious', the upshot of this rather maddening race being that the faith he was beginning to adopt, by default, was all too tenuous and fragile. At least his parents could take some solace in the fact that this wayward young man, who had been a thief and a scoundrel, among other things, was keeping up appearances. What's more, Augustine writes, 'even if I had not yet grasped the truth', being 'rescued from falsehood' (111) was no small accomplishment. He had thus moved on to a second moment of the developmental process, one which might be referred to as 'distanciation' (see Ricoeur 1981), which we can think of simply in terms of the need for divesting oneself of those modes of experience that, by virtue of their inadequacy, have prevented one from moving forward as readily as one might. To realize what one is not, while surely being a step in the right direction, is of course only a part of the developmental process. The far more arduous task of realizing what one is still remained.

LIVING IN THE MATERIAL WORLD

In the continued absence of some form of genuine faith in which to live, Augustine grew to be plagued by a profound sense of doubt. This is telling in itself, especially in relation to our earlier consideration of faith. For what we see here is that doubt and skepticism — as concerns the knowledge we allegedly *cannot* have, the truths we *cannot* attain, the selves we *cannot* be, and so forth — rely on a kind of anomie, a rootlessness and perhaps even a sense of disintegration at the very heart of things. Stated another way, one does not ordinarily doubt for purely philosophical reasons; one doubts because the tenuousness and fragility of the world call for it in some way. Along these lines, isn't it again possible to see in many of the intellectual battles presently being waged just that lack of faith in the steadiness of the world that can sometimes lead us to the conclusion that this world is somehow *by nature* shaky?

This is not the only reason for doubt, however. What is also often operative, in Augustine's case as well as in our own, is the fact that once the world becomes conceived fundamentally in terms of *matter*, alone — such that we are nothing more, ultimately, than physical bodies colliding in space, we hope according to some determinate principles at least — it becomes extraordinarily difficult to find an opening for those spirited concerns within which most of us exist. Can a being who is nothing more than a body traversing space ever bring forth a justifiable reason to be moral rather than immoral, to be good rather than bad, to love rather than hate? And can any of the allegedly wondrous things we surround ourselves with

– poetry, art, religion, philosophy – be anything more than merely human constructions, material things issuing from bodies, living in the material world? As I suggested a while back, there is a curious irony at work in these issues. For it may very well be that the contemporary refusal on the part of some to give credence to the 'self' or the 'subject' stems in part from an unwillingness – or inability – to conceive of them in other than predominantly materialistic terms: behaving bodies, the termini of language, culture, society, history, and so on. But there is a further question to be raised in this context. What sort of being is it who asks the sorts of questions that have just been raised? This, of course, is exactly what Augustine was trying to find out. Implicit, therefore, in the very question of whether indeed it might be useful to consider the possibility of a world *beyond* matter were the faint outlines of an answer.

His doubt was reaching a fever pitch. 'Anxiety about what I could believe as certain gnawed at my heart all the more sharply as I grew more and more ashamed that I had been misled and deluded by promises of certainty for so long, and had talked wildly, like an ignorant child, about so many unconfirmed theories as though they were beyond question' (115). Note what is happening here: Augustine's anxiety about certainty is being compounded by his shame in being duped by the falsity of these theories' promises. But what this means, we should recognize, is that certainty is by no means absent in this context: he is more than certain that he has been deluded. Can delusion be predicated without non-delusion?

Despite being on the way to recovery, Augustine was suffering essentially from a lack of trust; this earlier self, he writes, could be compared to a man who has been to so many bad doctors that when a good one comes along he can hardly be recognized. This too bespoke psychic defenses on his part: having been poisoned by illusion, he was reluctant to move forward, for fear that it might occur yet again.

When one took the time to think about it, though, there were a great many things that depended on trust. 'I began to realize', Augustine writes, 'that I believed countless things which I had never seen or which had taken place when I was not there to see – so many events in the history of the world, so many facts about places and towns which I had never seen, and so much that I believed on the word of friends or doctors or other people'. What would existence be like without these beliefs? 'Unless we took things on trust, we should accomplish absolutely nothing in this life' (117). The bottom line is, while we can surely flirt with skepticism in moments of philosophical reverie, Augustine reminds us that it is no easy task to live this way. Unless we are certain that the ground on which we walk is more or less stable and secure, we will be hesitant to take even the smallest step.

In addition to the more mundane certainties that Augustine became cognizant of, there was also the indubitable reality of death. It was a good thing he kept this in mind too, for in the midst of all of his existential quandaries he was still leading a dissolute life in his spare time; and this might have become a full-time occupation, he suggests, had it not been for his fear of the grim reaper and the consequences to follow (i.e. burning in hell evermore). Even though he wasn't living in faith quite yet, he had probably heard enough about eternal damnation to try to keep his impulses in check once in a while.

But it was Augustine's conviction in the materiality of the world and of God (even if His was a materiality like no other) that prevented him from carrying through the project he had begun. This conviction did begin to be shaken loose, however. Assuming for instance that God doesn't have a definite bodily shape but permeates all that is – Augustine could at least go this far in his consideration of the issue – there would still be some definite problems. Does an elephant have more God in it than a sparrow? The other issue that proved to be rather thorny for Augustine was that of evil. How could one sensibly account for its presence and still believe in a good and incorruptible God? The problem was not only a theological one but a psychological one as well. For if God wasn't responsible for evil, that must mean that *we* are. And this did not sit too well with Augustine. So *could* God be responsible for evil? A rather blasphemous question even to raise.

It finally dawned on Augustine that since God only made good things and since evil clearly did exist, it must not be a 'thing' at all, but rather a 'perversion of the will' that happens when we turn away from God's truth. So all is well and good: Augustine is starting to make a bit of headway into both the materiality issue and the question of the origin of evil, he loves God like he never has before, he sees that there exists a true eternity of truth, and he even begins to think about the soul, which takes the information we get through our senses and creates for us a coherent and sometimes beautiful world. Well, then, why wasn't he putting these ideas into practice?

Augustine remained betwixt and between, his rational consideration of these matters not quite sufficing to permit him to *live* his beliefs: 'Though I was thwarted by my wish to know more, I was conscious of what it was that my mind was too clouded to see' (152). During this phase of his development, he tells us, he not only began to see what is not but was beginning to acquire a sense of what is, even if in somewhat intellectualized form. He had therefore moved on to what can be regarded as a third phase of his developmental process, namely one of articulation; he had succeeded in giving a greater measure of form, definition, and clarity to the direction in which he knew he must proceed. What was still missing, however, was the motivation to go ahead and do what needed to be done: even with the lure of truth awaiting him in the future, it seemed that he couldn't bear to let go of his past, in all of its terrible comfort and security.

How strange it is, he must have said to himself, that even when we know beyond all shadow of a doubt where it is we need go to carry through the projects of our lives, we often find that there still remain unnamable forces keeping us back, lulling us into repetition. The only saving grace Augustine can see in retrospect was that by holding off on his finding and living the true path during this period of stasis and stagnation, the tension mounting all the while, it would be that much sweeter and more intense when he finally hit his stride. 'For the firmer our enemy the devil holds a man in his power, and the greater the number of others whom he holds captive through this man, the greater the victory when he is won back' (163). Augustine's suffering, as an integral part of the dialectical march of his redemption, will ultimately be seen, like a tortuous climb up a dangerous mountain, to have been well worthwhile. Indeed, it will have been necessary. If anything at all had become clear to him, it was that there were no short cuts to salvation.

KNOWLEDGE AND ACTION

Despite his intense longing to free himself from the shackles of his sordid past, Augustine found that he was unable to do so. He was well along the way; for that much he could be thankful.

> But the new will which had come to life in me and made me wish to serve you freely and enjoy you, my God, who are our only certain joy, was not yet strong enough to overcome the old, hardened as it was by the passage of time. So these two wills within me, one old, one new, one the servant of the flesh, the other of the spirit, were in conflict and between them they tore my soul apart.
>
> (164)

As Freud might have put it, this was a serious case of resistance. It simply isn't easy to give up one's old self, no matter how neurotically enchained one knows it to be. But why is this so? Why is it that even when every bit of evidence we can gather indicates clearly where we ought to be heading – a new job, a new mate, a new *self* – we often find ourselves paralyzed? Perhaps it is the death instinct that is responsible, a tendency to bask inertly in the confines of the given. It could also be, however, that this sort of paralysis, rather than representing an attempt to seek death – a death in life – is instead a way of avoiding it: no one likes to witness the death of a loved one, particularly if it is oneself. A bit more mundanely, could a man like Augustine really give up a life of wine and women for a life of chaste abstinence?

He is very honest about his situation: 'I could no longer claim', he writes, 'that I had no clear perception of the truth – the excuse which I used to make to myself for postponing my renunciation of the world and my entry into your service – for by now I was quite certain of it'. Nevertheless, 'Instead of fearing, as I ought, to be held back by all that encumbered me, I was frightened to be free of it'. He thus 'bore the burden of the world as contentedly as one sometimes bears a heavy load of sleep', and the fact that 'everyone rightly agrees that it is better to be awake' didn't much matter. 'Soon', he would say, 'Presently', 'Let me wait a little longer' (165). What a sluggard he was! Sleeping away his life, day in and day out. And let's not forget that even when he wasn't sleeping he would more than likely still be found in bed, the 'fetters of lust' not yet having been cast aside. 'Give me chastity and continence', he would pray, 'but not yet' (169).

Things were different. Whereas he used to turn a blind eye to himself, able to forget all too quickly the sacred vows he had made, enough had been happening (he had read some more books, met some more wise men, and so on) for him finally to appear 'naked' before himself, which left him with 'burning shame' over his deceit and inability to act; his old self, its arguments now exhausted, was 'silent and afraid'. He had even heard a story about a couple of men, with a lot less schooling than he himself had, who were able to 'stand up and storm the gates of heaven' (170), kicking away their earthly concerns and ascending into the heights of the divine. It was enough to make him boil in anger and self-hatred: 'I was beside myself with madness that would bring me sanity. I was dying a death that would bring me life' (171). He even went so far as to tear his hair out and beat his forehead with his fists. How is it that when the mind tells the body to do something it usually complies but when the mind tells *itself* to do something it often doesn't? Why doesn't it follow its own orders? The reason is, the orders could not have been fully given. Half bald and black and blue from his own merciless attack upon himself, Augustine was just too 'weighed down by habit' (172) – a counter-will battling against the will-to-truth – to pry himself loose from his old moorings. It was unfortunate that he had to abandon the evil-as-alien-substance defense; it really might have been useful during this painful time.

What eventually happened after this frightening attack, a 'great storm' having eventually broken within him, was that Augustine heard a child singing 'Take it and read, take it and read' (177), at which point, his book of Scripture laying close by, he did just that, reading the first passage upon which his eyes fell. What this passage said, in brief, was that it was high time that he stop being so lazy, profligate, and self-indulgent and dedicate himself to the Lord. As for his response, 'it was as though the light of confidence flooded into my heart and all the darkness of doubt was dispelled' (178). Finally! Augustine's mind was at last free, except of course from the memories that would remain with him and which would cause him to remain forever humble about his past. 'For there had been shadows and lies in the phantasms I had taken for the truth, and the memory of my past wrung many loud cries of sorrow from my lips' (187). There was no mistaking the source of the evil within which he had existed; it derived from himself and no other. Perhaps in time he would help all those other 'deaf corpses' out there, struggling to find their way in the world.

In this last, and final, moment of his development — with 'final' in this context meaning not the absolute end of a finite process, but the temporary culmination of an infinite one, an ending and a beginning, in one — Augustine had managed to resolve the conflict between his old and new selves in such a way that the latter gained ascendancy. Referring again to Ricoeur (1981), we might call this final moment of development 'appropriation'; after having articulated both the falsity of his previous vision and the truth of his present one, he had made the difference between the two his own through action — through practicing, as the saying goes, what he had been preaching. It is never enough, Augustine has told us, merely to know one's proper direction in life. As many of us have learned, knowledge without action is perhaps even more tragic, and certainly more painful, than the most profound ignorance. What needs to happen, in addition, is that one's own realizations and ends must somehow be woven into the fabric of subjectivity. Only then, when the mind has followed its own orders, will one be in possession of that sort of whole and undivided self which is able to step, undaunted, into the future.

RETROSPECTS AND PROSPECTS

As I have suggested above, the developmental process Augustine has undergone, far from being a terminal one leading to an absolute end, is at once a culmination and a new beginning; at the same time that he has appropriated the truth by living it, he has broken through the power of repetition and thus allowed himself to move forward, into a superior region of existence. There is a kind of paradox here, however. It is that this forward movement, to which we have given the name of development, is being predicated through memory, as Augustine looks back over the course of his life: prospects have emerged in retrospect. Is the idea of development, then, a fundamentally *retrospective* idea, founded on the basis of recollection, broadly taken? The answer, I am prepared to say, is 'Yes'. Is there any other way of talking about development than through the story of its process? And doesn't the 'end' of development, in this case Augustine's leap into faith, determine the meaning and significance of all that has led up to it? As I suggested in the previous chapter, had Augustine *not* been able to make the leap into faith, there really wouldn't have been much of a story to tell. There would merely have been an aimless and rather obsessive young man, who had made a few interesting discoveries about himself but who ultimately went nowhere. Fortunately, things turned out otherwise, and in place of what more than likely would have been no story at all, we have instead this passionate tale of coming into being.

Let us recount briefly the developmental trajectory Augustine has sketched for us. The first phase of his developmental process – the phase that has had conferred upon it the status of a beginning to the story he is about to tell – was that of *recognition*: stated simply, he came to realize, however dimly, that all was not well in his life, that there was a disjunction of sorts between the existence he was living and the one he might. By all indications, this is indeed the first phase of virtually all developmental processes, whether of the large-scale sort that Augustine has undergone – which may be seen as a kind of life project – or of those 'smaller' processes that we each undergo in making the transition from an inadequate mode of existence to a better one. What the foremost task is at this point, therefore, is precisely to determine just what it is about our present mode of experience that is inadequate. We need to gather together – to recollect – who and what we are and have been, toward the end of identifying the source of our alienation.

Now if in fact we do not succeed in identifying this source – if, that is, we simply go on, living as we have done – the story of development will already have been brought to an abrupt end; no future consequences will have conferred upon our malaise the dignity of a beginning, a provocation to work things through. In this first moment alone, then, there is already in evidence some two-way temporal traffic: we are speaking at once about what was, then and there, as well as about its rewritten meaning and significance, which emerges in line with the entire narrative of which it is a part. We thus find ourselves right smack in the middle of what is sometimes called the 'hermeneutic circle', where parts are read through the whole and the whole is read through the parts at one and the same time. What we also find, of course, is that the concept of development as such can only be predicated inside this very circle. How else would we know when a given story of development began except with reference to its outcome?

The second phase of Augustine's developmental process, which we call *distanciation*, had to do with both identifying tentatively the nature of his specific problems and conflicts, most of which seemed to be centered on his stubborn conviction in the materiality of the world, and with somehow 'separating' himself from them. As we said at the time, this was the period of his life when he began to see what he did *not* believe in, what he did not want to live and be. This second phase may also be seen as being intrinsic to the process of development as we are considering it here. This is because for every instance of self-gain, of moving forward into a new and superior region of existence, there is also inevitably self-loss: we must distance ourselves from that dimension of our lives that has been found wanting and see if there is a better way. Framed in more traditional developmental psychological terms, we are talking in this context about differentiation, a separation of self from self, such that the text of one's experience becomes transformed into an object of interpretation.

As Augustine's autobiography readily testifies, however, this task of beginning to 'name' one's inadequacies or determine what one is not, while integral to the process of development, is by no means the end of it. What must now occur in this third phase of development is *articulation*: of both the difference between one's old self and the one presently being projected as a future possibility, and of this projected self itself. In Augustine's case, the way this was manifested was in his realization of the truth about where he needed to go if he was to resolve the conflicts before him. At this point, he came to see quite clearly what sort of self he had to become; he had to not only distance himself from his old ways, but destroy them, leaving behind the countless lures of profane, earthly existence and commencing a life of true faith. There was no question whatsoever about the preferability of his projected self; the writing was on the wall. The only task that remained, therefore, was for Augustine to take what he now knew, indubitably, and put it into action.

In his final phase of development, that of *appropriation*, he did just that: having listened to the voice of the child bidding him to read, and having been urged miraculously by the Scriptures to change his evil ways, his knowledge became transformed into action, the result being that he had at last succeeded in calling a halt to his heretofore twisted life. Now appropriation, as we said earlier, may be seen as both an ending and a beginning: the former, in the sense of both the resolution of a conflict and the culmination of a project, and the latter, in the sense of freeing oneself from the stagnancy of repetition and thus opening the door to a new way of life. Along these lines, we can rightly say that Augustine, through this developmental process we have been discussing, has all but made himself over; he has taken the deformed self he had previously been and reconstructed it, thereby giving birth to a new and better one. This developmental movement, this shuttling back and forth between prospective and retrospective time, is precisely what is involved in the process of rewriting the self.

RECOLLECTION AND DEVELOPMENT

In his memory, Augustine writes, which is variously described as being like 'a great field', 'a spacious palace', 'a storehouse', and 'a vast cache', are 'the sky, the earth, and the sea, ready at my summons, together with everything I have ever perceived in them by my senses, except the things I have forgotten.' He also 'meets' himself as well: 'I remember myself and what I have done, when and where I did it, and the state of my mind at the time'. So far, he has offered us a classically materialistic conception of memory, the basic idea being that it is most aptly seen as a kind of container, a place, within which past experiences are kept. 'In my memory, too, are all the events that I remember', he continues, 'whether they are things that have happened to me or things that I have heard from others' (215).

Things are becoming a bit more ambiguous, it seems. As we will see in greater detail in the following chapter, memory now emerges as a fusion of our own past experience and texts of our own past experience supplied by others. *My* memory, in other words, may be thoroughly suffused with 'hearsay', which of course renders it somewhat more 'other' than Augustine had initially indicated. Furthermore, 'From the same source I can picture to myself all kinds of different images based either upon my own experience or upon *what I find credible because it tallies with my own experience*' (215, emphasis added). They can be fit into the 'general picture' of the past, and 'from them I can make a surmise of actions and events and hopes for the future' (215–16). Things are getting more complicated still. Who can plumb the depths of memory? he asks. Perhaps 'the mind is too narrow to contain itself entirely' (216). The mind's 'narrowness', it might be noted, is but one way of understanding this matter; given its finiteness, its limited capacities, it cannot quite capture its own interior workings. The other side of this, of course, is that the target of the capture – which is is also a part of mind – is too big and vast. So the mind, Augustine in effect maintains, is both too small and too large for total 'containment'. But might we not say, more appropriately, that the issue really isn't one of 'size' at all but is instead about the unsurpassability of interpretation, about the irrevocable need for *reading* the mind's contents, which, by their very nature, can never wholly be objectified?

Augustine himself moves in this direction. In addition to being conceived as a kind of container, filled with the inert artifacts of the past, he also conceives of memory as being composed of 'pictures', drawn in the present and comprised of both what he *knows* and what he *imagines*. All of this, he goes on to say, somehow gets 'fitted' into a 'general picture', which in turn projects itself into the contours of the future. So much for materialism! More important for present purposes, hasn't Augustine shown that one cannot possibly speak of either the self or of development apart from this 'general picture' one composes upon looking back from present to past? And isn't he himself also suggesting, in line with this general picture, that the issue is not so much the mind's 'narrowness' as it is its textual obscurity, its multiplicity of meaning? For all that Augustine's text embodies that 'metaphysics of presence' which many are interested in moving beyond, it also serves to undermine it at the very same time, keeping us in just that unsettled space between presence and absence within which, I suggest, we all dwell.

Consider again the word 'recollection' itself: while the 're' makes reference to the past, 'collection' makes reference to a present act, an act, as we put it earlier, of gathering together what might have been dispersed or lost. Framed another way, the word recollection holds within it reference to the two distinct ways we often speak about history: as the trail of past events or 'past presents' that have culminated in now and as the act of writing, the act of gathering them together, selectively and imaginatively, into a followable story. This in turn implies at least two things. First, without a trail of past events, there would be no story to tell. Second, without an act of the historical imagination, designed to give meaning and significance to these events and to glean the possible nexus of their interrelationship, there would be no past and indeed no *self*, but only a sequence of dispersed accidents.

Now following Foucault (e.g. 1973, 1977) and others (in developmental psychology, see, e.g. Gergen 1977, Neugarten 1969), there may be a great deal more that is accidental in both history in general and in our own life histories in particular than we might wish to avow. Perhaps we have reverted too often to a kind of wholistic fictionalization of the past, imposing unity and continuity on that which doesn't deserve it. Perhaps, therefore, we ought to be paying greater attention to 'discontinuities', 'ruptures', 'fissures', and so on than we have. But this does not mean abandoning narrative; it only means that in the interest of practicing something like fidelity to the twists and turns of the past, we ought to make sure that we do not foresake difference for the sake of identity, accident for the sake of a nice, smooth storyline. If any credence at all can be given to what Augustine has had to say, however, both in the story he has told as well as in his musings on recollection, there is no getting around the fact that narrative, like interpretation itself, is an unsurpassable feature of what we now think of as human self-understanding.

So too, I would hold, is the idea of development, taken here in the broad sense of moving forward into a superior region of being. But what can this really mean? If development isn't merely a self-aggrandizing fiction and if it isn't merely another spin on evolutionist thinking, in the sense of a virtual unfolding of an inchoate plan, a blueprint for the future, then what is it? For Augustine, development has led to his embracing God; the end, the telos, that restructures all that has come before is the process of giving himself up to the divinely Other. But this is surely not the only way to develop. There might be people, for instance, who go the exact opposite route and call it development; from living unreflectively under the spell of blind faith, of what they had taken to be divine authority, their own ends may have to do with breaking this spell and realizing their own authority and authorship. There are of course countless other ends that human beings might pursue as well, countless other ways in which they might improve their lot and move on to what they consider to be better ways of knowing and being and acting than what had existed previously. Are there in fact an infinite number of ways human beings may be said to develop?

In principle, I would say yes; there surely are. If there is no absolute end to the process of development, no singular telos that can plausibly be set forth as being *the* apex for all humanity, then development itself may be as various as the people who walk the earth. Moreover, I would also say that the process itself is in principle infinite, that is, that there can be something akin to human developmental 'betterment' as long as there is sentient life. Piaget, Freud, and others may have wished to call a halt to development once 'nature' had run its course, with the result that there appeared to be a ceiling of sorts, beyond which people could not go: formal operations, mature sexuality, and so on. In a broad sense, however, development – once it becomes 'denatured' – may be seen as a process that can go on forever. Don't even the most frail and wizened sometimes achieve renewed insight into who and what they are? It is true, of course, that they may not be developing in the same way as they did when they were children or adolescents, but doesn't this simply mean that we might want to devise ways of talking about development as it may occur beyond these earlier epochs?

Now in practice, there may not be quite so much variety in processes of development. Nor might these processes be quite so infinite, so unending, as we have just described; the worlds in which we live may indeed impose limits on what can be called development and on how far it can proceed. More generally, then, we can say that developmental processes and possibilities emerge in line with and as a function of these very worlds, the ends we pursue being irrevocably tied to extant conceptions of the good, the true, and the right. Within the context of these worlds, however, there is a fair amount of play and difference. Can we not say, in fact, that the process of rewriting the self, bound as it is to the unique constellation of experiences that have characterized a given life, will in turn yield a vast multiplicity of stories of development, each of them unique and unrepeatable in their own right? And is it not the case, furthermore, that these stories are indeed rooted in a kind of faith, in what it might mean to live well – a faith that, however labile and transient, we cannot live without?

Some might argue that this picture is a bit too individualistic, too tied to the idiosyncratic needs of wishes of specific selves. But hasn't it been implied here, particularly through Augustine's story, that development, far from being a matter of mere whimsical choice, is instead a matter of *devotion* to an idea or an ideal – or a God, as the case may be – that represents for us, in its very otherness from ourselves, an intimation of how life itself ought to be led? Even as recollection moves backward in time, gathering together anew the lineaments of selfhood, development exists on the horizon of the future, calling us forward, toward the self-to-be. The process of rewriting the self, in short, hovers in the space between recollection and development.

The perspective I am offering here needs to be articulated and defended further. For there are some very serious challenges to be met with along the way; and the most basic of these challenges – that of skepticism – often manages to exercise its power of attraction even on those who least expect it. Nevertheless, in the midst of trying to respond to the various challenges that are to come, we will be transforming and, if all goes well, enlarging our vision of the topic under consideration, which, felicitously enough, happens to be ourselves.

Chapter 3
In the name of the self

THE DANGER OF WRITING

'It is with a kind of fear', Helen Keller writes, in *The Story of My Life* (1988), 'that I begin to write the history of my life. I have, as it were, a superstitious hesitation in lifting the veil that clings about my childhood like a golden mist. The task of writing an autobiography is a difficult one. When I try to classify my earliest impressions, I find that fact and fancy look alike across the years that link the past with the present. The woman paints the child's experiences in her own fantasy' (3). Helen's fear, we will see, is multiply determined. For one, as she herself indicates, a significant portion of her past remains 'veiled', enshrouded in the dark silence of her lost senses. For another, in realizing that her past is comprised of both 'fact and fancy', there is the danger that the history she is writing is somehow suspect; where fact ends and fancy begins is anybody's guess, including her own. It is almost as if she is offering us a warning with these initial words: you must not believe all that I tell you.

To some extent, it might be argued, her fear is simply that of the autobiographer, whoever it may be: not only does self-disclosure have its dangers, but in many ways the veil of which Helen speaks is there for us all, our own distant pasts inevitably being a kind of abyss, deep, dark and amorphous. Freud took up this issue early on in his work, in the 'Three essays on the theory of sexuality' (1901–5b), considering what he called the 'infantile amnesia' to derive from our need to hide our threatening beginnings, particularly in the sphere of sexuality. Isn't it curious, he asks, that we feel no astonishment at the fact many of us 'retain nothing in our memory but a few unintelligible and fragmentary recollections'? We learn from others that 'we reacted in a lively manner to impressions, that we were capable of expressing pain and joy in a human fashion, that we gave evidence of love, jealousy and other passionate feelings by which we were strongly moved at the time, and even that we gave utterance to remarks which were regarded by adults as good evidence of our possessing insight and the beginnings of a capacity for judgement'. Yet 'of all this we, when we are grown up, have no knowledge of our own!' (174–5).

The situation, he notes, is not unlike that of neurotics, who also tend to 'withhold' certain features of their pasts. And for good reason: if we were to remember all that went on in those difficult years, the pains, the passions, and the wishes, we would be swallowed up in frustration and disappointment all our lives. Fortunately for some, unfortunately for others, we forget.

Ernest Schachtel extends Freud's ideas in his seminal essay, 'On memory and childhood amnesia' (1959). Instead of focusing primarily on the sphere of sexuality, however, Schachtel's idea is that there exists a more general and fundamental antagonism 'between reviving the past and actively participating in the present life of society' (281). As he goes on to argue, 'It is not merely the repression of a specific content, such as early sexual experience, that accounts for the general childhood amnesia.' Rather, 'the biologically, culturally, and socially influenced processes of memory organization result in the formation of categories (schemata) of memory which are not suitable vehicles to receive and reproduce experiences of the quality and intensity typical of early childhood' (284). Because we come to inhabit a vastly different world as adults, a world where language and convention come to achieve the upper hand in the formation of our experience, there is no returning to the earlier ways: to the extent that 'perception and experience themselves develop increasingly into the rubber stamps of conventional clichés' (288), Schachtel writes, memory follows in turn, the result being that much of what we remember is sadly bound up with what we are *supposed* to remember, what the social order tells us is significant.

But why is this so? Aside from what Schachtel refers to as the 'obscuring' function of language itself, why else might our earliest experience be hidden from us? The fact is, 'The world of modern Western civilization has no use for this type of experience. In fact, it cannot permit itself to have any use for it; it cannot permit the memory of it, because such memory, if universal, would explode the restrictive social order of this civilization' (284–5). From the sensuous immediacy of childhood, Schachtel tells us, we are steadily made to forget, to erase that endless well of emotions, in order that we can successfully carry on with the various tasks upon which the social order depends.

In short, childhood amnesia may not only be due to the traumatic nature of early events, as Freud maintained, but to the progressive schematization of experience along with the broader repressive forces of civilization as well. It is no wonder that we cannot recover the distant past in its immediacy and its fullness; the change we undergo from the pristine world of childhood – which, Schachtel implies, is the only true reality we will ever know – militates against it. For Helen, this change of which he speaks may have been especially salient owing to the unique transformation she eventually underwent: from a normal child, exploring the realm of the senses, to a deaf and blind one, suddenly being forced to grope her way through an alien world. But her inability to remember fully and adequately, as both Freud and Schachtel suggest, may still be seen as part and parcel of the seemingly unbridgeable gap between the child and the adult. In certain respects, therefore, her fate may not be vastly different from our own.

There is ample reason, I think, to question some of what these theorists have to say about the issue at hand, particularly in regard to the alleged pristineness of childhood and the inevitable fall into the deadened scripts of adult life. To be fair, Schachtel does in fact address the articulating function of language along with its obscuring function; he therefore knows that the movement of memory is not necessarily downhill, further and further away from the real. But the theme of loss and failure, the inevitable occlusion of reality wrought by the socially ratified designs we impose on our experience, remains paramount. In any case, whatever liabilities we may come to find in this formulation, the basic principle he offers us appears well worth considering: the changes that occur in our modes of figuring experience, from childhood to adulthood especially, render the notion of memory as 'recovery' highly suspect.

Returning to Helen, we also find in her initial words some possible confirming evidence for what Gusdorf had to say in the previous chapter. In recollecting the past through the eyes of the present, replete with its countless fantasies and desires, there does indeed exist the possibility that the story one is writing is more 'fanciful' than one might wish to avow. More than the mere description of what was, he told us, the autobiographical act may also serve as a vehicle for justifying what is, now, in the moment one commences to write. Schachtel and Gusdorf are thus of a piece on the main issue, however different their specific accounts may be: memory cannot help but deform the reality of the past. For the time being, however, let me reiterate that the disjunction between life as lived, moment to moment, and life as written, in the countless prejudices of the present, in no way *necessarily* entails the falsification of the past. As suggested in the previous chapter, it is inappropriate to conceive of ongoing immediate experience as a sort of yardstick or baseline against which to compare recollection. First, it is imperative to recognize that immediate experience is no less rooted in interpretation than memory is; in the very act of identifying our experience as possessing such and such a meaning, we are already in the thick of language. Second, and more important for our purposes, to understand recollection in relation to the aim of recovery is in fact to *mis*understand what it is all about: the positing of an intellible order to the past from the vantage point of the present. Indeed, the past – qua past – only exists in the present, in memory; it is not to be confused with the 'past presents' we formerly lived.

With these problems we have been considering in mind, it may be that Helen is doing little more in her introductory comments than offering a brief methodological commentary on what it means, generically, to undertake the project of writing an autobiography. We will be hearing much more about this in chapters to come. There is reason to believe, however, that significantly more is going on than meets the eye. Let us pursue the origins of Helen's fear a bit further.

LANGUAGE, THOUGHT, AND REALITY

'The beginning of my life', Helen notes, 'was simple and much like every other little life. I came, I saw, I conquered, as the first baby in the family always does' (5). Nothing out of the ordinary. 'I am told', she continues, 'that while I was still in long dresses I showed many signs of an eager, self-asserting disposition. Everything that I saw other people do I insisted upon imitating. At six months I could pipe out "How d'ye, " and one day I attracted everyone's attention by saying "Tea, tea, tea" quite plainly' (6).

Once again it would appear that there is nothing terribly unusual about Helen's situation, except perhaps her apparent precocity. It may be worth noting again (Augustine brought up a similar issue) that these beginning gestures are only hearsay, with others' renditions of her experience serving in lieu of her own memory, but by and large the situation would be the same for anyone else. Perhaps in dreams and the like there occasionally arise images that can plausibly be taken back to the earliest moments of life, to the primordial soup of our infancy. As a general rule, however, our histories begin not in memory, but in the stories told to us by others. Indeed, these *become* our pasts.

In any case, these idyllic childhood days were shortlived. 'One brief spring', Helen writes, 'musical with the song of robin and mockingbird, one summer rich in fruit and roses, one autumn of gold and crimson sped by and left their gifts at the feet of an eager, delighted child'. But then, 'in the dreary month of February, came the illness which closed my eyes and ears and plunged me into the unconsciousness of a newborn baby' (6). It was touch and go, she tells us; her doctor thought that she would certainly die. But one day, miraculously, Helen's fever left her, which was cause for great celebration in her family. Little did they know that she would never see or hear again.

> I fancy I still have confused recollections of that illness. I especially remember the tenderness with which my mother tried to soothe me in my waking hours of fret and pain, and the agony and bewilderment with which I awoke after a tossing half sleep, and turned my eyes, so dry and hot, to the wall, away from the once loved light, which came to me dim and yet more dim each day. But, except for these fleeting memories, if, indeed, they be memories, it all seems very unreal, like a nightmare.
> (6)

She gradually grew accustomed to her plight and in fact goes so far as to say that she 'forgot that it had ever been different, until', that is, 'she came – my teacher – who was to set my spirit free' (7). Whether Helen has forgotten the first nineteen months of her life or not, she is convinced that they remain very much with her still; she had 'caught glimpses of broad, green fields, a luminous sky, trees and flowers which the darkness that followed could not wholly blot out' (7).

Notice the mournful, elegiac quality of Helen's writing, the wondrous colors of nature serving as counterpoint to the colorless existence she was ultimately to lead. In line with what Gusdorf told us, she is doing more than merely recounting what was; she is instead telling the beginning of a story for which the outcome is already known. I mention this here only as a reminder for us to be aware of the narrational dimension of the project at hand: in the very act of remembering who and what she has been, Helen is placing her earlier experience within the fabric of narrative time, in line with who and what she is now, at the moment of writing.

Despite the difficulties that had beset her, Helen slowly but surely became engaged with the world. 'My hands felt every object and observed every motion, and in this way I learned to know many things.' She also 'felt the need of some communication with others and began to make crude signs' and, overall, 'understood a good deal of what was going on' about her (7). But there remained some serious difficulties as well, not the least of which included the fact that Helen had become a rather naughty little girl. She had even gone so far one morning as to lock her mother in the pantry, 'where she was obliged to remain three hours as the servants were in a detached part of the house. She kept pounding on the door, while I sat outside on the porch steps and laughed with glee as I felt the jar of the pounding' (11). Another time, upon discovering her little sister – 'to whom as yet no tie of love bound me' (12) – sleeping peacefully in a cradle reserved for one of Helen's favorite dolls, she immediately overturned it, nearly killing the baby in the process. Things were rapidly getting out of hand; someone had to teach this girl how to behave, her parents became convinced, and soon.

'Meanwhile, the desire to express myself grew. The few signs I used became less and less adequate, and my failures to make myself understood were invariably followed by outbursts of passion. I felt as if invisible hands were holding me, and I made frantic efforts to free myself' (13). This too lent no small measure of urgency to her parents' desire that a teacher be found.

Finally, in March 1887, Helen being almost 7 years old at this time, the famous Annie Sullivan arrived on the day that proved to be the most important one in her entire life. 'Have you ever been at sea in a dense fog', Helen asks, 'when it seemed as if a tangible white darkness shut you in, and the great ship, tense and anxious, groped her way toward the shore with plummet and sounding-line, and you waited with beating heart for something to happen?' Well, 'I was like that ship . . . "Light! give me light!" was the wordless cry of my soul, and the light of love shone on me in that very hour' (16).

Helen and Miss Sullivan struggled together for a good while, working especially on spelling out 'words' letter by letter, but progress was terribly slow. 'I did not know that I was spelling a word or even that words existed', Helen eventually realized; 'I was simply making my fingers go in monkey-like imitation.' Miss Sullivan's repeated attempts to move Helen beyond this 'uncomprehending way' were therefore met with a great deal of frustration. One day, in fact, Helen became so frustrated and impatient with her lesson that she seized her brand new doll and hurled it to the floor. 'Neither sorrow nor regret followed my passionate outburst', she admits. Quite the opposite: 'I was keenly delighted when I felt the fragments of the broken doll at my feet.' As Helen explains, she did not really know the meaning of love yet; there was 'no strong tenderness or sentiment' owing to the 'dark world' in which she continued to live (17). Miss Sullivan, meanwhile, swept aside the fragments of the broken doll and brought Helen her hat, which signalled that they would be going outside to take a break. 'This thought,' Helen writes, 'if a wordless sensation may be called a thought' (18), filled her with pleasure.

Then it happened. 'We walked down the path to the well-house, attracted by the fragrance of the honeysuckle with which it was covered. Someone was drawing water and my teacher placed my hand under the spout. As the cool stream gushed over one hand, she spelled into the other the word *water*, first slowly, then rapidly. I stood still, my whole attention fixed upon the motions of her fingers. Suddenly I felt a misty consciousness as of something forgotten – a thrill of returning thought; and somehow the mystery of language was revealed to me. I knew then', as if in a flash of insight, of revelation, of *thought*, 'that "w-a-t-e-r" meant the wonderful cool something that was flowing over my hand. That living word', she has come to believe, 'awakened my soul, gave it light, hope, joy, set it free!' (18).

But why? Why was it that something so apparently arbitrary as a word, a mere concatenation of letters, should set her soul free? Are we to assume, as Helen herself implies, that she had not really 'thought' until this time? Were her previous experiences with water essentially meaningless, 'wordless sensations' ultimately devoid of significance? Whatever the answers may be to these difficult questions, it would appear that the scene by the well was indeed a monumental one – particularly, perhaps, in retrospect. It would become clear soon enough that the space of her experience had become vastly enlarged.

Helen was immediately eager to learn, and as she returned to the house everything she touched 'seemed to quiver with life'. The only problem was the doll she had broken just moments before. 'I felt my way to the hearth and picked up the pieces. I tried vainly to put them together. Then my eyes filled with tears; for I realized what I had done, and for the first time I felt repentance and sorrow' (18). Remarkably enough, in this one brief moment Helen has apparently acquired not only the meaning of care and perhaps even love – the act of naming her little doll somehow rendering it nearer and dearer to her than it had ever been before – but the meaning of *meaning* itself: from wordless sensations there emerged genuine thought. Why, though, did there also emerge 'repentance' and 'sorrow'? The reason, it would seem, is that alongside the acquisition of language itself, what Helen also acquired was a sense of her own existence in time and thus of the narrative order of life itself: there suddenly emerged a *past*, to both celebrate and to grieve, a past that could be *rewritten* in the light of the consequences that followed from it. The doll was gone, and she had been responsible. Could it also be that her placement in the narrative order of life itself had suddenly given her an intimation of the finality of death?

The acquisition of language, she realized, entailed significantly more than merely attaching names to an already meaningful world. Rather, and by Helen's own account, language veritably created a world. But what had she really discovered? According to Cassirer (1944), she had discovered nothing less than the crucial difference between signs, which she had come to associate with specific things and events, and symbols, which had finally brought her into the realm of human culture. The associations between signs and things, even if repeated and amplified, Cassirer maintains, still fall short of an understanding of human language as such. What Helen needed to recognize, therefore, was that *everything* had a name, and moreover, 'that the symbolic function is not restricted to particular cases but is a principle of *universal* applicability which encompasses the whole field of human thought' (54).

For Cassirer, it should be noted, Helen's case is particularly important because it shows that the sort of progress in understanding she was able to make does not rely fundamentally on sense material: 'If the theories of sensationalism were right', he suggests, 'if every idea were nothing but a faint copy of an original sense impression, then the condition of a blind, deaf, and dumb child would indeed be desperate. For it would be deprived of the very sources of human knowledge; it would be, as it were, an exile from reality' (54–5). But what we see here, he says, is that human culture, including linguistic symbols, derives not from the content of sensory information per se, but from its form, its 'architectural structure': an interconnected edifice – a world – is built. 'The sign', Langer (1942) agrees, 'is something to act upon, or a means to command action; the symbol is an instrument of thought' (63), a means not merely of signifying something but of conceptualizing it, of 'fitting' it in some way: the symbol is 'coupled', as Langer puts it, with a conception that fits the object (see also Werner and Kaplan 1963).

In addition to veritably creating a world, though, what language also created, again by Helen's own account, was her very self, her 'soul's sudden awakening': she too had a name, and it was precisely this name, it seemed, that allowed her to make the all-important transition from awareness to self-awareness (see Bleich 1978). Again, alongside the birth of a meaningful objective world came Helen's own birth as a subject, as a continuous being which could now become the focus of reflection.

'Before my teacher came to me', Helen explains in another work (1908), 'I did not know that I am. I lived in a world that was a no-world. I cannot hope to describe adequately that unconscious, yet conscious time of nothingness . . . I was carried along to objects and acts by a certain blind natural impetus. I had a mind which caused me to feel anger, satisfaction, desire', and this led others to supposed that she had 'willed and thought'. But, she says, 'I never viewed anything beforehand or chose it'; and nor, she adds, 'did I feel that I loved or cared for anything'. Her inner life, in sum, had been little more than an empty flux of meaningless sensations, 'a blank without past, present, or future, without hope or anticipation, without wonder or joy or faith' (114).

All this changed. That year, she writes, 'I did nothing but explore with my hands and learn the name of every object that I touched; and the more I handled things and learned their names and uses, the more joyous and confident grew my sense of kinship with the rest of the world' (1988:19). Language, therefore, proved to be precisely the vehicle by which Helen grew to be at home in the world, to feel that it – and she – were indeed meaningful. Helen gradually learned to read as well and would sit in rapt attention as Annie described to her in vivid detail the wonders of reality. 'At the beginning I was only a little mass of possibilities. It was my teacher who unfolded and developed them. When she came, everything about me breathed love and joy and was full of meaning. She has never since let pass an opportunity to point out the beauty that is in everything, nor has she ceased trying in thought and action and example to make my life sweet and useful' (29). She and Annie were more than close, Helen goes on to say: 'My teacher is so near that I scarcely think of myself apart from her. How much of my delight in all beautiful things is innate, and how much is due to her influence, I can never tell. I feel that her being is inseparable from my own, and that the footsteps of my life are in hers. All the best of me belongs to her' (30).

All told, then, things were looking good. But who else, we can now ask, did Helen belong to? She herself – whoever 'she' may be – was forced, as it turned out, to raise this very sort of question. Rather than paying homage, however, as she did with Annie, she would eventually become bathed in fear, as if she was inhabited by the ghostly presence of others. Indeed, considering Helen's excitement and joy over the acquisition of language, it may be that much more surprising to find out that in many respects it proved to be the very bane of her existence. We skip ahead now some five years, to 1892, when Helen's honeymoon with words came to a startling halt.

WHOSE WORDS DO WE SPEAK AND WRITE?

'The winter of 1892', Helen writes, 'was darkened by the one cloud in my childhood's bright sky. Joy deserted my heart, and for a long, long time I lived in doubt, anxiety and fear. Books lost their charm for me, and even now the thought of those dreadful days chills my heart' (1988:47). What could possibly have happened to yield such powerful emotions? And how could Helen's great love of books, the very embodiments of the words that had so thoroughly opened up her relation to the world, have been brought to such an abrupt and terrible halt?

She had written a story, entitled 'The frost king', and sent it off to her beloved teacher, a Mr Anagnos of the Perkins Institution for the Blind, where it was published in one of the institution's regular reports. 'I wrote the story at home', she goes on to explain, 'the autumn after I had learned to speak. We had stayed up at Fern Quarry later than usual. While we were there, Miss Sullivan had described to me the beauties of the late foliage, and', judging by the outcome, which we will hear about shortly, 'it seems that her descriptions revived the memory of a story, which must have been read to me, and which I must have unconsciously retained' (47).

The event was terribly puzzling for Helen even still, at the time of writing her autobiography, for the entire process had seemed so natural and innocent.

> I thought then that I was 'making up a story,' as children say, and I eagerly sat down to write it before the ideas should slip from me. My thoughts flowed easily; I felt a sense of joy in the composition. Words and images came tripping to my finger ends, and as I thought out sentence after sentence, I wrote them on my braille slate.
>
> (47–8)

Phenomenologically speaking, then, she had been engaged in an act of the imagination, inhabited only by the muse; at the time, there was every reason to believe that those words and images tripping away were, fundamentally, hers alone. As for the result, the story appeared to be a remarkable, and remarkably original, achievement, and would no doubt have been deemed so even if the little girl who had written it could see and hear.

'At dinner', she writes, 'it was read to the assembled family, who were surprised that I could write so well'. The story was so good, in fact, that someone asked if she had read it in a book. 'This question surprised me very much', she notes, 'for I had not the faintest recollection of having had it read to me. I spoke up and said, "Oh, no, it is my story, and I have written it for Mr Anagnos."' It was to be a birthday present for him; and when she finally carried the story to the post office to send it his way, she felt as if she was walking on air. 'I little dreamed how cruelly I should pay for that birthday gift' (48).

It was eventually learned that there existed a story similar to the one Helen had written, 'The frost fairies', by Margaret T. Canby. 'The stories were so much alike in thought and language', Helen admits, 'that it was evident that Miss Canby's story had been read to me, and that mine was –

a plagiarism' (48–9). Although she had felt that she had been virtually inhabited by the muse, that she had suddenly become a medium for what could only be divine inspiration, it was indeed too good to be true. She had been a medium, all right, but her inspiration had been anything but divine: Helen's precocity turned out to be Miss Canby's maturity.

Now Miss Canby, it should be noted, wasn't particularly dismayed by this incident. In a letter she had written not too long after the discovery, she says,

> What a wonderfully active and retentive mind that gifted child must have! If she had remembered and written down accurately a short story, and that soon after hearing it, it would have been a marvel; but to have heard the story once, three years ago, and in such a way that neither her parents nor teacher could ever allude to it or refresh her memory about it, and then to have been able to reproduce it so vividly, even adding some touches of her own in perfect keeping with the rest, which really improve the original, is something that very few girls of riper age, and with every advantage of sight, hearing, and even great talents for composition, could have done as well, if at all. Indeed, under the circumstances, I do not see how any one can be so unkind as to call it a plagiarism; it is a wonderful feat of memory, and stands *alone*, as doubtless much of her work will in the future, if her mental powers grow and develop with her years as greatly as in the few years past.

There is but one thing to do in the present circumstances, Miss Canby concludes: 'Tell her there are a few bitter drops in every one's cup, and the only way is to take the bitter patiently, and the sweet thankfully' (cited in Keller 1974: 372).

Helen's initial response to the discovery was sheer bewilderment; having no concept of authorship whatsoever, in fact, she thought it was wonderful that two people should create stories so strikingly similar. 'I thought everybody had the same thought about the leaves', she had written in her diary shortly after the incident, 'but I do not know now' (386). A while later, in any case, after the severity of the incident was explained to her more fully, her wonder at the similarity of the stories turned into a profound sense of disgrace. She was 'astonished and grieved', she writes in her autobiography. 'No child ever drank deeper of the cup of bitterness than I did' (1988: 49). Notice her wording here: apparently those 'few bitter drops' that Miss Canby had warned her about had been taken to heart.

Now at first, Mr Anagnos, the man to whom the story had been sent, believed Helen's account. 'He was unusually tender and kind to me', Helen notes, 'and for a brief space the shadow lifted. To please him, I tried not to be unhappy, and to make myself as pretty as possible for the celebration of Washington's birthday, which took place very soon after I received the sad news' (49). So things were looking up. But then something strange happened. The night before this celebration, apparently, one of the teachers at Perkins has asked Helen a question about her story, and something she said seemed to be a confession that yes, indeed, the story had been lifted willfully. This teacher had misunderstood, Helen believed; there was no confession being made at all; she was innocent. But her protests came to naught. 'Mr Anagnos', meanwhile, 'who loved me tenderly', Helen writes, 'turned a deaf ear to the pleadings of love and innocence. He believed, or at least suspected, that Miss Sullivan and I had deliberately stolen the bright thoughts of another and imposed them on him to win his admiration' (49–50).

A court of investigation would try to determine the truth. It was a terrible time:

> I was questioned and cross-questioned with what seemed to be a determination on the part of my judges to force me to acknowledge that I remembered having had 'The frost fairies' read to me. I felt in every question the doubt and suspicion that was in their minds, and I felt, too, that a loved friend was looking at me reproachfully, although I could not have put all this into words. The blood pressed about my thumping heart, and I could scarcely speak, except in monosyllables.

And as she lay in bed that night, after this awful ordeal, 'I wept as I hope few children have wept. I felt so cold, I imagined I should die before morning, and the thought comforted me' (50). Miss Sullivan was exonerated. After some further investigation, it was learned that someone else had read Helen the original story some years back, while Miss Sullivan was on vacation. As for Helen, it was difficult to say whether or not she was guilty.

What *did* happen anyway? Let us turn first to Helen's own account. Interestingly enough, she notes,

> The stories had little or no meaning for me then; but the mere spelling of the strange words was sufficient to amuse a little girl who could do almost nothing to amuse herself; and although I do not recall a single circumstance connected with the reading of the stories, yet I cannot help thinking that I made a great effort to remember the words, with the intention of having my teacher explain them when she returned. One thing is certain: [Helen came to believe] the language was

ineffaceably stamped upon my brain, though for a long time no one knew it, least of all myself.

(51)

Strange. Despite the fact that Helen was read *stories* – at least in the eyes of those who knew what stories were, such as the woman doing the reading – she didn't experience them as such. She had simply experienced words, many of which were unfamiliar, strung in sequence, like beads on a necklace. If this is so, of course, it becomes extremely difficult, philosophically and legally, to determine what exactly was plagiarized, if anything. Lifting individual words would not seem particularly problematic; ultimately, neologisms aside, all words are 'lifted', as we noted earlier. Phrases, I suppose, would be a bit more troubling, though even here, it is important to note that many of the phrases we utter, even in our most personal moments, are derived from without. Lifting the entire story would be more troubling still, but there still remains the question of whether, if it is unintentional – which would render the meaning of 'lifting', as I've been using it, a bit different from how we ordinarily conceive of it – the accusation of plagiarism is at all appropriate.

We do have some other possibilities, of course, than the one Helen has offered us in her story. It could be, for instance, that without any concept of authorship, originality, proprietary rights, and so on, she thought it was perfectly acceptable to do what she did. This would presume that she knew what she did, in some sense – she had borrowed another's language – but had no idea that this was 'wrong'. Without having been exposed to all the ins and outs of modernity, with its strong emphasis on the ownership of ideas, perhaps she believed that words and phrases and stories were public property, take them as you wish.

Or, taking a more psychoanalytic approach to the issues at hand, it could be that Helen unconsciously lifted Miss Canby's story. Along these lines, perhaps she repressed having had the story read to her, since remembering would constitute an admission that she did indeed love Mr Anagnos and wanted to please him in whatever way she could. Here again, the accusation of plagiarism, it would seem, would not be quite appropriate; to the extent that her 'creative process' was fueled by desires of which she was unaware, her intentions ostensibly being buried somewhere in the dark corridors of her unconscious, it would be strange to claim that this was in fact an act of plagiarism. It all depends, I suppose, on how much credence we place in Freud.

Finally, it may be that, in light of her feelings for Mr Anagnos, she simply stole the story, consciously and willfully, in order to win his love and admiration, as he himself seemed to believe. In this case, of course, sacrilegious though it may sound, Helen would deserve to be called not only a plagiarizer but a liar as well.

My own feeling, given what I know of Helen's story, is that the mistake was probably an honest one. Needless to say, I can't prove this, but judging from her response to the incident as well as some of her subsequent speculations on the nature of mind, self, and so forth, there is good reason to believe that she was in fact innocent, at least at the level of intentions. The issues are more interesting if we assume so in any case. So let us proceed, cautiously, on the assumption that the story she has told us thus far approximates the truth.

ORIGIN/ALITY

What was her response to the incident once its immediate horror passed over? For one, she became terribly suspicious of her own apparent bursts of creativity. 'Now,' she writes, 'if words and images come to me without any effort, it is a pretty sure sign that they are not the offspring of my own mind, but stray waifs that I regretfully dismiss. At that time I eagerly absorbed everything I read without a thought of authorship'; in line with what was said earlier, she simply did not know that origins even mattered. But there was a further and somewhat more disconcerting realization as well. For 'even now', some ten years later, Helen adds, 'I cannot be quite sure of the boundary line between my ideas and those I find in books'. Perhaps this is so, she ventures, 'because so many of my impressions come to me through the medium of others's eyes and ears' (48). In any case, 'I have never played with words again for the mere pleasure of the game', she writes mournfully. 'Indeed, I have ever since been tortured by the fear that what I write is not my own'. Even when she wrote letters to her mother, she would be 'seized with a sudden feeling of terror' and 'would spell the sentences over and over' (51) to make sure they didn't originate elsewhere. But how could she ever know?

There is a sense, then, in which she came to feel that her own world was somehow secondhand; since nearly everything she learned came to her either through Annie Sullivan or through the numerous books she read, she couldn't escape the possibility that many of the thoughts that felt so very much like her own were in fact derived from others. Now as she herself suggests, it could be that this situation had much to do with the specific nature of her own disabilities, the implication being that her world was, of necessity, more secondhand than ours. After all, aside from what she was able to learn via those senses that had been spared – which was actually a great deal – she had to rely on what others, whether in person or through texts, told her. But here, of course, we must ask: How different, ultimately, *was* her situation? Are our own thoughts really any more firsthand than Helen's were?[1]

For some time after the plagiarism incident, Helen found herself confused not only by the nature of her own mind, which had turned out to be a rather curious amalgam of both her own thoughts and a variety of 'stray waifs', as she put it, but by the nature of her own originality as well. Fortunately, she received 'many messages of love and sympathy' from her friends, who continued to believe that Helen had fallen prey to nothing more than an honest mistake and that in due time she would find her own stride as a writer. For the fact of the matter was that despite her (apparently) unintentional theft of the Canby story, Helen had in fact gone considerably beyond the original version. As one commentator writes, in a supplemental account of Helen's life and work (in Keller 1974), 'The style of her version is in some respects even better than the style of Miss Canby's story. It has the imaginative credulity of a primitive folk-tale; whereas Miss Canby's story is evidently told for children by an older person, who adopts the manner of a fairy tale and cannot conceal the mature mood' that informs its writing. He refers to one passage in particular as a 'stroke of genius' and feels that 'there is beauty of rhythm throughout the child's narrative'. In his own estimation, then, the work was clearly original, 'in the same way that a poet's version of an old story is original' (391). There was thus every reason to believe that once Helen put her thoughts in order and succeeded in disentangling them from those of others, she would be able to mature into an authentic creative force.

Even Mr Anagnos had assumed as much. 'This habit of assimilating what pleased me and giving it out again as my own appears in much of my early correspondence and my first attempts at writing. In a composition I wrote about the old cities of Greece and Italy', for instance, 'I borrowed my glowing descriptions, with variations, from sources I have forgotten'. Knowing Mr Anagnos's 'great love of antiquity and his enthusiastic appreciation of all beautiful sentiments about Italy and Greece, I therefore gathered from all the books I read every bit of poetry or of history that I thought would give him pleasure'. And indeed it did: 'These ideas are poetic in their essence' (1988: 52), he had once said to her.

This too proved to be puzzling for Helen. 'I do not understand how he ever thought that a blind and deaf child of eleven could have invented them' (52). He was a fool, she seemed to be saying; he was so gullible as to believe that these poetic utterances were actually hers! She, being a young child, could be forgiven her gullibility; for all she knew, she *could* have been a great writer, a prodigy. But there was no excuse for him. Her words are spiced with contempt here. This man whom she had cared for so deeply has shown himself to be an easy mark. He had also spurned her, as she well knew, by refusing in the end to believe in her innocence. He had rejected her advances.

Then again, she qualifies, maybe he wasn't so gullible. After all, didn't others see some hints of talent too? 'I cannot think that because I did not originate the ideas, my little composition is therefore quite devoid of interest. It shows me that I could express my appreciation of beautiful and poetic ideas in clear and animated language' (52). Her story is getting a bit confused. While on the one hand it is amazing to Helen that a seemingly bright adult could find poetry in her ideas, she seems to feel that poetry really was there, in the form of appreciation. As a good many art experts the world over may well ask, isn't the capacity to appreciate itself testimony to the capacity, however unactualized, to create? Couldn't Helen be praised for at least having good taste? But how did she acquire this good taste anyway? Was her taste simply Mr Anagnos's taste, recycled? Had she satisfied her deepest wishes and fused with him, becoming as one?

Whatever the origins of her writing at the time, 'Those compositions were mental gymnastics', Helen admits. 'I was learning, as all young and inexperienced persons learn, by assimilation and imitation, to put ideas into words.' Part of her problem, then, may simply have been in her youth. 'The young writer . . . instinctively tries to copy whatever seems most admirable, and he shifts his admiration with astonishing versatility'. Consequently, 'it is only after years of this sort of practice that even great men have learned to marshal the legion of words which come thronging through every byway of the mind' (1988:52). Helen thus suggests that the writer, whoever he or she may be, must inevitably begin *derivatively*, borrowing, as it were, from those who have come before. Stated another way, one cannot simply commence to write de novo, out of nothing, but must instead master a tradition of some sort, the ultimate aim being to extend this tradition in some way; only by immersing oneself in what has come before will there exist the possibility of moving on to do something new and original.

Helen readily admits that she has 'not yet completed this process' (53); it is simply too early developmentally for her to have achieved the greatness and originality to which she aspires. This project of 'completion', therefore – whatever it might mean – must be deferred. For now, there is only hope, and not quite as much of it as she would like.

In addition to Helen's avowed artistic immaturity, though, there is a further, more significant problem, and it is one that she believes differentiates her from other young writers: 'It is certain', she notes again, 'that I cannot always distinguish my own thoughts from those I read, *because what I read becomes the very substance and texture of my mind*' (53, emphasis added). The problem, in short, was that virtually everything she wrote – indeed everything she *thought* – was somehow derivative; it owed its very existence to the texts that constituted her mind.[2] Whereas other young writers were at least able to begin to speak their own mind, Helen believes that she could not; there was simply no way to extricate herself from all of the other works she had been reading.

This does not mean that she had no concept of a world apart from texts, for she surely did; she smelled it, tasted it, and felt it. But beyond this most immediate realm of the senses, she suggests, there were only words, others' words, strewn together haphazardly. The result was that, 'in nearly everything I write, I produce something which very much resembles the crazy patchwork I used to make when I first learned to sew' (1988:53). Her writing was the very embodiment of heterogeneity and multiplicity, of the intermixing of the conscious and unconscious, of Helen – whoever she may be – and the others within her.

Helen can only hope that she will some day 'outgrow' these 'artificial, periwigged compositions', because it is only then, she believes, that her own thoughts and experiences 'will come to the surface' (53). Helen's formulation of the development of creativity, therefore, is approximately this: owing in part to her disabilities and her youth, both of which have left her rather cluttered up with the thoughts of others, she is still a second-rate, derivative writer. With some diligence, however, this will change and she will become an originating and original voice.

What she has also offered us here is a classic formulation of the notion of individuality: because she is young and impressionable, she is not yet her 'own person', so to speak (her thoughts and experiences, she implies, in the 'coming-to-the-surface' metaphor ostensibly being 'buried' for the time being); but if all goes well, if she manages to shed the thoughts and experiences of others, like so many social skins, she eventually will be. The implication, in other words, is that as of now, *she* is a crazy patchwork, just as her writing is; she is an amalgamation of others, a heterogeneous ensemble of parts, thrown together in a body. But all this, she believes, will change in due time, as she gradually comes into her own.

There is a kind of paradox here. What she says probably rings true to many of us. Somehow, we do manage to become our own persons over the course of time; we find that we become able to 'just be ourselves' rather than the imitative, other-driven beings we used to be. This is largely what is meant by the idea of identity. But isn't it also clear that the self of which

Helen speaks – this sovereign self, able to think thoughts that are fully her own – is an idealization, an imaginary vision of completion? Can we ever really become the authors of our own actions, our own selves?

AUTHORSHIP AND SELFHOOD

We may wish to ask further, with Michel Foucault (1977): What *is* an author? Among other things, the author is a designation, a means of classification, the function of which is 'to characterize the existence, circulation, and operation of certain discourses in a society' (124); it serves to locate works in relation to a point of origin. And far from being constant and universal, Foucault argues, the idea of the author has in fact arisen in history, being tied to the emergence of specific legal and institutional structures. How exactly does this 'author-function' emerge? It results, Foucault suggests, 'from a complex operation whose purpose is to construct the rational entity we call an author. Undoubtedly, this construction is assigned a "realistic" dimension as we speak of an individual's "profundity" or "creative" power, his intentions or the original inspiration manifested in writing'. But these are 'projections, in terms always more or less psychological, of our way of handling texts', Foucault maintains (127); they are extrapolations derived, in other words, from the process of reading itself.

Now the idea of an author – and, more generally, the idea of a subject – need not completely be abandoned, he notes, but 'reconsidered . . . to seize its functions, its intervention in discourse, and its system of dependencies'. Rather than asking, 'how does a free subject penetrate the density of things and endow them with meaning', perhaps we should ask questions like, 'under what conditions and through what forms can an entity like the subject appear in the order of discourse; what position does it occupy; what functions does it exhibit; and what rules does it follow in each type of discourse? In short,' Foucault concludes, 'the subject (and its substitutes) must be stripped of its creative role and analysed as a complex and variable function of discourse' (137–8). The bottom line, at any rate, is that the idea of the author as we know it ought to be considered anew; at the very least, we will have taken to task one more of humanism's idols and, by relegating it to its proper place in the order of discourse, tweaked in yet another way our own narcissism, hubris, and arrogance.

As Barthes (1977) goes on to elaborate, the author 'is a product of our society insofar as, emerging from the Middle Ages with English empiricism, French rationalism and the personal faith of the Reformation, it discovered the prestige of the individual, of, as it is more nobly put, the "human person'" (142–3). We see, therefore, that the two ideas with which we have been dealing, the creativity of the author and the individuality of the self, are intimately related; they are, we might say, two sides of the same coin. And they are both, again, deeply problematic. As Barthes puts it, 'it is language which speaks, not the author' (143); 'the author', he says, 'is never more than the instance writing, just as *I* [as was proposed earlier] is nothing other than the instance saying *I*' (145). The idea of the author as well as that of the 'I' are once more seen here as extrapolations, originating in language. As for the idea of a text, Barthes maintains that it is 'not a line of words releasing a single "theological" meaning (the "message" of the Author-God) but a multi-dimensional space in which a variety of writings, none of them original, blend and clash' (146) – the crazy patchwork Helen had described. For Barthes, however, and much to Helen's potential chagrin, this situation never really changes, appearances notwithstanding; even the greatest of writers 'can only imitate a gesture that is always anterior, never original. His only power is to mix writings, to counter the ones with the others, in such a way as never to rest on any one of them' (146). Thus the idea of the author, Barthes concludes, is one we can quite easily do without. All it does is stop the music, so to speak, constrict the field of things one might say about a text by tying its potential meanings back to a putatively sovereign place of origination, to an owner, a proprietor, who is thought to call the shots.

It is a shame that Helen was unable to benefit from the proclamations of Foucault and Barthes. Perhaps they would have made her feel less paranoid and guilty than she did. At the very least she might have been able to purge herself of the burden of her own perceived deficits, this originality she believed herself to have lacked.

But what about coming into one's own as an individual person, a self? Should we assume, given what has been said, that our very identities are illusory? That our experience of 'I', this supposedly continuous, integrated, originating being, is more a wish than a reality? 'Not only are selves conditional', John Updike has recently (1989) written, 'but they die. Each day, we wake slightly altered, and the person we were yesterday is dead' (211). Could it be that our conviction in our own unity as selves is a defense against our dis-unity, or a way of grieving over that part of us that dies each and every day? Or, more simply, is 'self' (or 'subject', 'person', 'Man', etc.) merely an artifact of language, here now, only to be erased perhaps at some future time, 'like a face drawn in sand at the edge of the sea'? (Foucault 1973: 387).

These sorts of questions are by no means new ones. Hume, for instance, in *A Treatise on Human Nature* (1874), notes that some philosophers 'imagine we are every moment intimately conscious of what we call our SELF; that we feel its existence; and are certain, beyond the evidence of a demonstration, both of its perfect identity and simplicity' (533). Unfortunately for them, however, says Hume, they are wrong. 'For from what impression could this idea be derived?' As he goes on to argue, 'If any impression gives rise to the idea of self, that impression must continue invariably the same, through the whole course of our lives; since self is supposed to exist after that manner. But there is no impression constant and invariable. Pain and pleasure, grief and joy, passions and sensations succeed each other, and never all exist at the same time. It cannot, therefore, be from any of these impressions, or from any other, that the idea of the self is derived; and consequently', he proclaims, 'there is no such idea' (533). Thus, 'The identity, which we ascribe to the mind of man, is only a fictitious one' (540); it is created, imagined, an extrapolation from the flux of experience which deludes us into positing an enduring substantiality when in fact there is not.

From other quarters entirely, Nietzsche (1968) discusses something quite similar. Descartes had essentially argued, Nietzsche writes, 'There is thinking: therefore there is something that thinks.' But really, he suggests, all we have 'is simply a formulation of our grammatical custom that adds a doer to every deed' (268). Who exactly is this doer? A soul? A nonmaterial substance? A control tower, calling out directions to be executed by the body? Not quite.

> The subject: this is the term for our belief in a unity underlying all the different impulses of the highest feeling of reality: we understand this belief as the *effect* of one cause – we believe so firmly in our belief that for its sake we imagine 'truth,' 'reality,' 'substantiality' in general. – 'The subject' is the fiction that many similar states in us are the effect of one substratum.
>
> (268–9)

Why 'fiction'? Once again, 'it is we who first created the "similarity" of these states'; and as such, 'our adjusting them and making them similar is the fact, not their similarity (which ought rather to be denied)' (269).

Where does this leave us? 'The assumption of one single subject is perhaps unnecessary; perhaps it is just as permissible to assume a multiplicity of subjects, whose interaction and struggle is the basis of our thought and our consciousness in general?' Nietzsche asks. Yes, he decides: 'The subject as multiplicity' (270).

Moving into different quarters still, as we learn from B. F. Skinner (1974; see also 1971): 'Complex contingencies of reinforcement create complex repertoires, and . . . different contingencies create different persons in the same skin, of which so-called multiple personalities are only an extreme manifestation' (1974:184–5). Again, not unlike Hume and Nietzsche: 'A person is not an originating agent; he is a locus, a point at which many genetic and environmental conditions come together in a joint effect.' This is not to say that we aren't unique, for as Skinner acknowledges, 'No one else (unless he has an identical twin) has his genetic endowment, and without exception no one else has his personal history' (185). This uniqueness, however, 'is inherent in the sources'. Consequently, 'There is no place in the scientific position for a self as a true originator or initiator of action' (247–8).

Now I would not suggest that Hume, Nietzsche, and Skinner would completely agree with each other; clearly, they have very different outlooks. But it is also clear that each of them, in their own respective ways, seeks to 'deconstruct' the idea of the self, or at least that version of it that arrogantly and mistakenly posits its own identity.[3] There are reasons for wanting to believe in this version, of course, and it may even be functional on some level, as many fictions are. It is no less necessary to recognize, however, that ideas may be perfectly functional while still being thoroughly false.[4] Had Helen stumbled upon just the sort of realizations that we have been considering here? Had she been led, precisely through her own confusion, to deconstruct not only her own self, but the very *idea* of the self? Is the self – not to mention the world – merely what we imagine it to be, a fictional extrapolation from the flux of experience, a name devised to stem the tide of the irreducible heterogeneity of things?

The answer here, I will suggest, is both yes and no: yes, self and world *are* fundamentally products of the imagination. But no, they are not to be thought of as *merely* imaginary, in the sense of being essentially fictional creations. Let me try to clarify this admittedly ambiguous position.

TO BUILD A WORLD

Helen continued to look forward to the day when she would become who she truly was. It would no doubt be an arduous task trying to separate out her own words from those of others, but this is what had to be done for her to be anything more than the simulation – indeed the impersonation – of an autonomous self. She had to be disencumbered; she had to slough off those layers of texts, texts upon texts, if she was to arrive at the real thing. She never quite said what this real thing might look like once it was found. Maybe now we know why.

In any event, there were plenty of things to occupy Helen's mind.

Indeed, she claims that within a year or so after the plagiarism incident she had almost forgotten it, electing instead to concentrate on a sketch of her life. 'When the ground was strewn with the crimson and golden leaves of autumn, and the musk-scented grapes that covered the arbor at the end of the garden were turning brown in the golden sunshine' (55), she began. But we might wish to pause for a moment here. It may strike the reader as somewhat sacrilegious to ask, but aside from the musk-scented grapes, why does Helen care about any of this? Just because she had been told that these sorts of scenes were beautiful ones? Helen is well aware of these questions. After describing her wonderful trip to Niagara Falls, for instance, she writes,

> It seems strange to some people that I should be impressed by the wonders and beauties of Niagara. They are always asking: 'What does this beauty or that music mean to you? You cannot see the waves rolling up the beach or hear their roar. What do they mean to you?'
>
> (56)

Later on in the book, she writes,

> 'I also enjoy canoeing, and I suppose you will smile when I say that I especially like it on moonlit nights. I cannot, it is true, see the moon climb up the sky behind the pines and steal softly across the heavens, making a shining path for us to follow; but I know she is there, and as I lie back among the pillows and put my hand in the water, I fancy that I feel the shimmer of her garments as she passes.
>
> (90)

Again, some might argue that Helen simply *knows* that these things are wondrous, precisely because others have told her so. In fact, if they are skeptical enough, they might go on to argue the same exact thing for each and every one of us. Judgments of beauty are merely products of convention; waterfalls and moonlit nights, far from being beautiful in themselves, are only deemed so because we've learned that they are: this will be Beautiful, that Ugly; this will evoke Passion, that Boredom; Shakespeare is Good, sitcoms are Bad. But who says? Do we somehow learn to see what is really *in* these things, or are we simply given particular – and ultimately arbitrary – evaluations, which then condition what it is we experience?

Helen grew to realize the significance of these questions firsthand. For interestingly and ironically enough she came to feel that one of the greatest deterrents to her own meaningful engagement with the world was that very institution which was allegedly designed to facilitate it, namely college. It simply was not the 'romantic lyceum', the 'universal Athens', she had thought it was. 'One goes to college to learn', she says cynically, 'not to think' (73). Another problem, however, was that Helen could not quite become connected to many of the works she was reading; they were somehow alien and distant. Somewhere along the line she had gathered the conviction that in college she would become still more deeply engaged in her pursuit of truth and wisdom, but sadly it seemed that they were forever placed at a remove from her.

> There, one does not meet the great and the wise face to face; one does not even feel their living touch. They are there, it is true; but they seem mummified. We must extract them from the crannied wall of learning and dissect and analyze them before we can be sure that we have a Milton or an Isaiah, and not merely a clever imitation.

As Helen goes on to note, 'It is possible to know a flower, root and stem and all, and all the processes of growth, and yet have no appreciation of the flower bathed in heaven's fresh dew' (78). Something was missing.

As Helen suggests, learning, however much it may be a prerequisite of deep and meaningful experience, a necessary condition of it, is not in itself sufficient to bring it about. As her alienated encounter with some of the 'classics' has demonstrated, *knowing* that the world is beautiful and *feeling* it are two quite different things. In sum, therefore, we ought not to suppose that we are merely instructed or socialized into being moved by classic works; there is something more going on.

But what? Consider this: many of the things that enrapture us, that send us into transcendent moments of pleasure and passion, such as a piece of music we listen to again and again, are likely to be thoroughly alien to many others; because that piece of music is not a part of their respective life-worlds, it does not, and indeed cannot, do for them what it does for us. We might also consider how our own tastes have changed with the years. Things that we had become ecstatic over become stale or silly or dead. We were caught up in a craze, we might conclude, swayed by the powers that be to believe that this was it, that there could never be another piece – or another person – quite like this one. Then it all changes. Isn't this relativity evidence for the learning thesis? If so much of what we appreciate is tied to culture, to our own place in the life course, and so on, then how else can we account for these phenomena?

Helen actually offers us several different possibilities. The first account is a kind of Jungian one. Given the depth of her appreciation of nature especially, she is led to surmise that 'there is in each of us a capacity to comprehend the impressions and emotions which have been experienced in mankind from the beginning. Each individual', she writes, 'has a subconscious memory of the green earth and the murmuring waters, and blindness and deafness cannot rob him of this gift from past generations. This inherited capacity', she believes, 'is a sort of sixth sense – a soul-sense which sees, hears, feels, all in one' (92). So she's talking here about a kind of spiritually-based synesthesia, which makes use of our archaic heritage in fashioning a meaningful world. Whatever may be learned, therefore, simply serves to reawaken what was already there.

Second, and relatedly, she also entertains (in a work referred to on p. 57, called *The World I Live In* (1908)) an account reminiscent of Chomsky's. 'The deaf-blind child', she suggests, 'has inherited the mind of seeing and hearing ancestors – a mind measured to five senses. Therefore he must be influenced, even if it be unknown to himself, by the light, color, song which have been transmitted through the language he is taught, for the chambers of the mind are ready to receive that language. The brain of the race is so permeated with color', she says, 'that it dyes even the speech of the blind' (123–4). She even goes so far at one point as to compare her experience to the phenomenon of the phantom limb: 'When a man loses his leg', she writes, 'his brain persists in impelling him to use what he has not and yet feels to be there. Can it be', she asks, 'that the brain is so constituted that it will continue the activity which animates the sight and hearing, after the eye and ear have been destroyed?' (86–7). Here, then, she is raising the possibility of deep structure not only at the linguistic level but at the sensory level as well: perhaps we are born to use each of the five senses and to experience the world in their terms, even in the event that some of them are missing.

The third account of her experience, again related to the other two in certain ways, has more to do with the idea of metaphor. 'If the mental consciousness of the deaf-blind person were absolutely dissimilar to that of his fellows', she notes, 'he would have no means of imagining what they think. Since the mind of the sightless is', however, 'essentially the same as that of the seeing in that it admits of no lack, it must supply some sort of equivalent for missing physical sensations.' How does it do this? 'It must perceive a likeness between things outward and things inward, a correspondence', as she puts it, 'between the seen and the unseen' (124–5).

> The flash of thought and its swiftness explain the lightning flash and the sweep of the comet through the heavens. My mental sky opens to me the vast celestial spaces, and I proceed to fill them with the images of my spiritual stars. I recognize truth by the clearness and guidance that it gives my thought, and, knowing what that clearness is, I can imagine what light is to the eye. It is not a convention of language, but a forcible

feeling of the reality, that at times makes me start when I say, 'Oh, I see my mistake!' or 'How dark, cheerless is this life!'

(125–6)

Acknowledging the simplicity (and perhaps untenability) of this correspondence theory, at least to the extent that inner and outer are taken to be mere mirrors of the other, it may still be that there is something to what Helen says in this context. For, 'Deny me this correspondence, confine me to the fragmentary, incoherent touch-world, and lo, I become as a bat which wanders about on the wing'. Indeed, she continues, if she were to omit 'all words of seeing, hearing, color, light, landscape, the thousand phenomena, instruments and beauties connected with them', she would 'suffer a great diminution of the wonder and delight of attaining knowledge'. Furthermore, her emotions would be 'blunted, so that I could not be touched by things unseen' (127). There is an interesting twist to the ideas Helen is raising here. It is sometimes thought that we use metaphors referring to the outer world to articulate the inner, as in 'Love is a rose' (see especially Lakoff and Johnson 1980). But Helen actually does the exact opposite, using the inner to articulate the outer. In any case, what is most important here is this notion of correspondence between the world within and the world without, a kind of isomorphism between the psychical and the material.

As an aside, it should be mentioned that from the perspective just offered, it may be that we can see an inroad into resolving the dilemma we posed earlier regarding the fact that many of the things that move us deeply are decidedly 'local' phenomena, inaccessible to those living at other times or in other places. That piece of music we listen to time and time again, for instance, the one that seems to correspond so well to our inner world, may not affect these others for the simple reason that it fails to correspond to *their* inner worlds; it fails to do justice to the sphere of life they have come to inhabit. So it is that they may surround themselves with entirely different objects to contemplate from ours. What this means, therefore, is that however local our appreciation of the phenomena of the world may be, however relative to our own culture, there is no need to reduce the transcendent experiences we have to mere instruction or indoctrination. This is because the forms transcendence takes depend, as a general rule, on our own specific life-worlds, our own unique modes of being, for their very existence: they occur in history. The long and short of this point is that we can still talk about something like representation and correspondence without being simplistically objectivistic or universalistic about it.

Think for a moment about the debate that continues to rage on about the status of so-called 'classics'.[5] On one side of this debate, the classic may be seen as embodying a timeless essence, and its appreciation signals the fact that the reality of which it speaks is enduring, objective, and universal. This is not to say that every last person who encounters these sorts of works will have exactly the same wondrous experience, since appreciation often requires a good deal of nurturance, only that these works contain within them specifiable meanings, able, with the proper tools, to be found. Given these specifiable meanings, it follows that these works contain within them intrinsic values as well: there are good works and there are bad ones and perhaps even an identifiable hierarchy in between. This is why, it is sometimes argued, we have read Plato, Aristotle, Shakespeare and the rest for many generations and will no doubt continue to do so in the future.

But who exactly is this 'we'? The second group of debaters, seeing full well that there are lots of people who just don't *like* these works, and who opt instead for other works that are more suited to their respective stations in life, can only conclude that appreciation is indeed a function of what one has been taught, of the reigning ideology that says: 'This, you must see, is good.' Taking this argument (in its most extreme version) one step further, it follows that no one work of art – or bottle of wine, or scene in nature, or person – is 'intrinsically' preferable to any other; and thus everything, in the end, is equivalent to everything else.

But haven't we raised the possibility that there might be another way of thinking of these issues altogether? Might it not be that art, wine, and person appreciation, rather than being a function of what is objectively and enduringly *there*, as in group one, or what is merely inculcated through learning, as in group two, is instead a function of culture, of that languaged world we all live in? Again, the fact that the specific forms our appreciation of things take may well be relative to time and place, in part at least, in no way entails the further supposition that they are arbitrary. Our own process of living in the world, in history, in language, may be precisely the condition of possibility for our authentic engagement with the phenomena we encounter. Hasn't Helen told us as much?

The final idea Helen sets forth, which brings together nicely much of what we have been discussing, is that the quite real world Helen inhabits, along with ourselves, is constituted in and through the imagination – that in fact, paradoxically enough, the world *becomes* real, just as it did at that fateful scene by the well, precisely to the extent that it issues from the imaginary. 'I tread the solid earth', Helen writes; 'I breathe the scented air', and 'Out of these two experiences I form numberless associations and correspondences. I observe, I feel, I think, I imagine. I associate the countless varied impressions, experiences, concepts.' And what happens, she believes, is that 'Out of these materials Fancy, the cunning artisan of the brain, welds an image which the skeptic would deny me' (1908: 128).

In this respect, Helen suggests, her own situation is no different from anyone else's. For the fact of the matter is: 'The bulk of the world's knowledge is an imaginary construction.' By extension, of course, so is the world itself. However, we need not equate the imaginary with the *merely* imaginary. 'History', for instance, 'is but a mode of imagining, of making us see civilizations that no longer appear on the earth.' Moreover, 'Some of the most significant discoveries of modern science owe their origin to the imagination of men who had neither accurate knowledge nor exact instruments to demonstrate their beliefs' (1908:89–90). But it would be silly, she implies – rightly, I think – to regard historical or scientific knowledge as *merely* imaginary.

None of what has been said here should be taken to mean that the sensory information Helen receives is irrelevant.

> Without the shy, fugitive, often unobserved sensations and the certainties which taste, smell, and touch give me, I should be obliged to take my conception of the world wholly from others . . . The sensuous reality which interthreads and supports all the gropings of my imagination would be shattered. The solid earth would melt from under my feet and disperse itself into space. The objects dear to my hands would become formless, dead things, and I should walk among them as among invisible ghosts.
>
> (1908:76–7)

Sensory information, therefore, is of the utmost importance in Helen's being able to construct a meaningful world. But this information alone, she believes, would amount to nothing: only with the inclusion of the imagination is a meaningful world possible.

Let us consider an example. 'In other people's houses', Helen notes, 'I can touch only what is shown me – the chief objects of interest, carvings on the wall, or a curious architectural feature, exhibited like the family album.' A house with which she is unfamiliar, therefore, has, 'at first, no general effect or harmony of detail. It is not a complete conception, but a collection of object impressions which, as they come to me, are disconnected and isolated. But my mind', she explains, 'is full of associations, sensations, theories, and with them it constructs the house.' It is not unlike 'the building of Solomon's temple, where was neither saw, nor hammer, nor any tool heard while the stones were being laid one upon another.

The silent worker is the imagination which decrees reality out of chaos' (12–13).

So let us assume, then, that Helen's experience of the world, rather than being merely a function of hearsay, is instead a function of her imagination, which synthesizes the information she receives and, in conjunction with language, creates for her an integrated reality, no more secondhand than our own. With these ideas in mind, might it not be said that the world itself is something akin to the house she constructs in her imagination, a house within which – after it's been constructed – she lives? More generally, do we not all live in such a house, the very reality we inhabit issuing from our own constructive imaginings?

Some might argue that this conception comes perilously close to solipsism. If we, as interpreters, have such a big part in construing reality, then how are we to talk about what is there and what isn't? Are we perceiving the world or just our own subjective interpretations, which would ultimately render it nothing more than a narcissistic mirror of ourselves? It may be unsettling to think in this way about reality. Many may still wish, in the interest of objectivity, to disavow their own participation in the construal of reality. But what we need to recognize is that this participation is by no means equivalent to solipsism or idealism or an uncritical brand of relativism. All we have learned is that our construal of reality, along with our beliefs about it and our evaluations of it, relies, of necessity, on the most fundamental modes of being and knowing that are part of the particular world in which we live.

There are of course some serious challenges presented by this point of view. Most centrally, in avowing our own imaginative participation in the construal of reality, there is the need to ensure as best we can that we are *not* succumbing to solipsism and that our interpretations are *not* merely subjective. Contrary to popular belief, it is still perfectly possible both to avow the primacy of interpretation and to misconstrue the phenomena with which we are concerned; in projecting our own idiosyncratic designs and desires upon the things we encounter, we can in fact fail to abide by what is there, on the page, or on the canvas, or in the person. But what is there, we must recognize, far from being a self-enclosed, static, obdurate thing, able to be captured wholly and unequivocally, is always already saturated in language, verbal or other; it is already *in* the world we inhabit. It is thus nothing other than language itself that prevents us from solipsism; it is this, above all else, that allows us to make sense of things and, occasionally, to share this sense with others. Let us not, therefore, rush hastily to the side of those skeptics who wish to deny Helen her reality, who consider her to be nothing more than a mere vessel for others' words.

In principle at least, her own situation is no different from theirs. But what about this self over which she continues to be so confused? How was she ever to transform this crazy patchwork into something more smooth and coherent?

LOOKING TOWARD THE FUTURE, IN ANTICIPATION

In reflecting on the college experience, Helen still finds that her mind is terribly cluttered up, just as it used to be, though perhaps for somewhat different reasons. 'It is impossible', she argues, 'to read in one day four or five different books in different languages and treating of widely different subjects, and not lose sight of the very ends for which one reads'. There is so much to learn in college, so much to take in, and so little time to do it! It can also get annoying after a while. 'When one reads hurriedly and nervously, having in mind written tests and examinations, one's brain become encumbered with a lot of choice bric-à-brac for which there seems to be little use. At the present time my mind is so full of heterogeneous matter that I almost despair of ever being able to put it in order' (1988: 77). How will I ever manage to find my own thoughts, my own true self, she in effect asks, when all I do is read?

This thought makes Helen not only confused and full of despair, but angry:

> Whenever I enter the region that was the kingdom of my mind I feel like the proverbial bull in the china shop. A thousand odds and ends of knowledge come crashing about my head like hailstones, and when I try to escape them, theme-goblins and college nixies of all sorts pursue me, until I wish – oh, may I be forgiven the wicked wish! – that I might smash the idols I came to worship.
>
> (77)

Much to her dismay, the hole of Helen's heterogeneity was being dug deeper and deeper, the prospect of her ever becoming one with herself growing more and more remote. She was sick and tired of putting everything that was important to her on hold. Everything was always later.

But who was it, we must finally ask, that was growing sick and tired of this incessant deferral? Who was this 'I' doing all of this lamenting, and where did it come from? Again, if it was 'Helen', then how did it manage to escape the clutches of others' thoughts? Had she been born into a world where there were believed to exist autonomous 'selves', who had their own thoughts and could distinguish them from others and who became angry when their autonomy was denied? Or had she just read somewhere that anger was the most appropriate response to having the process of her own coming-into-being deferred? But then who was this 'she' doing the reading? And on and on and on. No wonder everything was so confusing!

Whoever this person was, it seems to have become painfully clear to her that the genesis of her self, rather than culminating in some discrete end, was indeed an end-less project. Stated another way, the self, unlike the house – a thing, that she could gradually piece together bit by bit – was no *thing* (which is not to say nothing) at all; there wasn't anything quite there for Helen to touch, or smell, or taste, and thus no way for her to root her experience of self in a sensuous reality. She therefore couldn't create an image of her self – and nor can we – that was at all like this house of which we have spoken. It was rather a kind of shadowy construct emerging through interpretation, an imaginary vision of completion, as we put it earlier, that quite unlike the house, would have to be refigured, endlessly, in line with the various experiences that were to come her way throughout the course of her life.

Yet she kept on, as she knew she must, realizing perhaps that this process of deferral, even if it was destined to go on forever, as of course it was, was nothing really to fret over; one could still move forward – one could continue to *develop* – without necessarily assuming that it was in the direction of an already specified end. Nor did she need to fret over her disabilities. For the most part, she was just like all the others, overcome by heterogeneity and looking forward to the day when they could justifiably feel that they had come into their own.

One important set of questions remains for us to consider before concluding our discussion of Helen's life. Is the story she has been relating to us an *autobiography*? Or is it ultimately a biography, written by Annie Sullivan and whoever else brought the world to Helen's hands? More generally, we can ask: Is autobiography itself – the telling of 'our own' life story – really possible? Isn't the very determination of what is significant and worth telling and what is not made by others, particularly in the form of the words, modes of understanding, and genres they send our way?

My own conviction is that it is perfectly justified to call what Helen has done an autobiography, even if it is the case that she is inevitably working with 'hand-me-downs', so to speak, derivatives of what has come before; in telling your own story, you can only work with what is available, in the way of words, genres, storylines, and so on. There is no other way, no other means of capturing the 'really real', outside of language and culture, simply because the 'really real', in all of its multiplicity and changeability, is constituted as such *inside* language and culture, inside that 'world' we keep on referring to. Thus, autobiographies, biographies, and histories –

not to mention scientific theories – far from capturing reality 'in itself', can only aspire to disclose that which has already assumed its specific form in and through language. These hand-me-downs, therefore, are themselves unsurpassable; they can never completely be left behind.

But let me be quick to add that nothing whatsoever has been said about the uses to which these hand-me-downs may be put. Some people will appropriate them as they are; they will remain within the established idiom of their respective worlds and merely repeat what has already been. They will thus remain second-rate writers and perhaps rather boring, somewhat self-less selves. Others – Helen among them – seem to want to break the stronghold of the old altogether; they want to find images or words or thoughts or *selves* that are strictly their own. To a certain extent, they may be able to do this. But their ultimate goal – that of somehow creating their very own universe of language and meaning – must inevitably be thwarted by the fact that they are always already in a world whose contours have been supplied prior to their entry. Others still will try to seize upon what is and, precisely through attempting to rework the old, the established idiom, succeed in creating something – or someone – new and original.

While others' words inevitably speak through us, therefore, it is not quite fair to say that we are merely dummies, sitting on the laps of ventriloquists, mouthing their words. This may sometimes be the case, but not always. This is because as much as we ourselves are 'written' by the various texts we read, we are not done so without remainder. Helen herself demonstrates this point well: despite the fact that she continued to be plagued by the bric-à-brac in her mind, so much of which had come to her through the texts she read, she was still able to give out, in her own writing and in her own self, more than she took in.

She was probably able to do this even better as time wore on, given the vigilance she had learned to keep over her own work. In the end, she might have felt humbled by the fact that she could never completely leave behind the texts she had read, and that consequently, she could never completely be an original and originating voice, an author. But she might also have taken some solace in the fact that this incessant deferral of her own goal of becoming herself was, at the very least, a sign of life.

Chapter 4
Living to tell about it

PURE IMAGINATION

In certain important respects, we will be picking up where we left off by inquiring still further into the relationship between the lives we live and the narratives we come to tell about them. Things will be a bit different here, however, in that instead of drawing on a work of autobiography, as in previous chapters, we will be looking at a work of fiction, namely Jean-Paul Sartre's *Nausea* (1964). Interestingly enough, our basic mode of exploring this work will probably not seem very different from that which we have employed so far. If only in this minimal sense, therefore, there is not all that much separating the interpretation of supposedly 'true' stories from fictional ones.

There is, however, at least one important methodological distinction to be made. That is, whereas in the previous books we did in fact try to learn something about the authors themselves, since it was they who were doing the narrating, in the present case, we will be doing no such thing: there is not much to be learned about Sartre himself, on the basis of his imaginary creations. This route could be taken by placing the present novel in relation to all the other things Sartre wrote, by learning about his own life, and so on, but that would be a very different task from the one at hand; it would be largely psychobiographical, the text being seen as a pointer of sorts to its place of origin, the author. But this is not at all what we will be doing here. Instead, we will be dealing mainly with the 'narrator' of this 'story' – it will become evident soon enough why these words are inside quotation marks – in order to inquire more comprehensively still into a number of the problems we have considered in the previous chapters.

The narrator, Antoine Roquentin, seems to know all too well many of these problems. The novel takes the form of a kind of metaphysical journal in which Roquentin aims to record in piecemeal fashion the goings-on of his life. This indeed is what he ought to be doing, he believes: 'The best thing', he says, 'would be to write down events from day to day. Keep a diary to see clearly – let none of the nuances or small happenings escape even though they might seem to mean nothing. And above all', he goes on, they must be classified: 'I must tell how I see this table, this street, the people, my packet of tobacco, since *those* are the things which have changed.' Moreover, he 'must determine the exact extent and nature of this change' (1964:1).

Nothing, therefore, will escape from Roquentin's gaze, no matter how small and insignificant it may appear to be; he will prevent himself from succumbing to the insidious process of ordering his experience by refusing to deal with it selectively, claiming this is meaningful, that is not. In this manner, he suggests, he will try to remain as close to the real as he possibly can. Recall in this context what was said in the first chapter in regard to the relationship between lives and texts; in the second chapter, in regard to the 'illusoriness' of narrating one's life; and in the third chapter, in regard to the schematization of experience through language. There was a distinct sense, throughout each of these discussions, in which we tried to work through some of the difficulties attendant on seeking the real and the true via narrative. Might it not be preferable to abandon narrative altogether, to refuse to be that further step removed from life itself, to embrace instead the untidiness of ongoing present moments? This is precisely what Roquentin seems to have in mind.

His project isn't without its own difficulties, however, for there is still a definite 'danger' in keeping a diary of this sort. The fact is, 'you exaggerate everything. You continually force the truth because you're always looking for something' (1). Simply put, what Roquentin tells us is that writing, even in the minimal fashion he has chosen, is not living; rather, it is an act, in which consciousness is somehow added on to the experience one wishes to write about, the result being that the very act itself, the attempt to record faithfully what it is that is going on, cannot help but alter the experience itself. Even the writing of a diary, therefore – indeed, even conscious reflection itself – will subtly transform what is being considered. It is a kind of cat-and-mouse game, we might say: even as I try to capture the thing itself, my very act of trying leads it to recede. But isn't this still the 'best thing' one could do?

'Naturally, I can write nothing definite about this Saturday and the day-before-yesterday business. I am already too far away from it; the only thing I can say is that in neither case was there anything which would ordinarily be called an event' (2). Roquentin isn't about to reify the flux of his past experience into something it was not by conferring upon it the dubious status of an 'event'. He could conjure up some memories of this and that, to be sure, and he could also invent accounts of some of the things that happened on those less-than-fateful days, but more than anything, he believes, there was just a series of 'coincidences', strewn together, that he really 'can't explain' to himself. Even if he could explain these coincidences, moreover, why should he? What purpose would it serve, other than to delude him into thinking that life did indeed have some rhyme and reason?

Roquentin will therefore resist the desire to falsify and distort his experience, however powerful it may be. He will resist those conventional markers and signposts we often employ in trying to come to terms with our experience, toward the end of remaining true to life. Rather than assuming the role of 'autobiographer', therefore, he will assume the role of a reporter, a witness, who will tell it as it is. Should 'as it is' prove to be rather aimless and haphazard, a kaleidoscopic stroll through disconnected vagaries and accidents, so much the better: at least we will have met the void head on, without the crude consolations of our narrative designs. 'The thing is', he says, 'I rarely think'. What happens instead is that 'a crowd of small metamorphoses accumulate in me without my noticing it, and then, one fine day, a veritable revolution takes place'. This is exactly why his life has been given 'such a jerky, incoherent aspect' (5). Notice the implication here. Were he to *think*, a bit more than he does, his life might not be so thoroughly jerky and incoherent; he would be creating meaningful interconnections, smoothing over all of the rough edges, thereby giving it some semblance of wholeness and unity. Living as he does largely in the moment, however, the possibility for this is essentially obviated.

Roquentin is different from others in another way as well. Whereas most people have their own ostensibly continuous identities confirmed, mirrored, and supported by others, he lives 'alone, entirely alone' (6). Thoughts of others do indeed cross his mind every now and then, words flow through him, but 'I fix nothing. I let it go.' He thus marvels at all the young people sitting in cafés, drinking coffee, and telling such 'clear, plausible stories'. If he were in their place, he believes, he'd be hopelessly confused: without people asking him how he spends his time, like they do, he has all but forgotten how to respond. 'When you live alone', he says, 'you no longer know what it is to tell something: the plausible disappears at the same time as the friends'. All he does in this solitary existence, then, is 'let events flow past; suddenly you see people pop up who speak and who go away, you plunge into stories without beginning or end' (7). He would make a 'terrible witness', of course, if he was forced into the position of accounting for a coherent constellation of events, as happens in courtrooms and the like. For what could he possibly say that would be of value? Existing in the now, with nobody ever there to call forth the events of his life, he simply moves forward in time, on and on and on, into the future. Would there exist narratives, would there exist *selves*, without demands for accounts, either from others or from oneself? Couldn't these simply be artifactual responses to questions that might be better left unposed? In any case, 'I am not in the habit of telling myself what happens to me', he explains, 'so I cannot quite recapture the succession of events, I cannot distinguish what is important' (9). Maybe in due time he will get better at all this.

One of the further problems Roquentin faces is that he is presently writing a book, a history book no less, about a man named Rollebon, and it is a project requiring an entirely different attitude from the one he has adopted in writing his diary: whereas in the former narrative ordering is often considered to be of the essence, in the latter, as we have seen, it is largely to be avoided. Yet the specific difficulties he faces in writing are in certain respects much the same. There is no lack of documents, he notes; there may in fact be too many. Instead, 'What is lacking is firmness and consistency'. How exactly is he supposed to be able to take this massive quantity of heterogeneous information and make any sense of it? It's not that the documents contradict one another; but neither do they agree. If he was truly honest, in fact, he would have to admit that 'they do not seem to be about the same person'. But don't other historians face exactly the same task, of somehow creating a measure of order and coherence out of the disparate materials before them? 'How do they do it? Am I more scrupulous', he asks, 'or less intelligent?' Is he so faithful to the heterogeneity of these documents that the prospect of synthesizing them into a continuous narrative can't help but feel dishonest? Or is he simply too blind to see what's there? 'In truth', he must ask, 'what am I looking for?' The honest answer is, 'I don't know' (13).

It would be easy enough to raise some hypotheses about what is connected with what, but Roquentin is terribly skeptical about their validity. Indeed, he says, 'I am beginning to believe that nothing can ever be proved.' True enough, he continues, 'These are honest hypotheses which take the facts into account.' At the same time, however, 'I sense so definitely that they come from me, and that they are simply a way of unifying my own knowledge' that it is all but impossible to forge ahead in good faith. 'Not a glimmer comes from Rollebon's side'; all he was doing was living, and thus he could not possibly have had access – at least not access of the same sort – to the kinds of designs Roquentin has now, in the present: 'Slow, lazy, sulky, the facts adapt themselves to the rigour of the order I wish to give them; but it remains outside of them.' Is it any wonder he has the feeling 'of doing a work of pure imagination'? (13).

Perhaps some historians could rest comfortably with their hypotheses, believing that they were sufficiently 'data-driven' to be deemed probable. They could of course be wrong about these hypotheses, but apparently it isn't any great problem for them to assume that something like a true story could be told. For Roquentin, however, it would seem that the very idea of a true story could be nothing short of oxymoronic, a contradiction in terms.[1] We thus return, albeit in a somewhat different context, to a question posed earlier: since stories move backward in time and life itself moves forward, how could they possibly be called 'true'? It doesn't matter one whit how meticulous, objective, and 'faithful' an historian tries to be, Roquentin implies; once he or she starts making connections, the truth will be out of reach. How then can he go on with this project, knowing as he does that the very moment he tries to make sense of the data he will inevitably be corrupting them by transforming them into something they never were? The very condition for writing history, he might say, is to *lie*. For given that the past qua past only exists now, in present consciousness, what other conclusion could possibly be drawn? This will not be an easy book to write at all, not at least unless he starts thinking about the entire process in a radically different fashion from how he has so far. Can he?

FACE TO FACE

Staring into the mirror beholding the image before him, Roquentin can understand 'nothing'. He is pleased that he has nice red hair, so definite, so concrete and real, but aside from this there is little. 'Obviously there are a nose, two eyes and a mouth', he says (he's not completely out of touch with reality!), 'but none of it makes sense, there is not even a human expression' (16). Moving still closer, touching the mirror finally, even these fade and disappear, until 'nothing human is left' (17). Should we not say, ultimately, that the capacity to perceive human expression is itself a work of pure imagination? Move close enough and it disappears; a new perspective has been adopted. What is really there except a kind of strange topography of things – bumps and holes and hair and skin, each simply existing by themselves, alone? 'Perhaps it is impossible to understand one's own face'. Or, again, the problem could be his solitude: 'People who live in society have learned how to see themselves in mirrors as they appear to their friends' (18); they see themselves through the eyes of others. And it is just this, he has told us, that he cannot do. What is it that one feels, looking out at the world, face to face, as it swoons dizzily along, one thing after another, drunk on its own cheap events? A bit nauseated.

Only the music he hears – a piece of jazz, like a band of steel, solid and hard – can manage to cut through this weird, vertiginous existence. 'It seems inevitable', Roquentin says, 'so strong is the necessity of this music: nothing can interrupt it, nothing which comes from this time in which the world has fallen; it will stop by itself, as if by order'. Then a voice enters in amidst the din of sounds, 'as if it were the event for which so many notes were preparing, from so far away, dying that it might be born'. At long last, '*something has happened*' (22), something palpable, connected, and real, the parts of which do indeed belong together in a relationship of necessity: a melody, a kind of ideal object, able to exist still even when all material traces of it have vanished.

It was a far cry from the flimsy and manifestly *un*necessary relationships he had often created in examining both his own life and Rollebon's. Isn't it odd, he might have thought, that a piece of music should seem so much more there, so much more present, than anything else? If only life itself were a melody! But it isn't. Instead it is filled with pitiful gestures to order the flux, like those of an acquaintance of Roquentin's, the Self-Taught Man, who moves from book to book in alphabetical order. Perhaps he ought not be too hard on the man, though: at least with a sense of where he needed to go in his quest for knowledge he could avoid the ghastly stomach problems that Roquentin himself faced. 'There is a universe behind and before him' (30), and for this the Self-Taught Man is undoubtedly thankful; though of course it goes without saying that when he finally exhausts 'Z', he will be hurled into the void in a rather big way. One can only postpone this kind of encounter for so long.

As for Roquentin, who continues occasionally to let himself be 'caught' in the snares of memory, the encounter looms large. 'My memories', he feels, 'are like coins in the devil's purse: when you open it you find only dead leaves.' An image comes into his mind of a day long past, but he does not really know where he was; and even though if he closes his eyes he can recreate a scene – 'a tree in the distance, a short dingy figure runs towards me' – he knows better than to trust it. He is 'inventing all this to make out a case'. Yes, of course, 'certain details, somewhat curtailed, live in my memory'; there is no denying that there are indeed things very much like traces of the past, fragments of images, within us. 'But I don't *see* anything anymore. I can search the past in vain, I can only find these scraps of images and I am not sure what they represent, whether they are memories or just fiction' (32).

Are these images merely random flutterings on the winds of the past?

Are they telling in any way, like the 'screen memories' of which Freud (1899, 1901) has written, in which fragments of both the real and the imagined become fused together into the deceptive – but no less telling – guise of history? According to Freud, the images such as those entering Roquentin's mind are probably important for the simple reason that if they weren't, they wouldn't be recollected. Yet little importance is attached to these images. Could it therefore be that they stand for something else, something more important, that has been omitted from consciousness owing to the threat it presents? Is this something else inside Roquentin somewhere, exercising its secret schemes and plots by dressing itself up in the drab garments of the insignificant? No. Roquentin must catch himself here; he must not immerse himself in these deep waters. 'I could still tell stories, tell them all too well, . . . but these are only the skeletons. There's the story of a person who does this, does that, but it isn't I, I have nothing in common with him.' In addition to images, there are words aplenty; it would be no trouble at all, therefore, for him to attach meanings to these memories surging into consciousness. But they would not really be *his* meanings, he feels; rather, they would be those of the imaginary character in his mind. *I*, he suggests, am right here now, remembering. And if I am here, how can I be somewhere else as well? It must not, indeed it cannot, be me, he concludes; it is an-other. 'New images are born in me, images such as people create from books who have never travelled.' As for the words that come to mind: 'My words are dreams, that is all' (33).

Yet Roquentin remains ambivalent about remembering; he cannot quite bring himself to stop. 'For a hundred dead stories', he admits, 'there still remain one or two living ones'. These, of course, he must evoke 'with caution, occasionally, not too often'; they are precious and he doesn't want to wear them out. But they too can easily become defiled: 'I stop suddenly: there is a flaw, I have seen a word pierce through the web of sensations', and it may very well be 'that this word will soon take the place of several images I love'. He must therefore 'stop quickly and think of something else'. But it may be too late, for 'the next time I evoke them a good part will be congealed' (33).

Reminiscent of Schachtel's (1959) perspective, as discussed in the previous chapter, the idea here is that on some level language cannot help but deform and distort one's memories of the past; it replaces them, by putting something else in their stead. Experience, Schachtel writes, 'is always fuller and richer than the articulate formula by which we try to be aware of it or recover it'. But as time wears on, it is this formula, which itself becomes 'increasingly flat and conventionalized', that stands in place of the original. Thus we come to suffer a kind of alienation from the real itself, our perception and experience, trapped in the formulaic designs of the civilized adult world, growing deadened, a step removed from the immediacy of life. As for memory, it is 'even more governed by conventional patterns than are perception and experience' (291). Indeed, given what Schachtel has to say about the schematization and conventionalization of memory, about the inability to recall the experiences of early childhood especially 'in their freshness, in the real significance which they had at that time' (294), much of our past is 'condemned to oblivion' (296). The gap between experience itself and the words we employ to describe it can never be bridged.

Annie Dillard (1987a) makes a similar point in noting that the very act of writing a memoir, which she has recently done, is perhaps the surest way to 'lose' one's memories; you're 'cannibalizing your life for parts' (70). Indeed, after you've written, 'you can no longer remember anything but the writing. However true you make that writing, you've created a monster.' So it is that her memories — which, like Roquentin's, are best seen as 'elusive, fragmentary, patches of color and feeling' — die in the process of committing them to words. 'The work is a sort of changeling on the doorstep — not your baby, but someone else's rather like it, different in some way that you can't pinpoint, and yours has vanished' (71). The only difference between Roquentin and Dillard is that for Roquentin there is no need to await a concrete act of writing for his memories to become deformed, congealed, and lost; all this happens in the act of remembering itself once words slip in, only to erect a hopelessly and irretrievably dense barrier to the reality of the past. Remembering for Roquentin is thus implicitly seen as a kind of writing, which, rather than being a re-presentation of the past, refigures it in and through consciousness.

It may seem that there is nothing especially new about the point we are now considering. We have already spoken on several occasions of rewriting both the past as well as the self itself. Indeed, we have described it as a condition of self-understanding: only when the past is rewritten, such that new interpretations are made to emerge, does there exist the possibility for an enlarged understanding; 're-presentation' or 're-production', we noted — which is exactly what Roquentin and Dillard seem to long for, in the form of those precious fragments, untainted by the vicious prism of the present — could never really serve this end. Let me try to clarify this issue. In no way would I want to fault an autobiographical work, like Dillard's for instance, for its attempt to be faithful to the past; this is largely what a memoir (if not an autobiographical narrative)[2] tries to do. I therefore do not accuse her, or Roquentin for that matter, of getting things all wrong. Her own work (see *An American Childhood* (1987b)) is simply not a story about the movement of self-understanding per se. In fact the subject of the book, as she has stated, is not really *her* at all, but rather – again not unlike in Roquentin's case – the changing world through which she has moved.

We must nevertheless ask of both of them: Do we indeed 'lose' some-thing in the act of remembering or writing? In some sense, I suppose, we do, if only for the fact that once we let our present consciousness 'intrude' in any way, the past that was *is* no longer. This is always the case to some degree. That is, the images one recalls – however pristine, pure, and seemingly self-existent they may appear to be – are inevitably permeated by present consciousness. Memories are thus never to be seen as discrete *things*, but acts: I remember. With this in mind, perhaps we might convince Roquentin and Dillard that the images of which they speak are no less untouched by the present than those that are thoroughly bathed in language and interpretation. By being *images*, in short, they are still to be considered *imaginings*, the products of a conscious being bringing to mind what is not present.

For argument's sake, however, and for the sake of preventing ourselves from too much quibbling over philosophical details, let us assume there do in fact exist something like the untouched, unadorned images Roquentin and Dillard speak of. On a phenomenological level, and following the lead of Proust and others, some of what they have to say does ring true: every now and then an image – or a smell or a taste or a feeling – happens along that all but transports us into the past, almost like a kind of time travel. There still remain some important questions for us to consider, however. For even if we assume that such images do exist and that they are real 'fragments' of the past, must we conclude that the memories subsequently formed are merely pale and shadowy replicas, unreal substitutes for reality itself? Must we conclude furthermore that the very process of enlarging our own understanding of the past via rewriting is tantamount to its deformation and, ultimately, destruction? We often suppose in retrospect that we have finally gained access to a 'truth' we had never known before, one that was unavailable in the flux of experience. But is untruth therefore to be seen as the very *condition* of truth? Does it make sense to think about these issues in this way? Why should we not speak of transformation rather than replacement, of reconstruction rather than destruction, of gain rather than loss?

According to Roquentin, the 'I' he is right now, so full and fleshy (even if nauseous), is the pre-eminent reality. Hence, the characters who are the actors of his memories are seen as just that: *actors*, shrunken substitutes for the real thing. Likewise, as concerns these memories themselves, only the ones that are crisp and clean, unsullied by words, truly deserve to be called real; anything else is un-. But why? What makes those characters we imagine ourselves to have been, however different they may be from this full and fleshy 'I', any less real? The 'psychical', Freud has argued, may well need to be distinguished from the 'material', but is it not the case that they are both quite real? Perhaps Roquentin and Dillard (and the young Augustine as well) are so caught up in the perdurable trappings of the material world – the world presented, as if nakedly, when one gazes into a mirror, and when images from the past, hard and concrete, flash before one's eyes, like comets cutting through the dark – that they cannot see beyond it. It might therefore be wise for them to remember: the task of beholding oneself face to face is in no way reserved for mirrors alone.

THE START OF SOMETHING BIG

We nonetheless have before us another challenge – and it is a serious one – to the idea of rewriting the self. Alongside the overarching problem of narrative, as we discussed it in the case of Augustine, as well as the more fundamental problem of language, as we discussed it in the case of Helen Keller, there is again this problem of memory, which is in certain important respects the place where the two meet: the moment we try to do anything more than call up a former experience, it has been argued, we are imagining and thus fictionalizing, the monuments of the past suddenly becoming congealed into 'monsters' that we will never be quite able to shake. What's more, it follows from this perspective that each and every time we return to the past, an entirely new monster will have been created; what had already been rewritten will have been rewritten yet again, the latest version thus being another step away from the original, now long gone, dead, and never to be resurrected. The result? All we have are memories of memories of memories; and the longer we live, it would seem, the more fictional our pasts – and, of course, we ourselves – will have to be. So it goes.

It should be noted that Freud, among others, had a quite different way of understanding these issues. Our experiences, he suggested, were in some sense to be regarded as discrete and bounded entities, as artifacts, able to be retrieved given the proper archeological tools. This is not to say that he ignored the idea that the past could be rewritten, that memory could confer new meaning and significance upon one's previous experience; much of the work of psychoanalysis was based upon exactly this fact. Nevertheless, rather than seeing earlier mental formations as being wholly superseded and replaced by new ones, he saw them instead as 'overlaid'. What this means, he argued, is that no matter how far we develop into adulthood, nothing ever perishes. Hence the metaphor of archeology: the project of analysis was precisely to cut through the countless versions of the past that had been 'written' in memory and to behold the originals from whence they supposedly sprang.³

It could be, therefore, that Roquentin and company are wrong about proclaiming that owing to the machinations of memory, the past 'in itself' must die; perhaps, à la Freud, it is merely buried and overlaid by rewriting, there but inaccessible. It could also be that Freud is wrong, of course. Perhaps he entered into the materialism of his time a bit too wholeheartedly, thereby coming to conceptualize as 'things' phenomena that were best thought of in other terms. Indeed, it could be that the entire project of conceiving of psychoanalysis as archeology is the result of his misplaced concretism and is thus fundamentally flawed (see especially Schafer 1983, Spence 1982). We will discuss this issue further in Chapter 6 of the present book. For now, we will simply note that the verdict is not yet in.

The problem with which we began still remains. I have suggested that both memories and narratives, however removed they may be from our previous experience, still deserve to be considered real and potentially important as sources of information about ourselves and our pasts. I have also suggested that Roquentin and Dillard might have something of a fetish for the material world; because our memories are not nearly so full and fleshy as life itself, they were regarded, problematically by my account, as inferior and shadowy derivatives. But why should I have faith that they are anything more? And why should anyone?

Let us return to Roquentin as he examines an old picture of a woman he had once loved, unable to recognize her. 'I have never had such a strong feeling', he writes, 'that I was devoid of secret dimensions, confined within the limits of my body, from which airy thoughts float up like bubbles'. Once more: 'I build memories with my present self. I am cast out, forsaken in the present: I vainly try to rejoin the past: I cannot escape' (33). How could he ever 'rejoin' her? All he has is an image of an image as he sits now and looks. What good are photographs anyway? Common-sense wisdom has it that they preserve our memories or some such thing. But don't they really do just the opposite? Don't they serve *in lieu* of memories, serving as reminders not so much of that which lives on but that which is dead? We sometimes cry when we look at them, so moved are we by the ancient treasures we are beholding. But aren't we also grieving over that which we will never see again? A photograph: an attempt to freeze time, a material substitute for the real, an image of what is not. How tragic, Roquentin might say – all those scrapbooks, filled with nothing.

The Self-Taught Man had wanted to see some of these photographs. It is not surprising; his motivation is much the same as that which has led him to pore alphabetically through the stacks of the library. Obsessed in his desire for order and coherence, for a reason to get up every day and feel that he knows what has to be done, he's no doubt expecting some pathetic travelogue, where one magically transforms the mundane occurrences of everyday life into an adventure, into something worth telling about. 'He can go to Hell' (33).

Think of all of the things that can happen when one travels, says the Self-Taught Man: 'Getting on the wrong train. Stopping in an unknown city. Losing your briefcase, being arrested by mistake, spending the night in prison' (35). Wonderful, isn't it? Ah, the wondrous 'magic' of travel, of adventure. Has Roquentin had any? A few, he answers. But no sooner than he does is he 'seized with contrition; it seems as though I am lying, that I have never had the slightest adventure in my life, or rather, that I don't even know what the word means anymore' (36).

As Scheibe (1986) has suggested, people often seem to require adventures in order to convince themselves, consciously or unconsciously, that their lives have been full and abundant; in our own culture especially, replete as it is with individuals bent on doing different and unique things, it is important that one have something interesting to say when asked the sort of question the Self-Taught Man asks Roquentin. Now this does not mean, Scheibe recognizes, that adventures are necessarily regarded as such at the time of experience; the main thing is that one be able to see, through what he calls 'retrospective narrative enrichment', that one's life has indeed been worthwhile. Don't we want our own stories to be as full and rich and eventful as those we read about?

The relationship between adventure and memorability can be framed in two distinct ways. On the one hand, it may be that an 'objectively' adventurous life, filled with great events of one sort or another, culminates, as a function of the value conferred upon it, in memorability: it's clearly been well worth the trek, one might say. But on the other hand (namely Roquentin's), it may be that the need for memorability – which is itself a value conferred by our culture – is what leads to the positing of an adventurous past. Whereas the first account looks forward in time, the second looks back, the need for notable endings resulting in notable beginnings. It is exactly this need that Roquentin wants no part of. Thus, when the Self-Taught Man begins to ask him to recount 'one of those famous tales', he refuses to comply. 'No', Roquentin says to himself upon his companion's departure; 'I haven't had any adventures' (1964: 36).

Lots of things have happened through the years, but to call them adventures – even that time when he was almost stabbed by a knife-wielding attacker – would surely be stretching things beyond their true limits. Is he just fussing over words, stubbornly refusing to call a spade a spade? No, he insists; it is more than this. You see, he explains, 'I had imagined that at certain times my life could take on a rare and precious quality.' Suddenly, though, and 'without any apparent reason' (reasons are fictions too), he realized that he had been 'lying' to himself. He has no particular problem admitting that 'everything they tell about in books can happen in real life', at the level of events at any rate, 'but not in the same way' (36). He had nevertheless 'clung' to a belief in the identity of the two.

'The beginnings', Roquentin explains further, 'would have had to be real beginnings'. Yes, that is what he had wanted. 'Real beginnings are like a fanfare of trumpets, like the first notes of a jazz tune, cutting short tedium, making for continuity.' The start of something big, as it were. But consider this: 'Something is beginning in order to end: adventure does not let itself be drawn out; it only makes sense when dead' (37). Thus 'this beautiful melodious form sinks entirely into the past', never to return. Roquentin still wishes life could be announced and then announced again by this fanfare of trumpets, just like the jazz tune: 'what summits would I not reach if *my own life* made the subject of the melody'. The idea is very much 'still there, unnameable' (38). But there is something just too self-indulgent and unreal about the whole business; adventures are parts of monuments that he is no longer willing to build.

As an aside, we can venture that Roquentin is not especially interested in what might be called 'narrative emotions' either, like pride or humility or regret. Each of these refer to states of mind that can only be predicated in relation to the past: with pride, to all of the things I have been or done, for which I am grateful; with humility, to all of the things I might have thought I had been or done, which I now look back on with quiet disbelief; with regret, to all the things I haven't been or done, which calls forth a grievous sense of missed opportunities. It wouldn't be easy for Roquentin to dispense completely with these sorts of states of mind, of course; they are woven into our lexicon and, for many, into consciousness as well. But he would no doubt try all the same. For what each of them points toward, in different ways, is again the culturally-based value that is placed upon the dignity and worth of the individual as well as the tendency of the individual to conceive of his or her life in terms of narrative. In other words, the moment I reflect on the difference between then and now and feel certain things on account of it, I have already proclaimed my continuity as a subject, my worth as an object of reflection, and the virtue of making narrative sense of the difference at hand. What I also do, Roquentin might add, is immediately plunge into illusion: rather than say that good things have happened, I say I am proud and that I was somehow responsible for them; rather than point to my ignorance, I say I am humbled and that I ought to have known; rather than refer to the vagaries of my life, I say I am filled with regret and that I ought to have been able to seize the moment. But there is no reason, one could argue, to reward or punish oneself for the happenings of the past; if they could have been different, they would have been. Whether we imagine the beginning of a trajectory of events to be something big or something small is of no consequence. The principle is the same: I look back and confer meaning on something that simply didn't have it at the time. Why not let bygones be bygones?

'What is found at the historical beginning of things is not the inviolable identity of their origin', Foucault (1977) has written; rather, 'it is the dissension of the things. It is disparity' (142). Not unlike Roquentin, Foucault is suggesting here that we ought not to conceive of the inception of a trajectory of events as the inauguration of a story, the beginning of that fluid and continuous narrative that will lead, as if inevitably, to the outcomes one wishes to explain. This is often how histories get written, he implies; they commence with exactly that sort of fanfare that Roquentin seeks to cast into question. But they ought to be doing the opposite, Foucault believes: rather than trying to erect foundations, history ought to be in the service of disturbing and dismantling them. History must, in a sense, be anti-historical, charting the saccadic path of events in genealogical rather than narrative fashion. Only then will the edge of inevitability be removed, and only then will we render the human past less momentous and precious than we may wish it to be.

NARRATIVE DELUSION AND THE (META)HISTORICAL IMAGINATION

As Roquentin goes on to write, in support of this idea, 'for the most banal event to become an adventure, you must (and this is enough) begin to recount it. This is what fools people: a man is always a teller of tales, he lives surrounded by his stories and the stories of others, he sees everything that happens to him through them; and he tries to live his own life as if he were telling a story.' The thing is, though, 'you have to choose: live or tell' (1964:39).

He proceeds to recount an incident. He had once been with a woman for a few days, having a good enough time. But one evening, when she excused herself to go to the ladies' room, he began to reflect on what had been happening, which, in turn, began to assume the form of an adventure. Upon her return, however, he suddenly found that he hated her, but without quite knowing why. Now he believes he knows: the adventure was ending even as she sat down by his side; they were simply living again, and the banality of it all, juxtaposed against the romantic images he had conjured up in those brief moments she was away, was enough to deaden whatever they might have had together. Had he prevented himself from *thinking* about what had been happening, all would have been well; she would simply have reinserted herself into the ongoing flow of moments: 'Ah, you're back.' Instead, he had transformed her into a character, an actress in the fantastic theater of his imagination: 'Oh, it's you . . . '

If we were really honest with ourselves, Roquentin believes, we would be forced to admit: 'Nothing really happens when you live. The scenery changes, people come in and go out, that's all. There are no beginnings. Days are tacked on to days without rhyme or reason, an interminable monotonous addition' (39). From this perspective, there is nothing really connected or whole or sensible about the movement of our lives except what is created in consciousness; there are no intrinsic or immanent relations between the various things that happen. Thus any and all 'metahistorical' accounts of the past (see White 1973, 1978) – accounts, that is, that seek to contain all of the heterogeneous things that have gone on in some global and coherent narrative picture – must necessarily do damage to these things themselves; they make them out to be something they clearly were not.

Indeed, 'considered as potential elements of a story', White (1978) writes, 'historical events are value-neutral' (84); whether they emerge as components of a tale of tragedy or comedy or irony or satire depends on the historian who is doing the telling, how he or she decides to 'emplot' the events in question. Along these lines, 'Histories are not only about events but also about the possible sets of relationships that those events can be demonstrated to figure. These sets of relationships are not, however, immanent in the events themselves', he argues; rather, 'they exist only in the mind of the historian reflecting upon them' (94). Leaving aside for the moment the question of whether the events of the Holocaust, say, could plausibly be emplotted as comedy, we see that Roquentin and White are fundamentally of a piece on these issues: 'No one and nothing *lives* a story' (111), White insists; a story is instead something one creates in imagination upon pausing to reflect on the ostensibly neutral events of the past.

Even though 'everything changes' when one begins to tell about life, says Roquentin, 'it's a change no one notices'; they think they're telling 'true stories'. But they are of course mistaken: 'As if there could possibly be true stories; things happen one way and we tell about them in the opposite sense' (39). To return to an earlier point, the most fundamental trick one is perpetrating in the very act of telling is the idea of starting at the beginning, when in reality 'you have started at the end'. Stories thus move in the opposite direction from linear time: 'instants have stopped piling themselves in a lighthearted way one on top of the other, they are snapped up by the end of the story which draws them and each one of them in turn, draws out the preceding instant' (40). The information we are receiving, in other words, we know we will come to appreciate later on as the telling of subsequent events retroactively transfigures the seemingly banal and profane into the significant and sacred.[4]

From this perspective, therefore, there is a problem in that we forget, all too easily, that nothing at all was being announced at the time of occurrence, no pointers, no directions, no intimations of the things to come; 'the future was not yet there', except in the form of a vague and shapeless apparition. How arrogant Roquentin had been: 'I wanted the moments of my life to follow and order themselves like those of a life remembered.' He wanted to be immortalized, as it were, by living a life that deserved to be called memorable. But there is also something markedly defensive about this desire, Roquentin suggests. For isn't this attempt to step out of the flow of life by reversing the steady march of time a useful way of blinding oneself to the end, moving ever closer? Those who live in the moment know all too well that their time will come; the clock keeps ticking on and on. Those who seek to occupy the misty regions of the past, however, who want to enshrine themselves through the stories they tell, can take comfort in the fact that these stories – like melodies – will live forever. Might it not be, therefore, Roquentin in effect asks, that the desire to narrate, to immortalize onself through stories, is an attempt to deny death itself?

THE BANALITY OF EXISTENCE

People congregate in bars and restaurants, or they eat 'copious' Sunday meals, only to rise from their tables sluggishly to get dressed and go out on the town; they hear familiar Sunday noise, as they wait in a line to see a movie, which 'would speak and dream for them'; they all seem afraid somehow, at the core, afraid that their precious day would be spoiled. 'Soon, as every Sunday, they would be disappointed' (50); the movie would fail to match their expectations, they'd be surrounded by degenerates, and those whom they might have hoped would speak and exist, connectedly, would be alone and distant, lost in the void of the day's stifling aimlessness. 'Soon, as on every Sunday, small, mute rages would grow in the darkened hall' (51), as if people were ready to burst from the silence.

You could also go to the cemetery to visit the dead, or to your parents' house, or take a walk somewhere Lovely.

There is a bit more of a 'mixture', Roquentin notices, in the afternoon than in the morning; the 'fine social hierarchy' that had landed people at their respective luncheon tables is now largely gone; out on the street, everyone comes together in their mutual estrangement, passing and then fading. All is calm, if not quite well. Soon, they would all return home for another gathering of some sort. 'For the moment it seemed they wanted to live with the least expenditure, economize words, gestures, thoughts, float: they had only one day in which to smooth out their wrinkles, their crow's feet, the bitter lines made by a hard week's work.' But then, of course, as often happens, time starts wasting away; it is nearing the end of this fine day. Would they be able, Roquentin asks, 'to store up enough youth' to begin again tomorrow? 'They filled their lungs because the sea air vivifies: only their breathing, deep and regular as that of sleepers, still testified that they were alive' (52). Roquentin doesn't know quite what to make of all of this, what with his 'hard, vigorous body in the midst of the tragic, relaxed crowd' (53); it's just another day for him, and there is no need for consolations.

There is something ironic about Sundays. For just as people seize upon this fine day, this supposed break from the steady routines of the workaday world designed for enjoyment and relaxation, they often find themselves encountering head-on a kind of emptiness. After all the frantic energy of the week gone by, the manifest desire is often to take it slow and easy, to put a gentle salve on the wounds recently incurred. What they really need, however, is more busyness and activity, something to fill up the void that has suddenly been left. Only rarely do they succeed.

But what is happening here? Is it that people are finally face to face with the awful fact of how empty life can be in the absence of order and structure? Are they suddenly discovering what life is really like when they are left to their own devices, free to do as they please? Perhaps it is freedom itself that incites this emptiness: all dressed up and nowhere to go. Or could it be that the pleasantness of Sundays, set against the surrounding weeks, calls out all too loudly the difference between what life might be, if there could only be time enough to enjoy it, and what it usually is? It is curious that pleasure can sometimes be so tragic. But isn't it the case that pleasure sometimes gets buried in a kind of grief, owing to one's knowledge of just how ephemeral it is? It may be difficult to reconcile the realization that there is freedom and pleasure on but one measly day out of seven. Why should life be this way? Is it a matter of necessity, a function of scarce resources perhaps?

We need not decide whether the meaning of Sundays, as articulated by Roquentin, owes its existence to the pain of emptiness or the pleasure of abundance; they may not be so far apart and contradictory as we might suppose. In any case, Roquentin reminds himself, the Sunday he has been witnessing is theirs, not his; he is merely an observer, the days passing one by one 'in disorder'. He considers himself fortunate in this respect too; for even though his own life may be an aimless blur, rather formless and indistinct, at least he is not left with the 'taste of ashes' like all these others. With no expectations of what this fine day will bring and no need to sit at home at night and reflect wistfully on how nice it has all been, there will be no ending and thus no disappointment.

The problem with all of these people, it would appear, is that whether they opt for relaxation or adventure, what is most important is that they have done something that can be called worthwhile after all is said and done; they need to be sure that they have not wasted this precious day. But they must of course pay the price for this story they so desperately want to be able to tell. The price is that the story must end. Thus another Sunday fades away for them into oblivion, dying its slow death, until finally, before the day is even done, it is all in the past. It's just not worth it, Roquentin seems to say. If the price for trying to live one's life in story-like fashion is ashes, he would rather have no part of it.

The very next morning, however, he realizes that he has been gloating over everyone's despair. 'At heart', he says, 'what disgusts me is having been so sublime last evening'. When he was 20, he goes on to note, he used to get drunk, rogue-style. He knew even then that he was playing the role of hero, the romantic sod burying himself merrily or sadly in drink so as to take on the world's woes. But that was all right; that's what 20-year-olds did. The following morning he would find himself sick nonetheless, and not merely on account of all he had drunk, but on account of his pretenses, his desire to live in the shape of an image. Now, however, there is no excuse; 'I got excited like an imbecile'. He thus needs to wash himself clean 'with abstract thoughts, transparent as water' (56). Despite his best efforts, he had fallen prey to making himself precious by imagining himself as the one who could heroically escape from the tawdry stories others were telling, but in the very process he was doing exactly the same thing as they were. Wasn't he doing it right now, in fact, as well? It comes as no surprise that he feels dirty: the ashes are upon him too.

ACCIDENTS WILL HAPPEN

It appears that there is something inescapable about this desire to tell.

Roquentin pauses for a moment to reflect again on the historical figure, Rollebon, he has been writing about. 'I could imagine him so well', he says, 'if I let myself go'. The fact is, a character has indeed begun to emerge from his researches, a personality, characterized by 'rascality', as 'candid, spontaneous', and 'sincere as his love of virtue' (58). There is no denying, therefore, that Roquentin could, if he wished, bring together all of the information at hand into a serviceable unity. But why not go all the way? If this is where the information leads him, he might as well write a novel. But again, wouldn't he then be guilty of warding off the threat of 'real life', in all of its contingency, heterogeneity, and difference? Aren't stories ultimately defensive delusions, created as a means of defying the onslaught of time, with its accidents, its unforeseen and unforeseeable consequences, its nameless and unending future?

Lest we suppose that these concerns are those of existential philosophers alone, consider what the social and developmental psychologist Kenneth Gergen argued not very long ago (1977, 1980). Despite the heartfelt desires of a good many researchers and theorists to extend the domain of developmental psychology to the entire life course, including adulthood and old age, many of them have had their desires thwarted by their discovery that lawful and predictable relationships are only rarely forthcoming. As opposed to the earlier years of childhood and adolescence, when things are apparently a bit more orderly and regular, once we emerge into adulthood we seem to become as various and different as the situations we live through.

This realization, it should be noted, tends to go against the grain of a good deal of prior developmental thought. Freud, for instance, among others, had tended to assume that the adult years were more or less continuous with the earlier ones, that what we became were essentially variations on set themes, echoes of the distant past. But what Gergen is telling us here (see also Neugarten 1969) is that this assumption of continuity may well be off the empirical mark. So it is that he elected to adopt what he termed an 'aleatoric' perspective on adult 'development': rather than assuming order and stability, we should be on the lookout instead for chance and change, for the random rather than the predictable, for difference rather than identity. There is a further implication to this perspective as well: it is that the idea of development itself, which presumes not only the existence of a continuous subject but the progressive movement of this subject over the course of time, may in fact be outdated and obsolete, a stale leftover from those romantic days when people were thought to be whole, enduring, and headed somewhere good.

Like Roquentin, therefore, Gergen, in positing the random walk of life events rather than the supposedly ordered progression of a unitary subject, casts into question many of the ideas that have served as the very foundation of developmental psychology. While I am basically sympathetic with much of what Gergen has to say, at least as concerns the relative dearth of predictable relationships in adulthood and the need for adopting other models than the ones that tend to be employed, there is nonetheless one fundamental problem with the formulation just discussed that continues to plague me. The problem is that lamentation over the failure to achieve a respectable degree of predictability and so on remains intimately tied to precisely the same prospectively-oriented 'lens' that is rendering extant models suspect: because we cannot predict, he in effect argues, we must conclude that the movement of life is best characterized by chance; and consequently, whatever order we might confer upon this movement must necessarily assume the status of an imposition, a unity created rather than discovered. In this respect too, therefore, Roquentin and Gergen are thoroughly compatible. But must we conclude that just because our lives are unpredictable, they possess no order at all? Or that whatever order they do possess can only be an imposition, a way of fighting the flux? Why, in short, must we always look *forward* in our attempt to assess whether or not life has any continuity?

Consider another example. According to Donald Spence (1988), who has written extensively on the idea of narrative in psychoanalysis (see also 1982; for a critique, see Freeman 1985b), perhaps the most central problem of Freud's approach to interpretation is that it proceeds on the assumption that the world, including the psychic world, is in fact lawful and determinate, and that consequently, it is indeed possible to *find* meaning in it. Spence is for the most part right about this: when Freud interprets a dream or a slip of the tongue or an action, he is usually convinced that, rather than 'reading into it' (as many of his empiricist critics contend), he is discovering what was there, only buried. Recall again the metaphor of archeology in this context, the notion that there exist discrete traces, artifacts, able to be 'recovered' through the tools of analysis. Now while this may sometimes be true, Spence suggests – memories do indeed sometimes seem to get 'unearthed' through analysis – it is much better to assume that it is not. As such, we should adopt what he calls a 'Know-Nothing' world-view, which, because it is based upon a 'clear-eyed, honest, and truthful description of everyday events' (1988: 64), is equivalent to an admission that the world – à la Roquentin and Gergen – is much more random than we might like to think.

In line with the view being offered, the problem with most psychoanalytic research, Spence continues, is that 'it poses as discovery', when in fact it 'is only interested in confirmation'. In other words, because this research presumes that psychic events are lawful, there is a further tendency to presume that meanings are being found rather than made. What many psychoanalysts are thus engaged in is 'pseudo-confirmation and, ultimately, in pseudo-science' (67). Given their 'deep-seated faith in patterning' – their conviction that there must be and is a measure of order to the data they are interpreting – what follows is a 'general readiness . . . to accept almost any explanation' (68).

Why this readiness, this conviction in order and the possibility for discovering meaning? The basic problem for Spence is that analysts tend to fall in all too easily with the idea of the unconscious, which 'conflicts directly with the null hypothesis that chaos is everywhere'. If indeed the unconscious is always presumed to be operative, then randomness is out of the question; meaning is there, somewhere, and we must do our best to find it. Much the same kind of argument, Spence notes, arose in the Middle Ages in conjunction with the treatment of disbelievers: 'If the ways of God seemed inscrutable or baffling or perverse, the problem lay with us, the sinners, and in our lack of faith; what was apparently random on the surface stemmed only from a misguided reading of the natural order.' And the natural order, of course, was beyond doubt – at least until the goal of explaining the world via the Hand of God was exposed as an empty exercise owing to the fact that *everything* could be explained in this manner. Sad to say, but 'much the same problem holds with the present-day concept of the Unconscious' (70). This is surely a caricature of Freud, in my own estimation at any rate; he was well aware of the problem of validity in interpretation and did his best to articulate criteria that would ensure that he did *not* succumb to imposing meaning on what didn't deserve it.

But let us assume for the moment that some credence could be given to Spence's portrayal. What are we to do about the problem at hand? We must make sure, Spence argues, that our attempts at interpretation are paired with the assumption of a random universe; only this, he believes, will prevent interpretation from becoming hopelessly circular. How we are to go about interpreting a random universe he does not say. The reason, of course, is that it is impossible: one cannot *interpret* a random universe at all because it is essentially meaningless. Shades of Roquentin, once again.

Now I do not mean to suggest here that Freud's work is devoid of difficulties; all too often, in fact, he seemed to want to efface his own role in the process of interpretation under the pretenses of merely digging out what was there, already formed, waiting for his magic wand to make it appear. Nor am I suggesting that the process of interpretation more generally is to be understood simply as one of finding self-enclosed, thing-like meanings; much that I have already said in this book argues against this conception. But we must ask again: Why should we be so quick to assume that the order we often locate in texts, dreams, and people's lives is little more than the outdated assumption of determinacy in operation, running wild with pseudo-hypotheses about the way things are? Randomness, for Spence, reigns supreme; poor correlations and the like show this. What else is there but the null hypothesis in a null and void world?

For both Gergen and Spence, following in the footsteps of Roquentin, it is essential for us both to recognize and avow the fact that, appearances notwithstanding, the world is decidedly less orderly than we often suppose. Now to be fair to both of them, they are not maintaining that the world is wholly without order (though at times they come close); empirical science, if undertaken painstakingly and meticulously enough, can in fact continue to tell us many of the things we want to know. Indeed, by and large, it is precisely empirical science that has suggested to them that randomness may well have some primacy over order. There is significantly more to their assertions, however, than the usual empiricist caution against finding order where there is none. The aleatoric perspective Gergen had advocated (he has since made some changes – see e.g. Gergen 1991, Gergen and Gergen 1986) and the Know-Nothing view of which Spence speaks each contain within them a profound sense of skepticism as well: it is time to move beyond those brands of faith – in the idea of development and in the idea of the unconscious, both of which may conceivably owe their existence to a secret allegiance with the (alleged) hand of God – that dupe us into thinking that things are more meaningful than they really are.

What is also important to recognize from this perspective is, again, that if indeed one posits order to a particular array of phenomena, it is more than likely that this order will be made rather than found. Yet this may be nothing to fret over. Following Spence especially, it may in fact be something to celebrate on some level: to the extent that we embrace 'hermeneutics' (which is thought to make meanings) rather than 'science' (which is thought to find them), perhaps we will free ourselves from all of those nasty validity claims that hard-nosed scientist-types continue to insist upon. But note the origin of this version of hermeneutics: owing to the difficulty of finding 'whatever patterns actually exist' (1988: 81), it may be necessary to abandon this project altogether and move instead toward a more aestheticized psychoanalytic perspective, wherein analysands are supplied stories – largely fictional, of course – they might live by. If the truth is so hard to come by, Spence in effect asks, why don't psychoanalysts just do something else? Aren't they really doing something else anyway, only refusing to admit it?

Think again of Roquentin's dilemma: if he's going to be making up the whole story of Rollebon anyway, by transforming all the heterogeneous data before him into a coherent thematic unity, why not dive in headlong and call it a novel? Wouldn't he, like Spence, then be freed from the nagging of his historian friends, who keep insisting that he tell the truth, which can't possibly be done anyway? Let us skip ahead to the end of Sartre's book and see how Roquentin tries to resolve this dilemma.

NARRATIVE DESIRE

'To think that there are idiots who get consolation from the fine arts', Roquentin writes. Someone dies, for instance, and they listen to some classical music as a way of consolation, a way of somehow giving shape to their suffering. His own response is quite different. When a song comes on the phonograph, the lilting notes of a saxophone cutting through the 'drab intimacy' of the world 'like a scythe', he feels ashamed. 'You must be like us', the notes seem to say, 'suffer in rhythm'. Of course he'd like to suffer that way. Who wouldn't? 'But is it my fault', he asks, 'if the beer at the bottom of my glass is warm, if there are brown stains on the mirror, if I am not wanted, if the sincerest of my suffering drags and weighs, with too much flesh and the skin too wide at the same time, like a sea-elephant, with bulging eyes, damp and touching and yet so ugly?' (Sartre 1964:174). How could a piece of music be compassionate when all it does is express what one is not?

This music, as we said earlier, cannot ever be destroyed either. Certainly, he could get up from his table and break the record in half; he could do this with every record that existed. But he could never reach '*it*. It is beyond — always beyond something, a voice, a violin note'. Somehow there is something 'behind' the sounds he hears, 'vibrations in the air which unveil it. It does not exist because it has nothing superfluous: it is all the rest which in relation to it is superfluous. It *is*' (175). This is exactly what leads him to feel ashamed as he sits and listens. All around him are accidents and contingencies, superfluous and unnecessary events, emerging and receding, being born only to die. Nothing seems to *be*; nothing endures through all that happens, no firm designs, no secret melodies.

What does Roquentin want most of all? He too wants to *be*, like the melody. The same desire keeps coming around: 'to drive existence out of me, to rid the passing moments of their fat, to twist them, dry them, purify them, harden myself, to give back at last the sharp, precise sound of a saxophone note' (175). But no; he's just sitting in a bistro in front of a warm glass of beer, fuzzy and imprecise, drifting along with time itself. All the while, the melody remains the same, 'young and firm, like a pitiless witness' (176).

But didn't someone – another human being, stumbling through life – write this melody? The image of this man moves Roquentin; it's the first time in years this has happened. He also feels a bit of envy; he'd like to be in the man's place. He is a hero, this man, 'like the heroes of a novel; they have washed themselves of the sin of existing'. Wouldn't it be nice, Roquentin says, if people would think of him – gently, and with a measure of envy – as he was now thinking of this man? Wouldn't it be nice if he could live in their memories somehow, even after he was long dead? 'This idea suddenly knocks me over'; it had been so long since he had such longing and hope. Something brushes against him, like a soft wind: 'a sort of joy'. He also feels 'extraordinarily intimidated' at the idea, not unlike a man who is 'completely frozen after a trek through the snow and who suddenly comes into a warm room' (177). Suddenly there is the prospect of some life, the shock of a possible future and a possible past. Is he up to it?

Perhaps he should write a book. But not a history book: he had wanted to 'resuscitate' Rollebon but found that he couldn't, that it was impossible; what's dead is dead. He will write another kind of book, one in which 'you would have to guess, behind the printed words, behind the pages, at something which would not exist, which would be above existence'. Perhaps he would write a story of some sort, 'something that could never happen, an adventure', a story that would be 'beautiful and hard as steel and make people ashamed of their existence'. He would take revenge on their ignorance and emptiness through art, timeless, more real in its own way than reality itself, even if it did not quite exist; and he, in turn, would become 'precious and almost legendary' (178).

More important, though, maybe some of the book's clarity and precision would eventually 'fall over' into the story of his past, such that he would be able to remember his life 'without repugnance'. Maybe some day in the future he would be able to look back on this fateful hour and say, 'That was the day, that was the hour, when it all started' (178). Maybe he would be better able to accept himself as well, to feel that he had finally, right then and there, stopped wasting his life.

Roquentin himself, therefore, seems to be in the process of beginning a new chapter in his life. He is not of course in the position of knowing yet what the meaning of this chapter is – that will have to await the future itself, which will, he hopes, be illustrious enough to confer upon this hour the status of a beginning – but he does at least have the sense that a new day, indeed a new kind of day, is dawning. He has a project before him, he is headed in a more or less clear direction rather than wandering about aimlessly, as he had been; and it is exactly this project, the contours of which are now coming into being, that confer upon the present an intimation, however fleeting, of being meaningful.

But what does it mean to say that Roquentin is now beginning a new chapter in his life? Is the idea here that even though we do not and cannot live stories, we might as well pretend that we do? Or has he revised his earlier position, the idea being that perhaps living and telling are not so far apart as he had supposed?

Roquentin has been telling us all along that living one's life moment to moment and consciously reflecting about it, whether through memory or through writing, are two quite different things. He is undoubtedly quite right about this on some level, if only in the simple sense that, phenomenologically speaking, what I am doing right now – busily trying to write a book, moving essentially forward in time with each new word – is not the same thing as I would be doing if I were to take a step back and try to reflect upon my life in some way.

Now it is true enough, of course, that when I write I do not *only* move forward in time because in the very process of figuring out just what it is I want to say, I need to reach back into my memories, drawing upon what I know, so that I don't talk gibberish; the very condition for my writing being at all intelligible, therefore, is in fact my ability to remember. Likewise, were I to take that step back and reflect upon my life, I would not only be moving backward, for my desire to do so would have derived from the present, in the form of a concern for the future. Indeed, oddly enough, I move forward in time even as I look backward; I proceed further into the future as I remember the trajectory of my past. So things aren't so simple.

All the same, and issues of temporality aside for the moment, it is clear enough that living and telling, at least to the extent that telling has to do with deliberate reflection on one's past, are indeed two quite different phenomena. It might be mentioned that this problem can sometimes be a troubling one for those interested in gathering life history information for research and the like. The reason for this is actually quite simple: even though the people with whom we speak may occasionally take time out from their lives to engage in the sort of interpretive reflection being considered here (as they try to understand, for instance, why they are facing the difficulties they presently are, or why they elected to marry the person they did, and so on), it may nonetheless be the case that they have never engaged in this reflective process in as all-encompassing a way as they are asked to do in the research setting. As such, it can plausibly be surmised in these cases that some of the 'connections' these people are making may be arising for the very first time: 'I guess that's why I'm here doing what I am.'

It is with these kinds of examples in mind that some researchers find life history information to be hopelessly spurious, the stories people tell being considered as little more than methodological artifacts, products of the interview situation itself, perhaps bearing no relationship whatsoever to the lives they had been leading before we, the researchers, stumbled into them. All I would want to say in response to this complaint is that while it is certainly true that information of this sort *can* be spurious (particularly if people are telling outright lies), there is no reason to assume that it is necessarily so: even if the stories they tell have never been told before and even if completely new connections are being made, the realizations that may be immanent within them – the 'causes' that are being born through reflection – may be quite valid and real.

To return briefly to an issue we have already touched upon on several occasions, it may be useful to consider the idea that these causes that are posited through reflection (for simplicity's sake, we will be using the word 'cause' in this context to include 'reason' and 'motive' as well) are neither strictly forward-looking (in the 'if–then' sense) nor strictly backward-looking. 'In the phenomenalism of the "inner world"', Nietzsche (1968) has written, 'we invert the chronological order of cause and effect. The fundamental fact of "inner experience" is that the cause is imagined after the effect has taken place' (265). The end, as we have already suggested, determines the beginning. At the same time, is it not plausible to suggest as well that that very beginning has culminated in, if not led to, that very end?

A friend of mine recently discussed with me the case of a woman who is now in the process of working through the fact that at the tender age of 13, she had been witness to a steady stream of young lovers entering her mother's door. Not surprisingly, she is greatly bothered by this and feels that in some way it has contributed to her present difficulties. Now on the one hand, of course, she herself is constituting these earlier events as being causally efficacious; if, therefore, she had no awareness at all of them (whether conscious or unconscious), they wouldn't be serving as 'problems'. In this respect, it can be said that she is creating a causal connection via her present vantage-point; knowing the kinds of difficulties she faces now – she is disgusted at the sight of younger men, say – she looks back upon her sordid past and confers upon it a meaning and significance it may not have had at the time. On the other hand, however, it also seems clear enough that these earlier events wrought some quite definite (even if unknown) changes in her, changes that 'evolved' steadily into certain personal characteristics, certain fears and passions, which have culminated in her present confusion and her desire to make more sense of it all than she had previously.

Freud's discussion of 'deferred action'[5] is relevant in this context. Early on in his work he discovered that although certain experiences may be undergone that are not traumatic at the time of occurrence (seductions perhaps), they often *became* so at some subsequent point as further psychosexual maturation made possible different understandings of what happened. There is also the famous case of the 'Wolf-Man' (1918), for whom a dream called forth the distinct possibility that he had earlier witnessed his parents making love; the dream, therefore, led retroactively to the positing of a cause which was then posited in turn as at least one of the sources of the dream itself. Is this alleged scene best conceived to be the *consequence* of the dream or its *origin*?

A tentative explanation: 'At the age of one and a half the child receives an impression to which he is unable to react adequately; he is only able to understand it and to be moved by it when the impression is revived in him at the age of four [at the time of the dream]; and only twenty years later, during the analysis, is he able to grasp with his conscious mental processes what was then going on in him' (45). This sounds sensible enough. There is no reason to attribute sophisticated judgments to the child because this sophistication is really that of the adult who is presently in analysis. While something may well in fact have happened, therefore, an 'impression' of some sort, it was only later that it could be understood. Freud is thus telling us, again, that this event *became* an origin; in the very process of becoming 'activated', as he puts it, in retroactive fashion, it became a beginning – which, indeed, it might never have been if the Wolf-Man hadn't dreamed as he did that awful night.

Given the account Freud has provided, does it make sense to say that this adult man in analysis was finally able to grasp what had *then* been going on? Hadn't the little boy merely received an impression? He was like that 13-year-old girl discussed just before, gazing confusedly at her mother's revolving door; something was going on, but it was hard to say at that time exactly what. Was there anything much really 'going on' with the Wolf-Man?

Freud's answer is quite straightforward: there clearly had to be *something* going on in the little boy's life or he wouldn't have dreamed that dream. Similarly, in the girl's case enough has apparently gone on psychically that she has been led to reconsider it and, if all goes well, to rewrite it, and thus lessen some of her present difficulties. 'The effects of the scene were deferred', Freud writes, 'but meanwhile it had lost none of its freshness in the interval between the ages of one and a half and four years' (44). '*Now* I know what was going on', the Wolf-Man might have said to himself. 'If only I could have understood it then; it might have spared me all this trouble.'

Now again, it could be that Freud is confusing things here by continuing to work with his archeological metaphor. It could be, in other words, that there was nothing really dug out from the Wolf-Man's past at all and that an event that could plausibly account for the phenomena in question was simply created. But let us assume for argument's sake that there really was a primal scene and that the chain of events was roughly as Freud described. The implication here is actually rather strange. As Lukacher (1986) succinctly puts the matter, 'One is forced to admit a double or "metaleptic" logic in which causes are both the causes of effects and the effects of effects' (35; see also Brooks 1985, Nehamas 1985): that which is seen to lead to a specific outcome, in other words, can only be posited after the outcome is known and is thus cause – in the sense of origin – and effect – in the sense of product of narrative reflection – at once. As Ricoeur (1980) has written, with similar issues in mind, 'By reading the end into the beginning and the beginning into the end, we learn to read time backward, as the recapitulation of the initial conditions of a course of actions in its terminal consequences' (179; see also 1984, 1985, 1988).

According to the theorists we have been discussing, it might be said that while the narratives we tell about ourselves do indeed transform the meaning of our previous experience, just as Roquentin himself had suggested, we need not go on to claim that the origins or causes of which they speak are mere constructions, issuing strictly from the designs and desires of the present. Stated another way, while these narratives are unquestionably *dependent* upon the present, they are not on that account strictly *bound* to it, which would make of them nothing more than the methodological artifacts referred to earlier. The reason for this, as was suggested earlier, is that the very idea of an origin or a cause partakes not of one dimension of temporality but two, backward and forward, at once: now and then becoming compatriots in the articulation of a story, able to make sense simultaneously of both. What this means in turn is that narratives, far from necessarily representing a defensive retreat from the threat of real life, may instead represent a desire to encounter it head-on, toward the end of understanding and explaining both one's past and present self better than had previously been possible.

Think of the person who suddenly understands – which is not to say merely believes – that her feelings of inadequacy derive in part from the limited future that had been planned by her parents; or the person who realizes that his apparent meekness and timidity have issued from the fact of others having found him entirely too loud and obnoxious when he was a child; or the one who, like Augustine, sees, as if in a flash, that the profligate life he has been leading has served to conceal his inner emptiness and desolation. In none of these cases are people merely projecting their newly-found understandings on to the past. Instead, they are seeing that, largely unbeknownst to them, the trajectory of their lives has acquired a certain shape on account of the experiences through which they have been living, a certain directedness and thematic coherence. This shape, directedness, and coherence has only become perceivable now, in the present, from what Gusdorf (1980) called the 'aerial view' of memory. But this aerial view, rather than necessarily being in the service of falsifying the past, may instead be in the service of truth: there is now a greater consciousness of one's previous experience and a greater capacity to see the way in which all of the different parts of one's life have become orchestrated into a whole pattern, episodes in a still-evolving narrative.

Notice the significance of the idea of orchestration here: things do not ordinarily just 'happen' to us, Roquentin-style, only to fade away thereafter. What happens instead, when we meet someone new or read a good book or fall into some fortuitous occurrence, is that we often seek to integrate it in some fashion, to find a suitable place for it in our lives. This is not to say that we know exactly *how* they will be so integrated; that is left for the future to decide. But can't we say that each of these events are in some sense like the notes of a melody, only one whose shape we are not yet able to hear? More generally, even though we may seldom stop to narrate our lives in the sort of conscious, deliberate fashion discussed earlier, isn't it still the case that we are in the midst of creating stories even as we live? Some events will be experienced as consonant with who we are, others dissonant; some events will manage to carry our respective projects forward, others not; some events will emerge as parts of much the same story we have been living, while others may require that a different story altogether begins to be told. Perhaps living isn't so far from telling after all.

Early in the novel *Anna Karenina*, Kundera notes in his own book, *The Unbearable Lightness of Being* (1984), there is an encounter between two characters, Anna and Vronsky, in which they witness the event of someone being crushed by a train. At the end of the novel, the same thing happens, only this time the victim is Anna herself, in an act of suicide. 'This symmetrical composition', Kundera's narrator suggests, 'may seem quite "novelistic" to you, and I am willing to agree, but only on condition that you refrain from reading such notions as "fictive", "fabricated", and "untrue to life" into the word "novelistic"'. Why? 'Because human lives are composed in precisely such a fashion.' Indeed, the narrator continues, 'They are composed like music. Guided by his sense of beauty, an individual transforms a fortuitous occurrence . . . into a motif, which then assumes a permanent place in the composition of the individual's life.' Anna could have died any number of different ways, it is noted. 'But the motif of death and the railway station, unforgettably bound to the birth of love, enticed her in her hour of despair with its dark beauty'. Even in the midst of this profound pain, therefore, she was adhering to the 'laws of beauty'. It may well be unnecessary, then – and wrong – 'to chide the novel for being fascinated by mysterious coincidences'. It may, however, be quite right 'to chide man for being blind to such coincidences in his daily life'. For in being blind to them, or in refusing to recognize them for what they manifestly are – the notes through which a life is in the process of being composed – 'he thereby deprives his life of a dimension of beauty' (52).

Wasn't this Roquentin's main problem? Hadn't he taken a decidedly unnatural path in leading his life precisely by *refusing* to entertain its narrative dimensions? To live without narrative, it would appear, is to live in an essentially meaningless perpetual present, devoid of form and coherence; it is to experience the world as disconnected and fragmented, as an endless series of things that happen. *This*, Roquentin had suggested, was the reality of our existence; anything else was to be understood as simply the product of our imagination. But what he failed to see is that the very project of living itself is no less imaginative and no less bound to narrative than the alleged fictions we create when we reflect upon or write about our lives.

Perhaps Roquentin would be comfortable with this point of view. You're right, he might say: not only are autobiographies, histories, and so forth fictions, but so is everything else, including those nauseatingly fleshy moments. But then, of course, we would be forced to ask: What is it that deserves to be called real? The answer, of course, could only be: nothing.

As MacIntyre (1981) has suggested in his own consideration of the idea of narrative, in order to carry out the most basic task of identifying and trying to understand what someone (including ourself) is doing at any given moment in time, there is inevitably the need to place the action in a narrative context, the reason being that 'action itself has a basically historical character'. Thus, contra Roquentin and company, MacIntyre argues that stories, apart from works of fiction, are in fact 'lived before they are told'. Now this does not mean that the stories one eventually tells merely reproduce those that have already been lived; we have already adduced numerous reasons for why this cannot be. What it does mean is that we can quite easily conceive of narrative form without assuming that it necessarily involves 'disguise' or 'decoration'. It is rather part and parcel of intelligible human experience as such.

Of Roquentin, therefore, it may plausibly be said that despite his apparently noble intentions to look 'real life' straight in the eye and thus escape the terrible lure of narrative delusion, he has in fact done just the opposite: he has thrown himself instead into the land of unreality, where nothing begins and nothing ends. In attempting to strip away the historical character of life itself, then, he has not only deprived himself of a dimension of beauty, but of the very stuff of which human lives are made. Lest we wish to emulate him in this sort of anti-quest, fundamentally bereft of narrative form and order, we would be wise to think twice before relegating the stories we both live and tell to the realm of the wholly imaginary.

Very well, then. Let us assume that we have arrived at an adequate, even if incomplete, response to the challenge Roquentin has posed by concluding that the idea of 'true stories' is not necessarily as oxymoronic as he had suggested. Now by 'true', it must be emphasized, we are not speaking of correspondence with a former reality; again, there has been more than ample reason to reject this way of conceiving of the issue. We will have to assume, therefore, that in speaking of the possibility of there existing true stories, we are speaking about truth in terms other than those of correspondence. This in itself makes things a bit difficult. It also poses another challenge for us: if, indeed, we cannot judge the truth value of a narrative strictly by virtue of its correspondence to the past, then how – if at all – can we begin to differentiate true stories from false ones? It is to this challenge we will now turn.

Chapter 5

Fact and fiction

WHAT ARE THE FACTS OF HISTORY?

We will here be pursuing a rather different path from the one we, along with Roquentin, took in the previous chapter. Roquentin seemed to have decided in the end to make the move from history to fiction, largely in the interest of embracing more fully the imaginative and the artful; tired of the demand – and the pretense – of having to tell the truth by sticking close to the facts, it had become time to let things fly, to become carried away into that region of existence that went beyond the facts. Philip Roth, on the other hand, who will be the focus of the present chapter, has also grown a bit tired, but of something quite different: he will finally attempt to tell, as meticulously as he can, his very own story.

As we have seen in Helen Keller's case especially, this is an extremely difficult task, particularly since what is 'our own' is so thoroughly bound up with language, with words and genres that were on the scene well before we were. In Roth's case, however, there is yet another challenge to be confronted, for he will have to try in this very task he has set for himself to leave behind his own natural inclination to step into his usual role as fiction writer. Can he do it? Can he – can we – write a personal history unadorned with fiction? We have already noted, in the very first chapter of this book, that the 'fictive' – the making of sense and meaning – is indeed part and parcel of both historical understanding and of interpretation more generally. But can one abide by this demand for the fictive imagination without slipping into the creation of wholesale fictions? More to the point still, how does one begin to distinguish between what might be called 'true fictions' and false ones?

Roth begins his recent work, *The Facts* (1988), with a letter to one of his fictional creations, Nathan Zuckerman. Finally, after so many years of clothing the real with his imagination, he has chosen to write an autobiography and thus get down to the bare facts of his personal past. His project, then, is precisely the opposite of Roquentin's: rather than letting his imagination continue to carry him away into the comfortable enclosure of fiction, it is time now for Roth to confront himself head on, to take the terrible leap into the real.

Since Zuckerman has been so very important to him through the years, Roth is concerned with what his response to this unusual project will be. He writes,

> In the past, as you know, the facts have always been notebook jottings, my way of springing into fiction. For me, as for most novelists, every genuine imaginative event begins down there, with the facts, with the specific, and not with the philosophical, the ideological, or the abstract. Yet, to my surprise, I now appear to have gone about writing a book absolutely backward, taking what I have already imagined and, as it were, desiccating it, so as to restore my experience to the original, prefictionalized factuality.
>
> (3)

A strange and difficult turnabout, therefore, for Roth the fiction writer. Whereas fiction, he suggests, involves the transformation of the real into the imagined, autobiography involves the exact opposite, the attempt being in effect to denude one's imagination so as to behold the pristine origins from which it sprang. It is an act of 'desiccation', he tells us, an act of wringing out his own fertile mind toward the end of seeing what remains of his past, which lays buried beneath the countless layers of fiction he has written over the course of his life.[1]

Notice first what Roth is saying about fiction. Even in the most imaginative works, the concrete specifics of the author's reality are at the very heart of what is written. This is not to say that every work of fiction is a disguise for the author's life story, such that it would ultimately be a kind of cryptic autobiography in itself.[2] The idea is simply that one can only imagine from the vantage point of the life that has been lived.[3] Along these lines, then, we can say that although fiction suppresses what Ricoeur (1983) has termed a 'first-order' reference to the real world, in that what is being depicted is manifestly *un*real, it does so in order to pave the way toward a 'second-order' reference which may in some sense be even more real than (prefictionalized) reality itself: a generic portrayal of what *is*, within some particular sphere of life.

But right away a number of questions must be raised. Acknowledging the most obvious distinction to be made between autobiography and fiction (it doesn't, after all, take too much philosophical daring to say that the first tends to be about things that actually happened, the second not), is it always justifiable to claim that autobiography – along with other forms of history – is more 'particularized' than fiction? Why read a given autobiography or work of history unless it embodies some vision not only of how things were, but how they are or can be? 'The true stories of the past', Ricoeur (1983) writes, 'expose the potentialities of the present' (16). Aren't these sorts of stories every bit as much about the possible as the actual? Why is Roth writing this autobiography anyway? Why the interest in trying to 'restore' what he has been? Why search for 'the original, prefictionalized factuality' of one's former existence? 'To prove that there is a significant gap between the autobiographical writer that I am thought to be and the autobiographical writer I am? To prove that the information that I drew from my life was, in the fiction, incomplete?' (Roth 1988:3)

In large measure, he finally offers, the reason is to inform the present. We all go through spaces of darkness where the self becomes virtually opaque, and it is at times like these that 'you need ways of making yourself visible to yourself'. A number of months back, Roth had found that he could no longer understand what had once been obvious:

> 'why I do what I do, why I live where I live, why I share my life with the one I do. My desk had become a frightening, foreign place and, unlike similar moments earlier in life when the old strategies didn't work anymore – either for the pragmatic business of daily living . . . or for the specialized problems of writing – and I had energetically resolved on a course of renewal, I came to believe that I just could not make myself over again. Far from feeling capable of remaking myself, I felt myself coming undone.
>
> (4–5)

He appeared to be having something of a breakdown.[4]

Shortly thereafter, Roth suddenly found himself focusing on his past. 'If you lose something, you say, "Okay, let's retrace the steps. I came in the house, took off my coat, went into the kitchen", etc., etc. In order to recover what I had lost', he explains, 'I had to go back to the moment of origin' (5). Here, then, we find one of the prime provocations for rewriting the self: its fragmentation and dispersion, the patchwork 'coming undone', the hope of that ever-deferred sense of the whole effectively being erased by the perceived inability to 'remake' oneself. He was thus sent hurtling backward, almost as if by force, in order to rechart the terrain of his misplaced self.

In some ways this attempt to return to the origin, to a stable and enduring 'moment', was frustrated, and for no other reason than it simply did not exist. 'I found no one moment of origin but a series of moments, a history of multiple origins, and that's what I have written here in the effort to repossess life' (5). Not unlike what Roquentin had to say concerning the problem of positing beginnings, Roth is avowing the difficulty, indeed the untenability, of assuming that we can trace the trajectory of our lives back to *the* place where it all began. To do so, he implies, would be to succumb to much the same sort of narrative delusion that Roquentin feared and despised: that fanfare of trumpets announcing, illusorily, that a life – a precious life – was beginning. In any case, what Roth came to understand was that rather than there being a unitary foundation to his life, there was instead a vast array of possible starting places, dispersed and heterogeneous. As Freud might put it, he learned that he was 'overdetermined', the multiple origins of his life being fundamentally irreducible.

Rather than trying to transform this multiplicity into a single unified story, therefore, Roth has apparently decided to let it speak on its own terms. Hence this attempt at 'rendering experience untransformed' (5), what Roth calls the 'bare bones, the structure of a life without the fiction': the facts. Indeed, 'If this manuscript conveys anything', he writes, 'it's my exhaustion with masks, disguises, distortions and lies' (6); it was time to become real, particularly since his psychological health was at stake. 'I needed clarification, as much as I could get – demythologizing to induce depathologizing' (7).

This is of course a classic formula for the progress of self-knowledge: in order to become healthy, to 'depathologize' oneself, as he puts it, there is the need to strip away the various fictions and myths though which one has been living, the supposition being that when this stripping-away goes deep enough the true self will happily emerge. Perhaps this is an especially salient problem for the author (not to mention the actor or actress) who, in creating fictions all the time, can all too easily slip into becoming one him- or herself.[5] We may nevertheless want to ask again at this point: Is it possible to live one's life *without* fictions and myths? And if so, what might such a life look like?

It was indeed difficult for Roth to write this book. There was the need 'to resist the impulse to dramatize untruthfully the insufficiently dramatic, to complicate the essentially simple, to charge with implication what implied very little – the temptation to abandon the facts when those facts were not so compelling as others I might imagine if I could somehow steel myself to overcome fiction-fatigue' (7). Alongside the problem of becoming a kind of fiction himself, therefore, Roth suggests that the lure of the imagination can serve as an obstruction to the search for the real and the true; all of the old habits of going beyond the facts, of telling about more than what actually was, continued to exert their duplicitous force.

Yet the project was easier than he thought it would be. 'Perhaps that's because in its uncompelling, unferocious way, the nonfictional approach has brought me closer to how experience actually *felt* than has turning the flame up under my life and smelting stories out of all I've known' (7). In emphasizing his ability to gain access to how he actually felt in the past, Roth is offering an historiographical perspective reminiscent of Dilthey (1976) and Collingwood (1946), both of whom tended to see the writing of history as being contingent upon immersing oneself in the thoughts and feelings of those in the distant past: upon 'reliving' it, as it were. This does not mean, they realized, that the past could be completely re-presented 'as it was', to paraphrase Ranke's famous statement to that effect, for this would imply that the role of the historian in comprehending the past could ultimately be effaced, thereby resulting in a purely objective portrait. Indeed, by calling attention to the importance of 'reliving', however problematic we might find it to be, their aim was precisely to reject this image of objectivity by avowing that the historian's role could never be so effaced: reliving takes place in the present, in the historian's own mind. Roth must surely know this as well. It is *he* who is doing the reliving; time travel is out of the question.

A qualification is however in order. 'I'm not arguing', he writes, 'that there's a kind of existence that exists in fiction that doesn't exist in life or vice versa but simply saying that a book that faithfully conforms to the facts, a distillation of the facts that leaves off with the imaginative fury, can unlock meanings that fictionalizing has obscured, distended, or even inverted and can drive home some sharp emotional nails' (7–8). This formulation sounds sensible enough. In writing fiction, again, there is apparently the need to clothe the facts on some level. In part, at least in Roth's case, this is done for the sake of disguise; it is an act of depersonalization, that allows for a measure of self-expression while at the same time removing the burden of self-disclosure. Although I am not particularly interested in reducing fiction writing to some sort of therapeutic motive, we can see how the element of disguise might be therapeutic in its own right. If you have ever gotten dressed up for a Halloween party, you probably know what I mean. But just as these parties may get old after a while, since there are limits to how much disclosure is possible, so it was with Roth's fiction; it no longer did what he needed it to do.

Another reason for clothing the facts, the more important one no doubt, has to do with the aesthetic dimension of writing. That is, in order for the work to be readable and to extend its reach beyond the particularities of real life, interesting though they may be, there is the need to 'dramatize' and 'complicate', as Roth puts it: to lie, as it were. And even if the lie is in some sense in the service of truth, by Roth's own account the writing of fiction is no less a lie for all that. He wants to do something different.

There is a problem here, however, and it is one we have already begun to consider in several of our previous discussions. It is that the 'facts' of which Roth writes, the 'multiple origins' he has discovered in his quest for the past, are themselves products of the imagination, for it is only through the act of remembering, in the present, that facts and origins take on meaning and significance. The task Roth faces, therefore, is not so much to reveal the facts of his life in and of themselves (acknowledging that even these would be shot through with interpretation), but to posit possible beginnings in light of the end. In short, the project at hand, however much it might aim toward the revelation of the wholly factual, is irrevocably narrational and fictive: what unites beginning and end is the process of writing itself, a fundamentally poetic act in which the twists and turns of what had formerly been present become figured into a story of the past.

Now it could be argued here that in remaining on the level of the facts, there is not necessarily a *story* being told at all. Perhaps Roth, not unlike some contemporary historians, is attempting to escape narrative, so as to explode the illusion of continuity and identity – to preserve the differences, as Foucault or Derrida might put it. Roquentin also flirted with this idea, the fundamental problem of writing history being to succumb to positing a kind of false immanence to the data at hand, such that events are made to belong together when rightfully they do not. At an extreme, in fact, history may be emplotted as a distinctly evolutionary movement, a whole process, a 'dialectic', spiralling toward an identifiable end, such as Absolute Spirit (Hegel) or revolution (Marx). Thus we can understand why there are some who want to get away from narrative, particularly to the extent that it holds within it some of the pitfalls of teleological thinking. It is nevertheless clear enough that facts alone do not a history make.

Roth realizes this. 'I recognize that I'm using the word "facts" here, in this letter, in its idealized form and in a much more simpleminded way than it's meant in the title. Obviously the facts are never just coming at you but are incorporated by an imagination that is formed by your previous experience' (8). Of central concern here, once again, is the act of remembering. 'Memories of the past', he goes on to say, 'are not memories of facts but memories of your imaginings of the facts' (8). So he is not about to negate or deny the sorts of problems that Roquentin revealed in his own consideration of memory; he is not so epistemologically naive as to suppose that he can just call up the past as it was and tell it faithfully. But problems remain.

Given his recognition of the 'simplemindedness' of his discussion thus far, Roth admits that 'There is something naive about a novelist... talking about presenting himself "undisguised" and depicting "a life without the fiction"'. In writing an autobiography, 'You search your past with certain questions on your mind – indeed, you search out your past to discover which events have led you to asking those specific questions. It isn't that you subordinate your ideas to the force of the facts in autobiography but that you construct a sequence of stories to bind up the facts with a persuasive *hypothesis* that unravels your history's meaning' (8).

From the perspective Roth is offering, therefore, the imagination comes into play primarily in the act of 'binding' facts together through narration, which, ultimately, is in the nature of a hypothetical synthesis geared toward 'unravelling' the truth of the past. The process is not unlike that which takes place in the practice of science, as customarily conceived: the results of inquiry become bound into theories, which ideally will approximate the truth. In this respect, and despite the earlier notion of somehow reliving the past, Roth's position is reminiscent of Hempel (1942, 1965) and the so-called 'covering law' theorists, who argued that history ought to be conceptualized as an enterprise fundamentally the same as any and all other forms of science. It is true enough, Hempel notes, that historical explanations are often incomplete, at least as compared to those offered in the hard sciences, but the operative principles and objectives are no different. The historian, he argues, must seize upon the available facts and try to explain the past in as lawful and exhaustive a manner as possible, with each stage of the historical process ideally being shown to '"lead to" to the next and thus be linked to its successor by virtue of some general principles which make the occurrence of the latter at least reasonably probable given the former' (1965: 449). In short, Hempel's position is founded upon a prospective causal framework rooted in the traditional scientific goals of prediction and control.[6]

For the time being, suffice it to say that the perspective Roth has offered us is questionable on at least three counts. The first is in the presumption that facts are separable from the 'persuasive hypothesis' that binds them together. As I will argue in greater detail later on, the autobiographer – as well as the biographer, the historian, and, last but not least, the scientist – does not simply bind together the available facts, because, as Roth himself implies, the very determination of what is to *count* as a fact derives from the questions (and the hypotheses) one brings to the task of inquiring. In selecting for inclusion in his story the facts he has rather than some others, he has already determined what sort of story he wants to tell. This doesn't mean, of course, that facts are irrelevant or that they are merely blank screens on to which we project our various prejudices about the world, only that facts acquire whatever sense they have as a function of the whole to which they contribute and of which they are a part. Referring once more to what is sometimes called the 'hermeneutical circle', Gadamer (1979) writes: 'the anticipated meaning of a whole is understood through the parts, but it is in light of the whole that the parts take on their illuminating function' (146). Along these lines, then, it can plausibly be said that there is a sense in which the narrative one writes or the theory one constructs is as much determinative of the facts as vice versa.

Second, and with this hermeneutical circle in mind, it is also necessary to reiterate the idea that when we speak about causation in history, we are always relying on a narrator, who, from the vantage point of the present, has undertaken the task of establishing meaningful connections between past events. More simply, we are only in the position of knowing what might have led to what *after* the data we are interpreting are in – that is, retrospectively[7] – which in turn renders the more traditional 'if-then' model of causation questionable.

Finally, it is also questionable whether the language of 'unravelling' is appropriate for our present concerns. Ordinarily, when we speak of unravelling there is the connotation of having arrived at an exhaustive solution, as in the unravelling of a mystery, for instance. At the end of a mystery, everything often comes together; all of the disparate pieces of the puzzle, all of the clues, the significances of which had been fundamentally unknown, suddenly make sense. We may well wish our lives were like this – mysteries that with sufficient patience and diligence could wholly be unravelled – but as a general rule they are not. There is an important implication to be reiterated here: no matter how successful we may believe ourselves to be in *explaining* the course of our own histories, the *interpretive* dimension of the venture remains unsurpassable.

The main point to be extracted from this brief digression into historiography in any case is that, overt differences aside, writing an autobiography may indeed be more like writing fiction than Roth initially suggests: it is 'a sequence of stories', as he himself puts it, that together encompass what the author believes his or her past to have been. To this extent, the project Roth has set for himself, rather than being a 'return', is, like all pro-jects, directed toward the future, toward that vision of the whole that calls us – teasingly on occasion – to understanding.

PRESENCE AND ABSENCE

Earlier in this chapter, when we tried with Roth to identify some of the possible differences between autobiography and fiction, we discussed the issue of disguise and how problematic it may become for the fiction writer. Roth was tired of disguise, he told us, tired of having to clothe, for others as well as for himself, the reality of his life. In writing an autobiography, he implied, there would again exist the possibility of really letting it fly: the facts, the truth. But can we really assume that an autobiography can be written without disguise? Isn't there still a need, whether conscious or unconscious, for a measure of decorum in this potentially threatening movement of revelation? And how much does the autobiographer – or anyone else for that matter – really know about his or her life anyway? We do stupid things. We form ugly relationships. We kick ourselves time and time again for not being able to see what nearly every other sentient being we know can see perfectly well. Aren't we sometimes the last to know?

Aside from the manifest reasons he has already offered, Roth admits that he doesn't really know why he has chosen to write this book:

> Though I can't be entirely sure, I wonder if this book was written not only out of exhaustion with making fictional self-legends and not only as a spontaneous response to my crackup but also as a palliative for the loss of a mother who still, in my mind, seems to have died inexplicably – at seventy-seven in 1981 – as well as to hearten me as I come closer and closer and closer to an eighty-six-year-old father viewing the end of life as a thing as near to his face as the mirror he shaves in.
>
> (8–9)

'I wonder', he continues, 'if a breakdown-induced eruption of parental longing in a fifty-five-year-old man isn't, in fact, the Rosetta stone to this manuscript' and 'if there hasn't been some consolation, particularly while recovering my equilibrium, in remembering that when the events narrated here were happening we were all there, nobody having gone away or been on the brink of going away, never to be seen again for hundreds of thousands of billions of years' and 'if I haven't drawn considerable consolation from reassigning myself as myself to a point in life when the grief that may issue from the death of parents needn't be contended with, when it is unperceivable and unsuspected, and one's own departure is unconceivable because they are there like a blockade' (9). Even in the midst of his attempt to recover the unvarnished facts of the past, the meaning of the fact of his doing so – which is to say the meaning of what exactly is being done through the writing of this book – remains open to question.

He is treading here on some difficult ground. It seems true enough, I think, that we can offer plausible explanations for many of the things we do: I know why I went to the store (to get some bread), I know why I took a shower (I needed one), and so on. But even as I am sitting here trying to think of examples of more or less certain explanations I find myself getting stumped. Do I really know why I came into work this morning? *Can* I know? Come on, you say, you wanted to work on this nifty book. But why? Why *this* book, for instance, and not some other?

These sorts of questions are what lead us to think about the the hidden underground of psychological life. As Freud and others have argued, if the reasons for our actions are not immediately forthcoming in consciousness, then perhaps we must search elsewhere; when understanding stops, we move toward explanation, toward asking why, with the hope that, if all goes well, we can begin understanding once again.[8] There is also often this supposition that, yes, there *is* an explanation for our actions, somewhere; it is simply not manifest. This is why we move into that subterranean realm Roth speaks of: there is a reason buried in me; let me see if I can find it. And sometimes we do. That is, after some time searching we seem to be able to come up with an account that really does seem to work; it resolves all of our previous uncertainties, returns us to the fold of understanding: *that's* why I did it. But can I ever, and can Roth ever, fully succeed in 'locating' the reasons for why we have elected to write the books we have? Is there some sort of discrete cluster of reasons – eight, twelve, twenty-seven – scattered about in our unconscious, waiting there, like animals in a cage, eager to be let out, if only we could find the key? This question, of course, can be extended to self-understanding more generally. Can we ever fully know how we got to be the people we are?

It could be that the problem here is simply one of access. Perhaps we are so thoroughly overdetermined, so totally overrun by such a huge quantity of factors that there is just too much going on for us ever to achieve a complete grasp (see Chapter 1, regarding Derrida's comments on the notion of 'totalization'). This is the assumption, I would offer, of much of social science, including psychology. There is a finite world out there, teeming with variables, that could, in principle, be completely captured. This does not mean that we ever will succeed in this task, not in this lifetime anyway, but the limits at hand are practical ones; there is just so much one can do. As a corollary to this assumption, there is also the familiar notion of scientific progress, the idea being that with diligence and patience we will at last approach the desired end: complete knowledge. In certain domains of scientific endeavor, these assumptions may well have a measure of validity to them. It could also be the case, however, that our 'failure' to arrive at complete knowledge, either of the outer world or the inner world, is not so much a function of there being 'too much' present, but because, as Derrida suggests, 'there is something missing': a 'center', which would ultimately allow interpretation to cease.

Along these lines, it may be that Roth, along with the rest of us, cannot fully know why he is doing what he is because there is no exhaustive set of reasons that could ever be articulated; origins, again, are irreducibly multiple, reasons essentially indeterminate. In avowing the essential indeterminacy of the meaning of the act of writing his autobiography, Roth thus undermines the very project he has undertaken: he knows he is doing something – that much is a fact – but he cannot say with any certainty exactly what. All the while, the project's possible origins clamor about, vying, futilely, for a chance to answer the unanswerable.

But let us not be skeptics. Let us continue to assume that something akin to self-knowledge is possible. We still need to determine more clearly what this can possibly mean and we will try to do so in due time, but for now we will go with our gut conviction (mine anyway) that we do occasionally gain some insight into who and what we are. But an important question remains. Namely, how do we *know* when we are knowing? That is, how do we know when we are gaining insight and when we aren't? Perhaps Roth will help us to begin to answer these questions.

For now, however, the question he must ask in his letter to Zuckerman is much more straightforward: 'Is the book any good?' Roth himself is in 'no real position to tell' (10). It is time now then to take a brief look at what he has to say, along with Zuckerman, and see for ourselves.

THE MANIFEST TEXT

Roth begins the text proper, as we have called it, with a prologue describing his father's brush with death back in 1944, due to a severe case of appendicitis. The surgeon, upon opening him up and seeing the extent of the problem, gave him less than a fifty–fifty chance to survive. But survive he did. 'Despite a raw emotional nature that makes him prey to intractable worry', Roth writes, 'his life has been distinguished by the power of resurgence' (12). If only it could go on forever, Roth muses. The fact is, however, that right now, in his pitiful infirmity, 'He is trying to die'. Not that he says this or thinks it, 'but that's his job now and, fight as he will to survive, he understands, as he always has, what the real work is' (17). As Roth continues, in true Freudian form, 'the link to my father was never so voluptuously tangible as the colossal bond to my mother's flesh' (18), and thus, 'To be at all is to be her Philip.' Nevertheless, 'in the embroilment with the buffetting world, my history', he writes, 'still takes its spin from beginning as his Roth' (19). Or so it seems now at any rate: beginning and end fused into one, compatriots in the eternal return.

Being Jewish in America comes next, particularly his encounter with the 'awesomely named gentiles' with whom his father, an insurance man, worked. He had been respectful and even admiring of these people, to be sure, but along with his father he also knew that they were the very ones responsible for preventing more than 'a few token Jews' from moving on to important positions within the firm. More intimidating still were the kids on the Jersey shore who would call Roth and his cohorts 'Dirty Jew' and try to beat them up merely for being who they were. It was vacation-time, that was all, and everybody minded their own business, but the 'irrational hatred' that was in the air was often all too palpable. Come to think of it, Roth notes, these kids weren't really all that different from the big executives with whom his father worked. 'Small wonder', he continues, 'that at twelve, when I was advised to begin to think seriously about what I would do when I grew up, I decided to oppose the injustices wreaked by the violent and the privileged by becoming a lawyer for the underdog' (25). This, as we know, changed; but the echoes of those frightful years still remains.

He recounts high school as being much the same, a football game, for instance, ending in a virtual 'pogrom', the bus being surrounded by the screaming gentile fans whose team had lost to a bunch of Jews, anxious to do some damage. It was through experiences like these, Roth writes, that he learned how to flee, from a crowd at least; there was just no sense colluding in the sort of 'bloodletting' Jews throughout the centuries had had to endure. He would live out his aggression by becoming a devotee of prizefighting instead; it was safer and easier. It wasn't as if these sorts of things happened that often, Roth admits. Generally, in fact, he sees his youth as having been rather quiet and comfortable. But no matter how infrequent these events were, they have apparently etched a firm place in both his memory and his identity.

In addition to being a Jew, however, Roth was also an American, getting together with his buddies, playing baseball, and learning the ways of the world. College began in unexceptional fashion as well: he was a pre-law student, eager to right the wrongs of society, in a local branch of the state university. Finding himself lunching casually with those gentiles who had earlier been little more than 'tough and generally superior adversaries' in sporting contests, he found his Americanness burgeoning still further. It seems he had become a part of the much-touted melting pot.

But he felt the need to get away, to be out on his own, especially to avoid the 'battle' a more and more independent young man was bound to have while still under the wing of his parents. The question was where to go. The Ivy League schools, he felt, weren't very different from his father's firm, particularly since some of them had Jewish quotas, a practice that disgusted him. They were costly too. Then there were all those schools whose football scores he heard on the radio. And then there was Bucknell University in Pennsylvania, where his friend Marty had decided to go, and who, in no time at all, seemed to have become a man of the world, poised and confident. Roth envied him greatly: even with a newly bought pipe and a condom in his wallet, Roth didn't yet feel that he himself was a man. So off to Bucknell he went with Marty.

Surprisingly enough, it turned out that he was actually invited to join not only the Jewish fraternity, Sigma Alpha Mu (whose members were referred to as the 'Sammies'), but a predominantly gentile one as well, Theta Chi. Unsure what to do, given the choice, he consulted his parents, who promptly and typically told him to do what made him happiest. There would definitely be some 'anthropological excitement' if he were to become a member of Theta Chi, but he was afraid, he says, of having to censor himself in what seemed to be a somewhat staid community of WASPS; he was something of a clown, apparently, and this, alongside his strong desire to avoid becoming 'encased in somebody else's idea of what I should be', led him to conclude that joining this fraternity 'could wind up being a far more conformist act than taking the seemingly conventional course of being with boys from backgrounds more like my own, who, just *because* their style was familiar, wouldn't have the power to inhibit my expressive yearnings' (51–2).

Not unlike Helen Keller, then, he desperately wanted to become his own person. So the Sammies it was: Roth, one of the 'coarse and uninhibited performers who ignited whatever improvisational satire flared up in the living room after dinner', who spun out 'spirited low-comedy concoctions' (53), and who eventually became a stellar example of that strain of 'Dadaesque Jewish showmanship' that culminated in such 'cultural-political deviants and cunningly anarchic entrepreneurs' (56) as Abbie Hoffman and Lenny Bruce, had found himself exactly that sort of comfortable niche that might allow him to soar.

His membership turned out to be relatively shortlived owing to the fact that he had befriended a couple of fellow students with similar passions for the literary life, which led to their helping to found *Et Cetera*, a magazine existing on its behalf. Somewhere along the line Roth had apparently become a humanist, seeing in literature rather than law a possible future.

It apparently began with his exposure to e.e. cummings by a penniless, unconventional English professor and his wife, both of whom were 'free (in the biggest and best sense), levelheaded Americans, respectable enough but unconcerned with position and appearances' (57). Without quite deserving the title of bohemians, they were their own people, who showed Roth how becoming his own person might be done with some class, integrity, and subtlety. 'They made being poor look so easy that I decided to follow their example and become poor myself someday, either as an English professor like Bob or as a serious writer who was so good that his books made no money' (57–8). He decided, in other words, to live out the myth of the struggling and poverty-stricken artist–intellectual, who would work away in terrible obscurity, seeking the existential solitude that only a life of deprivation could bring.

These early models of Roth's proved to be as much enamored of him, particularly when he jumped up from the dinner table to mimic his stereotypically Jewish relatives, as he was of them. Indeed, he notes tellingly, 'they were not merely entertained but interested' (59). Nevertheless, he goes on to say, it was inconceivable at that time that he might actually take some of these madcap antics and make a life out of them: 'it did not dawn on me that these anecdotes and observations might be made into literature, however fictionalized they'd already become in the telling'. As he asks, with the wisdom of hindsight, 'How could Art be rooted in a parochial Jewish Newark neighborhood having nothing to do with the enigma of time and space or good and evil or appearance and reality?' (59) He had been paving the way toward his own future without his even knowing it.

All the while, in fact, the stories he himself had begun writing – 'mournful little things about sensitive children, sensitive adolescents, and sensitive young men crushed by coarse life' (60), modelled after his 'titan', Thomas Wolfe – kept pathetically on. Here again we see the wisdom of hindsight, in the form of a profound sense of humility. 'I wanted to show that life was sad and poignant', he writes, 'even while I was experiencing it as heady and exhilarating; I wanted to demonstrate that I was "compassionate", a totally harmless person' (60). Good to be done, he in effect says, with that simpering, colorless little fool. Obviously there have been some changes since then.

Roth is not being overly judgmental about his past foibles, however. For the situation in which he had found himself back then was in no way an optimal one: 'if there had been some sort of worthy competition around', he writes, 'I might not have produced these unconscious personal allegories to begin with' (60). He had done what he could. But this does not mitigate the sense of humility, perhaps even shame, he presently feels. Memory is strange this way: even if in looking back on our pasts we realize that things could not have been other than what they were, it may be difficult to own fully all that we have been. 'Look at how naive I was', we say; 'it's hard to believe'.

Meanwhile, as editor of the literary magazine, improving his writing a bit as time wore on, Roth became defined (mainly by himself apparently) as the college's 'critical antagonist', spewing out socially and politically conscious venom designed to awaken his sleeping classmates, 'rather than a boy who secretly still possessed enough of his own "high school values" to want to be popular and admired' (65). He even went so far as to abuse publicly the editor of the student newspaper, a cheerleader, whose banal creations made his skin crawl. Although it could also be, Roth admits, that his unsuccessful courting of two of her fellow cheerleaders the year before had led him to want to retaliate. Perhaps his self-righteous literary politicality, in this case at least, was just a guise for his own failures. As for the result of his merciless attack, he was reprimanded severely by both the Dean and the college's Board of Publications, after which time he had run to one of his professor's houses, nearly in tears over what had happened.

Despite this unfortunate event, Roth was anything but defeated in his quest to become literary. 'This is how I will live', he had said to himself, as he attended an honors seminar at the home of his professor. 'I would be poor and I would be pure, a cross between a literary priest and a member of the intellectual resistance in Eisenhower's prospering pig heaven' (68). Assisting him in his vision, eventually, would be his girlfriend Polly, who chain-smoked, drank martinis, and, most important, was the most sardonic girl he knew. Together they initiated one another into the pleasures of love.

This too was shortlived, mainly because of a threat of pregnancy, which managed to put a damper on Roth's sense of commitment: 'Having narrowly escaped premature domesticity and its encumbering responsibilities, I abandoned myself to dreams of erotic adventures that I couldn't hope to encounter other than on my own' (77). This theme of abandonment, he believes, is nothing new. 'I had succesfully distanced myself at eighteen from my father's strictures, at nineteen from the meaningless affiliation to the Jewish fraternity, at twenty from the cozy ordinariness of the amiable student community; I had even begun to outgrow my own moralizing polemics. Now, at twenty-one, I wanted to be free from the exclusivity of monogamous love' (78). The facts are thus beginning to be bound together more clearly, as Roth had promised. The story he wishes to tell is coming into focus.

Rather than going to the University of Pennsylvania for graduate school, where his soon-to-be-ex-girlfriend had also been accepted, he decided to be off on his own, at the University of Chicago, where he would study literature, do some teaching, and, last but not least, encounter a woman whom he describes as the girl of his dreams. If only he had known what kind of dreams they would be.

She was the 'incarnation of a prototype', this woman, though of quite a different sort from the sardonic, sophisticated martini-drinker he had left behind. In the midst of his bourbon-induced post-faculty-party giddiness, this young lustful intellectual, who was already beginning to publish some short stories, was ready for something else. What he found was 'a small-town drunkard's angry daughter, a young woman already haunted by grim sexual memories and oppressed by an inextinguishable resentment over the injustice of her origins; hampered at every turn by her earliest mistakes and driven by fearsome need to bouts of desperate deviousness, she was a more likely fair-haired heroine for the scrutiny of Ingmar Bergman than for the sunny fantasies of M-G-M' (81). She wasn't like all the other gentile girls he had come to know at Bucknell and elsewhere. In fact, 'she was that world's *victim*, a dispossessed refugee from a sociobiological background to which my own was deemed, by both old- and new-world racial mythology, to be subservient, if not inferior' (82). To top things off, she was four years older than he, divorced, and had a couple of children too.

He had to have known, of course, that his family would be appalled at what this brash young man had dragged home, but that was their problem, he believed, and he would expose their narrow-minded clannishness by 'taming' this woman and thus demonstrating that their silly fears were unwarranted. All told, she was just what the doctor ordered: 'I was at last a man' (86). So he was. 'Our seemingly incompatible backgrounds', he goes on to write, 'attested to my freedom from the pressure of convention and my complete emancipation from the constraining boundaries protecting my preadult life'. Indeed, with this in mind, he could only believe: 'I was not only a man, I was a free man' (86–7). He had even forsaken one of his own along the way, a woman from 'Jewish New Jersey' who, however desirable and however passionate their affair, simply wasn't enough of a challenge. The story, of an independent and daring individual determined to make his life memorable, continues. Sad to say he had gotten everything 'backward'. 'Could I have been any more naive?' (90)

All the while, Roth and his mate, Josie, told one another stories about who they were, what their lives were like, if only to sharpen the differences. He writes,

> I was wooing her, I was wowing her, I was spiritedly charming her – motivated by an egoistic young lover's predilection for intimacy and sincerity, I was telling her who I thought I was and what I believed had formed me, but I was also engaged by a compelling form of narrative responsory. I was a countervoice, an antitheme, providing a naive challenge to the lurid view of human nature that emerged from her tales of victimized innocence.
>
> (93)

And he loved it, for a while anyway.

A brief two years later, they found themselves in the thick of 'the most grueling, draining, bewildering' fights (95). Perhaps he wasn't the hero he had thought he was, and perhaps she wasn't quite as salvageable as he had hoped. This is what probably led to Josie's near-breakdown and her flirtation with suicide and to Roth having to assume a responsibility he would much rather have done without. 'Fleeing and hiding were repugnant to me: I still believed that there were certain character traits distinguishing me from the *truly* wicked bastards out of her past' (101–2). So they endured. They were extremely lucky, Roth notes, that they didn't end up 'maimed' or 'dead' from doing so.

Meanwhile, just about everyone, particularly his mother, could see how awful and futile the whole thing was. The fact that Josie had tricked him into believing she was pregnant – she had apparently bought a urine specimen from a pregnant woman who lived in one of the local tenements – didn't help much either. Now here, Roth suggests, was someone who knew what fiction was all about. The details of her eventual 'abortion' were even more vivid still. How could he not be taken in? 'The wanton scenes she improvised! The sheer hyperbole of what she imagined! The self-certainty unleashed by her own deceit! The conviction behind those caricatures!' (111). What talent! 'Without doubt she was my worst enemy ever, but alas, she was also nothing less than the greatest creative-writing teacher of them all, specialist par excellence in the aesthetics of extremist fiction.' As for the terrible result: 'Reader', Roth proclaims stoically, 'I married her' (112).

For whatever reason (Roth himself claims innocence), meanwhile, a number of the stories Roth had been working on at the time struck certain of his Jewish readers as so anti-Semitic that he was accused of being a traitor to the cause. 'I'd had no intention as a writer', he feels, 'of coming to be known as "controversial" and, in the beginning, had no idea that my stories would prove repugnant to ordinary Jews. I had thought of myself as something of an authority on ordinary Jewish life, with its penchant for self-satire and hyperbolic comedy, and for a long time continued to be as bemused privately as I was unyielding publicly when confronted by Jewish challengers' (124–5). But hadn't he had a history of being controversial? Hadn't he been admonished before for a loose pen? Of course they hated him, he concluded, but this was because they were all so 'fanatically insecure' (129). Despite the fact that he had briefly contemplated looking elsewhere for the details of his fiction, he decided the exact opposite: he would bring the frenzy to a head by pursuing with renewed energy and commitment the very same literary path for which he had been branded.

Several years later he took up with another woman, one whose appearance was as 'indelibly stamped by privilege as Josie's had been by her provincial small town. The two women', he continues, 'were drastically different physical types from social backgrounds that couldn't have been much more dissimilar and, as women, so unlike as to seem like representatives of divergent genders' (132). At the same time, however, this new mate was, not unlike Josie, 'intriguingly estranged from the very strata of American society of which they were each such distinctively emblazoned offspring' (132–3). In her own way, she was another outsider, and in certain respects perhaps, another cause as well. But she was much more presentable than Josie, from whom he had separated, had been. Most important, in any case, was that she was the living embodiment of utter 'guilelessness', as real and true and 'sweet-tempered' as Josie had been un-real, false, and hateful; 'and it was from this that my frazzled virility took heart and my regeneration began' (135). Alongside his recovery not only from Josie but from a severe bout with appendicitis, he was, by most indications, in the process of being healed.

Not completely, however. For Josie steadfastly refused to divorce him, preferring instead to hound him in whatever pathetic way she could, until, that is, her sudden and violent death in a car accident. He had at first thought that the news of her death was a trick, another fiction perhaps, being sent his gullible way. He also couldn't believe that 'miracles' such as this one could really happen. But his visit to the funeral home indicated otherwise: '(H)er ineradicable need for a conscienceless, compassionless monster as a mate had at last been realized – I felt absolutely nothing about her dying at thirty-nine', Roth admits, 'other than immeasurable relief' (153). The fact was, 'I'd always understood that one of us would have to die for the damn thing ever to be over' (155). Fortunately, it was her.

'The Roth family menace, peritonitis, had failed to kill me, Josie was dead and I didn't do it, and a fourth book, unlike any I'd written before in both its exuberance and its design, had been completed in a burst of hard work' (156). All was well. With a big advance in hand, he and his sweet-tempered woman-friend, whom he eventually decided he would never marry, were off to Europe, seeking as much enjoyment as they could. Owing to the recent traumas he had suffered, some of it proved to be rather empty and aimless, but maybe this was how it had to be if all of that debris was to be cleared away. He returned more determined than ever 'to be an absolutely independent, self-sufficient man', striving to bring forth once more 'that exhilarating, adventurous sense of personal freedom' (160) that he had experienced some twelve years before, as the young literary rogue, on the make. It may seem a bit unlikely, but perhaps he would be able to get things right this time around.

These, then, are the 'facts' of Roth's life, a portion of it at least. In sum, he was a relatively unexceptional youth, though a bit oppressed by the strain of anti-Semitism he occasionally had to endure; he yearned desperately for independence and autonomy, which he eventually seemed to find to some extent at college; and he proceeded, wrong-headedly, to throw himself into a doomed relationship that he only began to outlive when his wife was dead, after which time he could resume the carefree, rakish existence he had always wanted. As I have intimated above, it is unclear whether we should understand this resumption as a comic ending or a tragic one – since we do not know what its consequences will be – but let us not be overly troubled by this. The main thing for now is, what does Zuckerman think about this story?

IN THE AFTERMATH

The sad truth is, he doesn't think much of it. First, because of the need to be discreet about the lives of the people Roth has written about, there is not enough being disclosed in the book. 'In the fiction', Zuckerman writes, 'you can be so much more truthful without worrying all the time about causing direct pain. You try to pass off here as frankness what looks to me like the dance of the seven veils – what's on the page is like a code for something missing' (162). The book is just too 'kind' and 'careful', and in its very selectivity it winds up being as much about what cannot be said as what can. In short, because of the minimalistic approach Roth has taken here, the book being little more than what Freud might call the manifest content of things, the reader is forced into the awkward position of having to examine the margins and interstices of his discourse in order to determine what this life might really have been about. Zuckerman's presumption, therefore, is that an autobiography ought to be more honest and complete.

The second problem, very much related to the first, is that the person of Roth himself is not given nearly as much attention as it ought to have. This of course makes perfect sense given his vocation. 'Your gift is not to personalize your experience', Zuckerman informs him, 'but to personify it, to embody it in the representation of a person who is *not* yourself. You are not an autobiographer, you're a personificator.' Indeed, Zuckerman ventures, 'My guess is that you've written metamorphoses of yourself so many times, you no longer have any idea what *you* are or ever were. By now what you are', he concludes, 'is a walking text' (162).

Once again, the presumption is that Roth is somehow dancing around who he is: rather than just coming right out and saying what he thinks and feels about the world he has experienced, he localizes himself in the figures of others; like his fictional creations, they exist as symbolic extensions of his own unspeakable inner world. Roth's treatment of himself is thus no less elliptical and circuitous in Zuckerman's eyes than the facts he has chosen to present. The result is that the reader, in yet another way, is relegated to the position of having to *interpret* what is going on in the book rather than just being *told*, 'This is me'.

Given the problems he has enumerated thus far, Zuckerman can only ask, not only of Roth but of autobiographers more generally: 'How close is the narration to the truth? Is the author hiding his or her motives, presenting his or actions and thoughts to lay bare the essential nature of conditions or trying to hide something, telling in order *not* to tell?' (164). These questions are difficult ones, for as Zuckerman himself realizes, 'In a way we always tell in order also not to tell.' But in the interest of truth, he continues, the 'governing motive' of autobiography being 'primarily ethical as against aesthetic', [9] there still exists the expectation that one will 'resist to the utmost the ordinary impulse to falsify, distort, and deny' (164). And he just doesn't believe that Roth has done this.

'Is this really "you",' Zuckerman asks, 'or is it what you want to look like to your readers at the age of fifty-five?' Isn't Roth aware of his fictional devices? 'Think of the exclusions, the selective nature of it, the very pose of the fact-facer' (164). How could he possibly pretend to be presenting us with the unvarnished truth? Here too Zuckerman had expected something different; he had been promised the facts and instead got just another work of fiction.

What's more, Zuckerman feels Roth's fiction is more exciting. Knowing what he does of Roth's imaginary worlds since he has been a longstanding participant in them, Zuckerman cannot help but juxtapose the intense and alive emotionality he has witnessed thus far with the staid and largely unexceptional story he has just been prodded into reading. He doesn't expect that there will be perfect coincidence between Roth's fictional characters and Roth himself, but the utter disjunction between the two makes him extremely uncomfortable, as if he is not being told all that is going on: 'Because if there wasn't a struggle, then it just doesn't seem like Philip Roth to me. It could be anybody, almost' (165).

There has simply got to be 'something in the romance of your childhood', especially, 'that you're not permitting yourself to talk about, though without it the rest of the book makes no sense' (169). Do you mean to say, Zuckerman in effect asks, that except for your nightmare with Josie, your life was as decorously boring as you've made it out to be? And what *about* Josie? In the span of a year, Roth had gone from a seemingly typical college student to someone immersed, deeply and irretrievably, in a 'pathologically tragic' relationship with a broken, beaten-down divorcee. 'Why? Why did you essentially mortify yourself in a passionate encounter with a woman who had a sign on her saying STAY AWAY KEEP OUT? There has to be some natural link between the beginning, between all that early easy success, culminating at Bucknell and Chicago, and the end, and there isn't' (170).

What has been omitted, Zuckerman believes, is the central motive that effected this transformation.[10] Hasn't there got to be a reason buried in there somewhere, something that would bring together these two selves, one happy-go-lucky and the other beleaguered and masochistic, into some sort of comprehensible relation? Aren't we determined beings, our beginnings, if only we could know them, foretelling the endings we will become? Come on, Roth, tell us what happened! 'Even if it's no more than one percent you've edited out, that's the one percent that counts – the one percent that's saved for your imagination and that changes everything. But this isn't unusual, really', Zuckerman acknowledges. 'With autobiography', he believes, 'there's always another text, a countertext, if you will, to the one presented.'[11] This is why it must be deemed 'the most manipulative of all literary forms' (172).

But even this insight cannot allay the most salient source of Zuckerman's discomfort: 'The truth you told about all this long ago' – in fiction – 'you now want to tell in a different way' (173). His complaint, in other words, is that Roth has succumbed to the lure of rewriting his self; he has left behind the harsh immediacy of the events that had fueled his earlier work and has given them new meaning through the distance that has been conferred by time. Fortunately, this complaint notwithstanding, Zuckerman is indeed able to see both the text and the countertext of what Roth has written. The biggest 'flaw' of the book, therefore, namely its tendency to conceal the supposed reality of the past, is at one and the same time the vehicle for its revelation.[12]

But this is not good enough for Zuckerman. Yes, he implies, I understand; of course you want to idealize your parents, for instance, given that one of them is dead and the other fast approaching death. In addition, it may be difficult to remember all of your earlier despair over the way of the world, its senselessness and hypocrisy. Finally, for the sake of your own self-preservation, it stands to reason that you would portray yourself as Josie's victim – 'Here I am, this innocent Jewish boy and American patriot, my mother's papoose and Miss Martin's favorite, brought up in these innocent landscapes, with all these well-meaning, innocent people, and I fall headlong into this trap' (174) – but how could Roth possibly negate his own part in all of this? Zuckerman, in short, wants everything in the text rather than the countertext; what he feels he has learned about Roth on the basis of his interpretations cannot lessen his frustration with this simplistic piece of self-disclosure. 'At the least', he writes, 'there is more ambiguity in your role than you are willing to acknowledge' (175).

There is some ambiguity about Zuckerman's *own* role as well, however. 'I'm not even sure any longer which of us he's set up as the straw man', he moans to his wife, who has just finished reading the book. 'I thought first it was him in his letter to me – now it feels like me in my letter to him. It's irrelevant to say I don't trust him when maneuvering is the message, I know, but I don't. Sure he talks so freely about all his soft spots, but only after choosing awfully carefully which soft spots to talk about' (192). But isn't Zuckerman himself doing the same thing? Might it not be the case that his own text, like the text proper, also has a countertext? Moving still further in this direction, couldn't this countertext have its own countertext? When does it ever stop?

It could be, of course, that this endless layering of text upon text is exactly what Roth wants to convey. That is, it could be that the facts themselves are so thoroughly indefinite and ambiguous that this multiplicity of possible interpretations is all that can be offered. After all, didn't he speak earlier about 'multiple origins'? Maybe this entire book is simply his way of saying: when it comes right down to it, who knows? Here are the facts, reader, do with them what you will. Some of you will see me as a victim, some as a perpetrator; some weak, others strong; some independent, others dependent. But couldn't his own positing of multiplicity also be a means of exonerating himself from his various wrongdoings? Couldn't he be basking, problematically, in the illusory comfort of indeterminacy?

Roth has unquestionably given us plenty to work with here, no less than three texts in fact: the letter, the text proper, and Zuckerman's response. Given this wealth of material, it would be easy enough for us to say, here is a fellow who has at least had the courage to cast into suspicion the meaning of his own account. Most autobiographers do not even go this far; instead, they tell us what their lives have been like and leave it essentially up to us to determine what sort of sense is to be made. But again, couldn't it be that Roth's 'courage' is really a way of *preventing* us from making sense of his own life? Recall the theme of abandonment we came across earlier. Is this book Roth's way of saying, 'You'll never touch me, I won't let you near enough'? If so, of course, he will have undermined – whether intentionally or not – his own aim: this triad of texts, in their apparent attempt to destabilize our understanding of who he is, may in fact be showing us the way.

I will not offer a definitive 'ur-text' able to encompass Roth's life. Several tentative conclusions might, however, be drawn in the light of the information we have before us. We might conclude, for instance, that he is a classically pseudo-independent male, who, upon forming attachments to others, cannot help but go on to break them, given both his need for autonomy and his fear of commitment. He can't quite go it alone, it appears, but neither is he able to be together with someone else; on some level, others inevitably seem to be obstructions to his selfish pursuits. Following Erikson, it could be that his own problems of intimacy are a function of the fact that he never really established an integrated identity. Didn't he seek to find himself *through* others, particularly Josie, who may be seen as little more than an instrument for his own aborted attempt at becoming an American and not just a Jew, one who could show the world how open and tolerant and caring he really was?

Or, taking this line of thinking one step further, we might conclude that he was never quite able to live down his Jewishness. He saw prejudice as a child, became determined to avoid it all costs, went off to a predominantly gentile school where he went out with predominantly gentile women, eventually took up with someone who was the complete antithesis of anything and everything his parents could have hoped for, and finally wrote anti-Semitic stories to show just how detached from his heritage he really was. Perhaps, then, his is a story about identifying with the aggressor and blaming the victim. Isn't this what his critics accused him of?

Or, it could be that he was simply an actor, a role-player, now the Jewish comic, with the predictably sardonic girlfriend; then the literary intellectual, churning out pathetically sensitive allegories about his own compassionate self; then the hard-drinking rogue, hungry for exactly that kind of degradation and middle-American emptiness that he was to find in Josie; and finally, the writer–star, anxious to kick everyone away and soak up some much-deserved glory.

Perhaps some common ground can be found between these interpretations. Acknowledging that the various scenarios we have just discussed are by no means mutually exclusive, let us say that the narrative one, the search for independence, is largely what Roth's triad of texts is about. We have now a theme, a storyline. Where do we go from here? That is, how do we begin to understand the emergence of this theme? Possibilities proliferate once again. Our task is still an interpretive one, of course, but this time on a more explanatory plane.

We could, for instance, be essentially psychological about it. We could look, for instance, for childhood precursors to Roth's burgeoning need. Maybe early on he was prevented from becoming as independent as he had wanted, owing to the close bond he had with his mother (whose presence is nevertheless largely suppressed in his story) and, on account of his frustration, became hell bent on becoming his own man, family and the rest be damned: 'You think you can keep me under your wing and create the dutiful Jewish son you undoubtedly hope for. Well, I'll show you!' Thus his botched attempts at intimacy may stem from his resolve never to be smothered again.

We could also try a more culturally-based analysis, focusing especially on the issue of his Jewishness. Maybe he was smothered not so much by doting parents, but by a way of life that seemed to him hopelessly clannish and old-fashioned. All that Jewish stuff was good for them, but not for him; he was much better off becoming an American, a participant in the melting pot, who would be spared the frustration of always having to defend the faith. Maybe he ultimately rejected this faith as well, becoming one of that strange breed of anti-Semitic Jew who simultaneously embraces and negates his or her origins.

On a more sociological level, it could be that Roth's need for independence is rooted in a fundamentally male ethos that dictates that intimacy is a kind of taboo, a compromise of one's masculinity. And perhaps this is further accentuated by his vocation as a writer, which dictates that he run around with lots of women, preferably those with whom genuine attachment is impossible, to ensure that he both has plenty to write about as well as avoids living that sort of humdrum bourgeois existence that is such an anathema to many of the literati. Gender and vocation aside, Roth may also be caught up in the ideology of individuality, which was particularly salient in the 1950s and 1960s, and which, in yet another way, dictated that he be freewheeling and uncommitted to anything but his own personal desires and interests.

We could go on and on and on: multiple texts, multiple origins. We need to reach our own conclusions about what exactly this book is. On the one hand, Roth-the-letter-writer's, it is a series of episodes – 'facts' – bound together, as he puts it, into an hypothesis, which has assumed the form of a narrative. Given the primacy of these facts, alongside the relative absence of interpretation – by his own account anyway – there is little for the reader to quarrel with: this is how it was; make of it what you will. On the other hand, however, namely Zuckerman's, these alleged facts are nothing more than a pretense for the illusory self-portrait Roth wants to paint now, in the present. They are fictions, he complains, and as far as he is concerned, not very good ones either. Had Roth-the-letter-writer been able to understand this, he might have come up with a better book, Zuckerman feels, one shorn of the pretenses of presenting the unvarnished truth.

As has already been implied, however, it may very well be that both Roth-the-letter-writer *and* Zuckerman are to be regarded as straw men. For while the first is reluctant to avow the fictive dimension of the project he has undertaken, the second is unable to see that the process of rewriting the self need not necessarily be construed as a falsification of what 'really was'. In a sense, in fact, they fall prey to much the same error. In speaking about the recovery and the falsification of the past respectively, they fail to see that a life history, far from being a mere repository of fundamentally dead things, lying in wait, to be used in the service of either truth or of fiction, is instead an open work, able to be reread and rewritten over the course of time.

To Roth-the-letter-writer, then, we can say that the goal of establishing the facts of his life, untainted by imagination, unmediated by writing, is misguided: once you have singled out this rather than that, indeed once you have even *begun*, the imagination – the historical imagination – is already at work, fashioning a story with just this beginning. As for Zuckerman, we can say to him that the observed disjunction between the former present that was lived and the past that is now being written does not necessarily mean that falsification has occurred. In fact, it may mean the exact opposite. As we have noted on several occasions, the 'aerial view' of the present may be precisely what affords one insight into the possible illusions of the past.

But is this what Roth was doing? That is, *was* he in fact gaining some insight into his life? Or was he enmeshed in another fiction? More generally, how can we ever be in a position to tell the difference between the two? In the case at hand, I'm sorry to say, I do not think we can arrive at the answer to this last question. We should feel free to make some guesses, of course, but it is unclear how we would arrive at a verdict. We do not have Roth-the-man before us, or even Roth-the-author. All we have are texts, and decidedly elliptical ones at that.

The more important question in any case is: What about ourselves? How do *we* know whether our latest rendition of who we are and what we have been is 'for real'? Can't we be fairly certain, in fact, that it's *not*, given that every last one we come up with gets replaced, again and again and again, thereby exposing the limits of what we had assumed was the truth? It is a strange situation we are in. For what is implied here is that the search for self-understanding is at one and the same time a search for self-*mis*understanding, for the inadequacy or the incompleteness or the duplicity of the way we are understanding right now. In some ways, then – and recall Augustine especially in this context – we actually seek our own death, being ever on the lookout for suitable replacements, for new selves, preferable to the old ones.

But we cannot, ever, I would argue, rest comfortable assuming that we have finally found it: the last word, the Truth. This is because in making this assumption, we will also have assumed that it is possible to step out of our own history, our own finite understanding, which we simply cannot do. Haven't we already noted that the process of understanding, whether of self or world, is an infinite task, able to continue as long as there is life? Isn't there always more to know? There surely is. But what does it really mean to know? And again, how do we know when we are doing it rather than something else altogether?

THE PROBLEM OF THE TEXT

We must see if there is a way out of the abyss. The question of the validity or invalidity of his interpretations aside for the time being, let us look a bit more closely at what Roth has done in this book. Think about some of the different, albeit largely implicit, explanations he has offered us and assume, again for argument's sake, that they are at least within the range of possibility: his Jewish background, his college experience, his awful marriage, and so forth. Surely these things have *something* to do with how he got to be the person he did, don't they?

But why not include the fly that was on the wall of his childhood bedroom? Why not the indigestion he might have suffered as an adolescent after eating too much spicy food? Why not a million other things that have happened to him through the years? We can only answer, with caution and with care, that the fly, the indigestion, and those million other things are plainly and simply *irrelevant* to the matters at hand. But how do we know this? We could say with the Gestalt psychologists, for instance, that human beings are just naturally capable of gaining insight into their affairs: partly owing to experience and partly owing to the sorts of beings we are, we just *know* some of these things. There is undoubtedly something to this idea, but it may be less than completely satisfactory.

Think about what Roth has done here. He has offered us an essentially historical–psychological account of his life, recounting those experiences he believes to have been formative in determining who he is. But isn't it likely that people from certain other cultures might offer completely different, unhistorical and unpsychological accounts of how they got to be who they are? Isn't it even likely that the very project of retracing one's steps may not even be conceivable to some people? Along these lines, couldn't it be argued that the accounts Roth is offering are just the conventionalized hypotheses and scripts presently possessing currency in our culture?

With these questions in mind, some might hold that the fly and the rest are deemed irrelevant simply because language says so. Who knows? It could be that the specific kinds of accounts Roth offers will be rendered obsolete at some point in the future, when new words come along and transform the world one more time. This may be humbling to think about, but it is undoubtedly so. Nevertheless, we can still say that the fly and the rest are deemed irrelevant exactly because they *are*: they are just not part of the stock of interpretive possibilities we *know*, through language, to be relevant.

Is it possible then that explanation-by-fly-on-the-wall will one day be seized upon as being wholly appropriate for answering the questions at hand? Possible? Yes (though our conceptions of flies will certainly have to change radically). Likely? Of course not. This is simply because the language we use to navigate through the world, however changeable it may be, is unquestionably constrained in its field of potential transformations by both the particular sorts of beings we are and, perhaps more important, by the legacy of prior language use itself. Now if we wish to persist in being skeptics, and insist that Roth's explanations are no more compelling than explanation-by-fly-on-the-wall, we may; skepticism clearly has its comforts. But we must also realize that even if the reality in which we live and think and question and answer is a changeable one, here one epoch and all but gone the next, it is not on that account any less real. Why should the world have to be transhistorical, transcultural, and so on in order to be proclaimed real?

It may of course be unsettling to reflect on the fact that there exists such great variation in the way reality is constituted, interpreted, and explained, and for some it may even imply that the specific ways we do so are fundamentally arbitrary: different fictions for different folks. But there is nothing arbitrary about this situation at all. All that is being said is that we interpret and explain in ways that are more or less consonant with the particular reality we inhabit. A beer commercial comes to mind in this context: this, it says, is as real as it gets.

Very well, then, let us say that we have begun to establish an appropriate range of possible accounts. We are not in the position of saying definitively who and what Roth is and how he might have gotten that way (nor will we ever be), but surely we can speak with some conviction about who and what he is not: he was not an abused child, now trying to work out his problems; he was not a rich boy, or a black boy, or a diseased boy or a whole lot of other things besides. So practically speaking, we can forget about all of these things, which, in itself, circumscribes what we might want to say about him. Texts are often amorphous, ambiguous, heterogeneous, and so on; that goes without saying at this point. It seems to me, though, that in the case of a given text, there are many, many things that it is just not about.

But how exactly does one go on to select from among the different possibilities that are within the appropriate range? The problem we are considering here, it should be emphasized, holds not only for the sort of interpretive task we are presently considering, but for any interpretive task. You gather a set of data, life histories say, and you immediately find that the people you are studying call forth a multiplicity of possible reasons for how and why they have become who they have. How do you begin to make sense of what they tell you?

In traditional empiricist fashion, you might decide that some sort of coding scheme is called for, or a 'content analysis'. As such, you could meticulously comb the text before you, looking for recurrent words or statements, and check them off one by one, after which time you would create certain categories: mother statements, father statements, whatever. After this meticulous cataloguing, you could then try to piece everything together and create a portrait designed to answer the questions you posed when you initially gathered the data. This strategy may be perfectly appropriate in some cases. But it also contains within it at least one troubling assumption. This is that the frequency of words or statements (or even, for that matter, themes and motifs) is a valid index of psychological significance. In some cases, it may be. In other cases, however, it clearly is not.

Another interpretive strategy sometimes called for is to see if one can determine the informant's or author's intentions (see Hirsch 1965, 1976). Simply stated, when you are interpreting a text, it would seem that one of the most sensible things you could do would be to work out what the author meant. In certain respects, this is what Freud tried to do; he looked at what it was that people were saying and tried to infer their intentions, however hidden they might be. More generally, it could be that interpretation requires immersing oneself, empathically, in (what seem to be) the thoughts and feelings of the other, in the manner of Dilthey and Collingwood, as discussed earlier.

There are problems here too, however. As concerns Freud's strategy, needless to say, it takes a good deal of time and expertise. Although it is easy enough on occasion to feel like an amateur psychoanalyst when interpreting interviews and the like, it is wise to be cautious in adopting the role; one or two interviews does not a psychoanalysis make, no matter how clinically astute we may be. As concerns empathy, the problem is a similar one: it is simply no easy task to divine the thoughts and feelings of the other. More importantly, these thoughts and feelings aren't there in any case; the text of what is being said is.

So how, we must now ask, do we determine what a text seems to say? Let us turn to Gadamer for some help. We proceed, he writes (1979), 'by a certain preliminary structuration which thus constitutes the groundwork for later understanding. This process is dominated by a global meaning we have in view, and is based on the relations which an earlier context affords us.' More simply, as we begin reading we gradually get some sense of what is being said; meanings slowly emerge. 'But, of course, this purely anticipatory global meaning awaits confirmation or amendment pending its ability to form a unified and consistent vision. Let us think of this structure in a dynamic way', Gadamer says; 'the effective unity of the anticipated meaning comes out as the comprehension is enlarged and renovated by concentric circles' (146). More simply again, meaning expands and (often) becomes more coherent and unified as we read on; we gather a progressively broader context within which to place the information we encounter.[13]

In line with what has been said thus far, Gadamer goes on to write, 'When we understand a text we do not put ourselves in the place of the other', and nor is it a matter of 'penetrating the spiritual activities of the author'. Rather, it is 'simply a question of grasping the meaning, significance, and aim of what is transmitted to us' (147). Notice what is being said here. In opposition to the empiricist vision of detachment and objectivity, often thought to be the prerequisites for interpretive validity, Gadamer is arguing that it is precisely our own anticipatory understanding of things that is needed, our own belongingness to a world, a 'tradition' we already know about.

Now as soon as we come across some 'initially understandable elements', we have in hand a preliminary sketch of the text. As such, 'Understanding the "thing" which arises there . . . is nothing other than elaborating a preliminary project which will be progressively corrected' (149) as our reading proceeds. The phenomenology of the process is actually quite a bit more complicated than this, Gadamer notes, but the present account will do in a pinch.

There are some problems, however. 'One who follows this course', Gadamer acknowledges, 'always risks falling under the suggestion of his own rough drafts; he runs the risk that the anticipation which he has prepared may not conform to what the thing is'. What this means, therefore, is that, 'The constant task of understanding lies in the elaboration of projects that are authentic and more appropriate to its object.' How exactly is this accomplished? 'Every textual interpretation', he answers, 'must begin . . . with the interpreter's reflection on the preconceptions which result from the "hermeneutical situation" in which he finds himself. He must legitimate them, that is, look for their origin and adequacy' (149–50). A formidable task, this, and decidedly easier said than done. But we will assume, for now, that it is possible.

But isn't there a sense in which Gadamer is advocating the same sort of detachment as the empiricists of whom he is critical? Isn't he asking us to forget our preconceptions? He replies: 'do not make me say what I have not in fact said; and I have *not* said that when we listen to someone or when we read we ought to forget our own opinions or shield ourselves against forming an anticipatory idea about the content of the communication. In reality, to be open to "other people's opinions, " to a text, and so forth, implies right off that they are *situated* in my system of opinions, or better, that I situate myself in relation to them' (151). What is needed most of all, in short, is our own genuine receptivity to the otherness of the text. 'Yet this receptivity', Gadamer emphasizes once more, 'is not acquired with an objectivist "neutrality": it is neither possible, necessary, nor desirable that we put ourselves within brackets. The hermeneutical attitude supposes only that we self-consciously designate our opinions and prejudices and qualify them as such, and in so doing strip them of their extreme character.' It is only then that we can 'grant the text the opportunity to appear as an authentically different being and to manifest its own truth, over and against our preconceived notions' (152).

We must recognize that Gadamer is not offering us a discrete method here; there is no fixed formula for understanding, no key that might be employed to unlock the meaning of texts. Rather, there is an attitude, an attitude that can be described not only in terms of receptivity but in terms of *respect* and, again, *devotion*: we need to care for and abide by what is being said. Only then does the possibility of 'replacement', as we put it earlier, the process by which new meanings can emerge 'over and against our preconceived notions', even exist. We must therefore attempt to distinguish 'between blind prejudices and those which illuminate, between false prejudices and true prejudices' (156).

But how, finally, do we accomplish this, other than by keeping a firm vigilance over our own notions of things? Receptivity and respect are certainly necessary conditions for valid interpretation, but are they sufficient? Can't we be receptive and respectful, not to mention loving and caring, and still get everything wrong? To the extent that unconscious motives and the like remain at work, certainly. Moreover, it may also be the case that by public, consensually-established standards, our interpretations may also be deemed faulty. Upon reading Shakespeare for the first time, for instance, we may come up with an interpretation that is so simplistic and superficial that compared to the finely honed work of Shakespeare scholars, it cannot help but appear inadequate. But might this not be a false comparison? Aren't we falling prey to substituting *their* own hermeneutical situation, which has a history of critical analysis behind it, for ours?

The idea of truth must clearly be relativized on some level; we cannot compare the thing-for-them to the thing-for-us; we live in two different worlds, two different hermeneutical situations. But where does this leave us? Are we to assume that a 10-year-old's reading is every bit as good as the mature scholar's? Doesn't this relativization of the idea of truth entail in the end a complete and total relativism, where every reading is as sound as every other? Not at all. For the fact of the matter is, as a general rule our ongoing engagement with the world changes and complexifies our own hermeneutical situation, which in turn changes and complexifies the qualities of the things we interpret: a new truth emerges.

We must still ask: Is this new truth necessarily 'better' or just different? It certainly could be just different sometimes: we get a new angle on a book we are reading, see it in a different way from how we had. But our new reading can surely be better as well. How do we know this? Precisely by its juxtaposition to the old one, which becomes exposed as inadequate in the very process of its being replaced. 'The "former" prejudice is not simply cast aside', therefore: 'whatever replaced it cannot present its credentials until the position under assault is itself unmasked and denounced as prejudice'. Thus, 'Every "new" position which replaces another continues to need the "former" because it cannot itself be explained so long as it knows neither *in* what nor *by* what it is opposed' (157).

The notion of 'better', therefore, derives not from a comparison of two readings held fundamentally apart from one another, but from their relationship, from the transformation of one into the other: 'Now', you might say, 'I have a more adequate – comprehensive, complex, differentiated, aware, integrated, whatever – understanding of this thing before me.' Needless to say, this too will change, and our humility, perhaps even our humiliation, will return once more: How could I have missed it? How could I have failed to see? How could I be so ignorant, stupid, naive, and just plain wrong? But we ought not move too far in this direction: again, our own hermeneutical situation has changed. Should we ever kick ourselves for our former foibles? Certainly, but only if there is good reason to believe that our own previous interpretations were inadequate given the situation we were in at the time.

We may still be a bit uncomfortable with this formulation, particularly in light of the relativization it has entailed. So we have this idea of truth now, and that is all well and good, since it occasionally seems that we are in fact able to acquire something like it, but it never quite stands still. It is always changing; there is never a point of arrival: understanding is, once more, end-less, not unlike the process of development, of which it is an integral part. There is another possible source of discomfort as well. There is the truth of the Shakespeare scholars, and then there is my truth; we can't compare them. So aren't I hopelessly alone, living solipsistically in a world that only *I* inhabit? Moreover, aren't there then as many different truths as there are people in the world? My thoughts, my understandings, my truths are *mine* and nobody else's. Is there a way out, into the world? Is there any common bond between us?

The bond that prevents the present formulation from devolving into solipsism or pure subjectivism is none other than the tradition, and more specifically the *language*, we hold in common. Now it is undoubtedly the case that there can never be a thought, an understanding, a truth quite like my own; in certain respects, my own hermeneutical situation *is* like no other. But you probably haven't escaped noticing that when you are together with others who inhabit roughly the same world as you do, interpreting a text for instance, you find that you are sometimes able to communicate with them, to share some ideas about the text's possible meaning and significance. This is not to say that you will reach perfect agreement, but you will at least be able to get some conversation started. If you are lucky, in fact, you might even challenge your own respective prejudices and provoke one another to a more adequate reading than either of you alone may have had.

Gadamer has, it must be hoped, been of some help in our attempt to articulate some idea of what it means to understand. Nevertheless, we may want to think about a few of the points he has raised a bit more critically. He spoke, for instance, about a 'global meaning' that 'dominates' the process of interpretation, a vision of the whole that is progressively corrected and refined as the process moves along. Now it could be that this vision of the whole is simply one of our human ways. We all seek 'fulfillment', Kermode (1979) has written; 'we all seek the center that will allow the senses to rest' (73). But what if, following Derrida (and perhaps Roth), there *is* no center? What if there *is* no global meaning to a text, but only a heterogeneous ensemble of multiple possibilities? Gadamer clearly has much to say that is useful and important; none of these questions are intended to challenge that. But it could very well be, I will suggest, that his own version of hermeneutics tends to underemphasize both the multiplicity of texts and, in parallel, the frequently dispersed and even fragmentary quality of the process of interpretation itself.

Although it may be that our desire to seek the center is part of our human ways, the situation could also be quite otherwise: rather than being a function of nature, this desire may be a function of culture, a 'logocentric' culture, as Derrida (1976) has put it, that persists in attempting to close the process of interpretation by imagining that there is an end in sight, a 'perfect coherence', deferred but visible.

I am not suggesting here that we either can or should completely abandon this desire, for there are unquestionably times – particularly when we interpret ourselves – when a vision of the whole, of a center, is appropriate and necessary. In the midst of my own occasional dispersion and fragmentation, I, not unlike Roth, may seek to establish a more integrated and coherent interpretation of who I am. But the quest for the whole, I would also argue, must not be undertaken at the expense of difference and multiplicity. Indeed, isn't the very recognition of this difference and multiplicity – in Roth's case, the feeling that he has come undone – precisely that which provokes us to move forward, to develop, with the hope of effecting a new vision of completion? Hasn't this in fact been the case with each of the characters we've discussed – from Augustine, with his terribly divided self; to Helen Keller, who had found herself so thoroughly fraught with heterogeneity; to Roquentin, who had wished that his life could assume the concreteness and solidity of a melody? Didn't each of these characters work toward establishing some semblance of identity in and through difference?

There is one further issue that needs to be addressed in conjunction with Gadamer. In addition to speaking about global meaning and so forth, Gadamer has in fact spoken about the 'thing' itself, along with the need for our anticipations to conform to it. Now given all that has been said here I am not about to accuse him of having a naive or simplistic conception of what a thing is; it would be audacious, as well as wrong, for me to do so. Gadamer in no way conceives of a thing, a text for instance, as a discrete object, able to be grasped in identical fashion by all who interpret it. Rather, a text for Gadamer is a compilation of words, an embodiment of language, whose very qualities of 'thingness' are inseparable from the specific interpretive community that is doing the reading. This again is why we can acknowledge the thingness of a text (or a work of art, a person, etc.) while at the same time acknowledging that it might be a completely different thing for someone else.

Gadamer also appears to realize that an interpretation cannot rightly be said to 'correspond' to a thing, and for much the same reasons suggested above. The qualities of a text are not just there, waiting in anonymity; instead, they emerge through reading itself, as a function of who we are and how we read. If we want to continue to use the language of correspondence and conformity, therefore, this may be all right (sometimes) – as long as we realize that our interpretations correspond or conform not to the anonymous thing of subject–object thinking but to the languaged thing, constituted in its specific form by us, the interpreters.

But as we asked much earlier, what exactly is the 'thing' when the text being interpreted is ourselves? In the case of a written text, we noted, there are at least words on a page. Without being crude about it, we can say that it is an object of sorts, outside of ourselves, written by someone else. Now there are some – 'reader response' critics, for instance (see Tomkins 1980) – who may want to quarrel with even this. For aren't we actually creating the text in the very process of reading itself? In some sense, I suppose, we do create what can thereafter be said to be there, but my own feeling is that we ought not take this position too far. Clearly, the words that exist, on the page, hold within them some constraints on our creativity. This is why when we read Shakespeare and debate what it all means, we do not customarily believe ourselves to be reading Dickens or Hemingway or Balzac or (Jackie) Collins. But are there any comparable 'traces' when the text is ourselves?[14] What exactly are we to do about this?

TO KNOW THYSELF

We have before us another rather thorny problem. The fact is, *we* ourselves are not texts; we are just people, who think, feel, say, and do lots and lots of different things. But perhaps we have a clue here as to where we might head in moving our discussion forward. Can't we still propose, following

Ricoeur (1981) especially, that all that we think, feel, say, and do are *themselves* texts (or at least 'quasi'-texts), requiring just the same vigilance, respect, and care that those texts that exist outside of ourselves require? Wasn't this Freud's claim as well? Indeed, what Ricoeur eventually came to realize, in significant part *through* Freud, were the limits of self-reflection understood in terms of direct access to consciousness: 'There is no direct apprehension of the self by the self, no internal apperception or appropriation of the self's desire to exist through the short-cut of consciousness, but only by the long road of the interpretation of signs' (Ricoeur 1974: 170). Self-understanding, in short, requires as its very condition of possibility precisely the same hermeneutic principles and forms of attention as textual understanding more generally.

The problem, however, is that in dealing with these different texts of the self, we remain in the difficult and rather precarious position, it seems, of being not only readers but authors as well. We interpret texts that we ourselves have fashioned: *our* thoughts, *our* feelings, *our* words, *our* actions. Even our memories, Roth reminds us, are imaginings, occurring now, as we reflect. Doesn't this mean then that we are hopelessly intertwined with exactly that which we wish to interpret? When I try to interpret my own memories, aren't I trying to come to terms with things that are *already* interpreted, already saturated in language, indeed in *my* language?

All this is true. When we try to interpret ourselves, we are undoubtedly dealing with something much less obdurate, much less present, than even the most elliptical of written texts. Perhaps this is why we are so often so thoroughly puzzling to ourselves – even more puzzling, in fact, than significant others in our midst. Them we can see and hear. But me? Do I really know what my own 'personality' is like? Do I really have a kind of whole picture of myself comparable to that which I have of others? 'You are the only one', writes Barthes (1989), 'who can never see yourself except as an image' (36).

Interestingly enough, when we try to interpret ourselves, we may often try to imagine the way these others might do it; we try to look at ourselves through *their* eyes, as best we can. 'One cannot really see one's own exterior and comprehend it', Bakhtin (1986) also notes, 'and no mirrors or photographs will help'. In fact, he argues, 'our real exterior can be seen and understood only by other people, because they are located outside us in space, and because they are *others*' (7). We must therefore emulate these others in some fashion. Sometimes, of course, we fail; we either come up with nothing or, in some cases, illusions. This is apparently what Zuckerman believes has happened in Roth's case; he has come up with an all too innocuous self-portrait, designed to be a kind of apologia for his sordid past. But don't we sometimes succeed as well? Don't we sometimes gain, through interpretation, a measure of insight into who and what we are? I said above that there exist many different texts issuing from ourselves. But can't we also say that new selves – selves that are better understood than the old ones – issue from these same texts?

Whether Roth has engaged in a process that has culminated in greater self-knowledge than he previously had, I do not know. What I do know, however – though, admittedly, I can never prove that it is so – is that for all its ambiguity, its lures and traps and holes, the possibility for self-knowledge surely exists. Now I am not talking about 'perfect' self-knowledge, and nor do I want to claim that things that I am virtually certain of now won't be displaced at some point in the future. In fact, I *hope* this will happen, for it will mean that I will have developed beyond where I am now. Just as we noted in regard to the idea of reality, there is no reason to assume that what can arguably be termed 'knowledge' is set in stone. But to deny the possibility of knowledge, whether of world or self, is, I would argue, to engage in a profound act of bad faith, the consequence of which can only be a deafening silence.

On some level, of course, we can virtually ignore the question of knowledge and truth, and create stories of ourselves that all but leap over the texts of our existence; we can simply ignore who and what we have been, and fashion that picture of ourselves that we would most like to own. Functionally speaking, this may sometimes work quite well for us – as long, that is, as the various 'facts' we have skipped over don't rear their ugly heads and punish us for all we have forgotten. But functionality and knowledge are by no means equivalent. Defenses, for instance, are often highly functional; they may allow us to take comfort in dangerous and threatening situations. But as a general rule they don't help us too much in knowing ourselves – at least not until they are exposed as such.

The bottom line is this: if we have any desire at all to abide by the admittedly elusive texts that comprise our existence, we are going to have to do some very careful reading. For the sake of security, we may occasionally fall back upon our old ways of looking at things, our old prejudices and preconceptions, and continue to see what we want to see. But if we are forthright in our venture, and receptive enough to our own otherness, we may well succeed in replacing these old ways with new, more adequate ones: a new self will have been written.

How, then, do we know when we are engaged in knowing? When I asked a friend of mine this question, he said the answer was simple: he feels bad. Jokes aside, there may be something to this idea. For the desire for self-knowledge, which is part and parcel of the process of development itself, is often a response to a problem of some sort, to a disjunction, as we put it earlier, between what is and what ought to be, however ill-articulated it is. What this means, therefore, is that the desire for self-knowledge is precisely in the nature of an exposure of – and perhaps assault upon – the inadequate selves we have been. So it is that he, and we, sometimes feel bad when we see what has been going on. Now admittedly, my friend went on to note that he is somewhat inclined toward self-punishment; he frequently feels that he deserves to feel bad. Thus the possibility exists that he is taking on burdens that are not rightfully his, alone.

What he needs to do, therefore – and this too is reminiscent of Freud, among others – is to take his new interpretations and see how well they cohere with and illuminate the various texts, his own and others', that continue to emerge throughout the course of his life. He needs to test them against these texts and see if they are able to make greater sense of things than had previously been possible – as in the idea of juxtaposition we spoke about earlier. If they are in fact so able, then perhaps he had been on to something. If not, then perhaps he had better return to the available information and see if there is another way. We must not speak facilely about this sort of process; defenses and the like will undoubtedly still be at work. The basic principles, however, still stand.

We said as much in conjunction with our discussion of Roth himself. He seemed to be convinced, toward the end of his presentation of the facts, that he was on an upward swing once again; he had apparently worked through some of the debilitating traumas that had come his way, and armed with his new knowledge, he would be able to forge ahead, healthy and free. But the whole thing could be one great big delusion as well: his new woman friend could be just another weird plaything, designed to satisfy his own perverse and immature needs; perhaps he would be too old and worn to resume the carefree, footloose existence he seemed to want; perhaps he would be haunted by Josie's gruesome death, and come to regard himself as nothing less than a murderer, who had wrought havoc on an innocent bystander. Perhaps his analyst has some clues about all this. But it may be too early still for Roth to find his way about the thickets of his life. Only time will tell.

Chapter 6
The primal scenes of selfhood

SECRECY AND SECRETS

In Frank Kermode's graceful book, *The Genesis of Secrecy* (1979), he refers to the 'radiant obscurity of narratives' (47). Whether the task is one of reading narratives, writing them, or more informally reflecting on the fabric of our lives, as much as we may hope to find just that key which will unlock the mystery of the text before us, what we often find instead is ambiguity and opacity: a resistance, on the part of the text itself, to yield to our desire for closure. 'The pleasures of interpretation', Kermode writes, 'are henceforth linked to loss and disappointment, so that most of us will find the task too hard, or simply repugnant; and then, abandoning meaning, we slip back into the old comfortable fictions of transparency, the single sense, the truth' (123). We assume, in other words, that there are secrets to be found in the texts we encounter, discrete kernels of meaning that, if we only work hard enough, we will succeed in discovering. As a rule, however, Kermode tells us, there is only secrecy, and we must therefore be bold enough and humble enough to remain in the surplus of meaning that exists.

There is much to recommend Kermode's point of view: the texts of our pasts are indeed regions of secrecy, whose meanings are never wholly to be discovered. The very primacy of interpretation militates against this. Along these lines, we can see why Freud, among others, has been taken to task for presuming that the secrets of the personal past could ultimately be pieced together, reconstructed, toward the end of fashioning an 'intelligible, consistent, and unbroken case history' (1901–5a:18). Despite his considerable emphasis on the process of interpretation, there is reason to believe that the 'old comfortable fictions of transparency' continued to work their insidious ways.

Now on some level, as I have suggested already, this sort of critique of Freud, particularly in regard to his metaphor of archeology, is quite right (see Freeman 1985b); there was a sense in which Freud seemed to suppose that, although interpretation was a necessary tool for the excavation of buried meanings, one could, in the end, move beyond it; interpretation was thus conceived essentially as a methodological instrument, a technique, that would lead to the discovery of data that could ultimately stand on their own. To this extent, the role of the interpreter-narrator was, upon piecing together the fragments of the past, effaced, and the hermeneutic circle broken. What Freud failed to see, therefore, as clearly as he might have at any rate, was that the history that ultimately emerged via interpretation was still bound to it, deriving its very intelligibility and consistency precisely on account of the process of narration itself.

It is time now to pay more serious attention to a question that has come up before in the course of our inquiry. Is the metaphor of archeology, along with the more general idea that there exist secrets to be discovered, just plain wrong? Despite the obvious difficulties of this metaphor and of Freud's conception of life history more generally, tied as they are to a fundamentally objectivist view of the personal past, my own inclination is nonetheless to answer this question, cautiously, in the negative. The reason is simply that there are unquestionably lives the very contours of which have been formed out of just those secrets that Freud was so concerned to reveal. I will not go so far as to claim here that each and every one of us harbors these secrets, and that if only we could discover them we would finally have in hand the aforementioned key that would unlock the door to the past; there is little reason to suppose that lurking beneath the manifest nature of things, there is always and inevitably a hidden reality and a hidden truth, pulling the strings of our lives like silent puppeteers, directing our futures in ways that are unbeknownst to us. At the same time, however, there do seem to be cases in which something not at all unlike this does seem to occur. Perhaps we can learn from one of these.

The first chapter of Sylvia Fraser's book, *My Father's House* (1987), which carries the subtitle of 'A Memoir of Incest and of Healing', is called, rather appropriately by all indications, 'Secrets'. It is the beginning of a story that Fraser was only able to tell sometime during her late forties, when she arrived at the startling realization that she had in fact been sexually abused by her father throughout her childhood and on into early adolescence. 'The story I have told in this book', Fraser writes, 'is autobiographical. As a result of amnesia, much of it was unknown to me until three years ago.' For the sake of clarity, she goes on to say, she has used italics 'to indicate thoughts, feelings, and experiences pieced together from recently recovered memories, and to indicate dreams'; and it is important that we, the readers, keep this device in mind as we read, mainly so that we acknowledge throughout that the story being told is the product of her own reconstruction.

Furthermore, in order to provide 'focus and structure', she admits to using many of the techniques of the novelist, and avows that 'No attempt has been made to create full or balanced characterizations', but 'only to portray such persons and myself as our lives relate to this difficult story'. Nevertheless, to the best of her knowledge, she says, 'I have not exaggerated or distorted or misrepresented the truth as I now understand it.' Finally, and for the sake of offering a response to those who would want to claim that she is either fantasizing or lying or simply writing fiction, Fraser closes her introductory comments by stating that the fact of her abuse by her father 'has been corroborated by outside sources' (1).

It should be noted as well at this point that the book is written in a rather curious way. For although she knows, at the time of writing, that she has in fact been the victim of incest, her decision is to tell her story in such a way that she is able to capture what was, at the time of experience, her utter confusion, her sense that something back then – it was unclear what – was indeed wrong. Even though the story she tells is informed by her realization, in other words (again, she will even be referring, in italics, to certain thoughts, feelings, and experiences that she has reconstructed in line with memories that emerged much later on), her attempt here is to try to re-present her life as it was lived at the time, in all of its uncertainty and indeterminacy. What she is doing, in short, is telling about her life as it *must* have been lived given the outcome.

Now I realize that this woman's claim to be telling the unvarnished truth does not necessarily make it so. I realize as well that there is something downright incredible about much of what she has to say, particularly regarding her profound amnesia. But let us try to suspend our incredulity, for a while at least, and see what it is that seems to have gone on in this woman's strange and difficult life.

Before proceeding, there is one 'methodological' problem that ought to be (re)acknowledged, and it has to do with the idea that the series of events and experiences that culminate in Fraser's realization and that lead subsequently to her reconstructing her previous life is itself a product of this same reconstruction. As such, the end of the story is, once again, contained in the beginning. We therefore hear a tale of ignorance and unawareness, of symptoms and clues that result only in mystification, of a life whose very shape was determined, in significant part, by a knowledge that manifestly did not exist. Had Fraser tried to tell her life story prior to her realization – which, not unlike Augustine, was a 'conversion' in its own right – it would no doubt have been vastly different; it would likely have been disconnected and fragmented, in much the same way that the stories initially told by Freud's patients were. There are thus no pretensions here concerning the kind of story that is being told: it is one of moving from unconsciousness to consciousness, her ability to predicate the former as such being precisely a function of the emergence of the latter. An interesting corollary follows from this: I cannot speak of that of which I *am* unconscious, but only that of which I *was*. Hence the narrational dimension of the notion of the unconscious itself.

The book begins with Fraser's recounting a number of rather neutral childhood events: sitting on Daddy's lap, playing ticktacktoe, going to nursery school for the first time, going to Granny's, to church, and so on. This is of course one of Fraser's fictional devices: on the surface, she suggests, hers was a childhood like any other. But it isn't too long after Fraser introduces these commonplaces of childhood that she recounts Daddy in his pajamas, giving her candy, giving her cookies, and her own feeling of being his uncontested favorite little girl. There are also her mother's admonitions of 'Filthy filthy!' when she touches herself in those private places, her young body becoming suffused with danger, such that she will be reluctant to speak when it becomes the object of another's wicked designs. Finally, there are those awful memories, which only now, in the wake of her discovery, can be inserted into the text of her past.

She would cry when her mother put her to bed. 'I didn't used to be afraid of the dark', she writes, assuming the voice of that frightened little child, 'but now I know that demons and monsters hide in the cubbyholes by my bed. I'm afraid one will jump out at me, and rub dirty dirty against me' (8). Alongside further commonplaces, like fun with Smoky, her new cat, there are also fits, in which she would turn blue and need to have her tongue held in place with a wood stick. There would be fear at these, and then rage. 'I kick my heels and scream', she writes, but 'I no longer remember quite why' (12). As for how it was that she managed to keep quiet about those terrible trysts with her father, her newly-found memories supply the answer to this too: '*My father needs a permanent seal for his lips*', Fraser writes (in italics), '*one that will murder all defiance. "If you say once more that you're going to tell"* ', he had apparently said, ' "*I'm sending that cat of yours to the pound for gassing!*" ' (12). That was all she needed to hear. It was easy to recall the magnitude of her hate; it had been right there, palpable and real, at the time it happened. The reason for it, however, would remain a secret, for many years to come.

DOUBLE TROUBLE

'When the conflict caused by my sexual relationship with my father became too acute to bear', Fraser surmises, 'I created a secret accomplice for my daddy by splitting my personality in two.' So it was that she devised 'another self', separate from the manifest one, 'whose existence was unknown' to her. As for her loss of memory, it was retroactive: 'I did not remember my daddy ever having touched my sexually. I did not remember ever seeing my daddy naked. I did not remember my daddy ever seeing me naked.' Thus, whenever he approached her sexually, Fraser again surmises, she turned into her 'other self', the result being that nothing at all of these experiences was remembered. 'Even now', she continues, 'I don't know the full truth of that other little girl I created to do the things I was too frightened, too ashamed, too repelled to do, the things my father made me do, the things I did to please him but which paid off with a precocious and dangerous power . . . She telegraphed messages to me through the dreams we shared' and 'leaked emotions to me through the body we shared', and her 'guilty face' would sometimes be glimpsed in the mirror. None of this, however, was even remotely evident at the time of experience. The only thing that was really feared was the house in which she lived, 'which by guilty association became the house that knew'. To this extent, 'the usual childhood reality was reversed. Inside my own house, among people I knew, was where danger lay. The familiar had proven to be treacherous, whereas the unfamiliar . . . still contained the seeds of hope' (15–16).

Things are getting a bit complicated here. What had happened, apparently – and the word 'apparently' is certainly appropriate in this context, given that this 'other' and her activities are strictly (and avowedly) constructions – was that little Sylvia Fraser had somehow dissociated herself from her dangerous encounters, such that she could be both present and absent at the same time; as cognizant as she was of virtually everything else that was going on in her young life, these encounters were immediately and spontaneously banished from consciousness, in true repressive fashion. Furthermore, as a correlate of this act of repression, there was (apparently) also a significant measure of displacement as well, her terrible fears of her father having been transformed into a profound aversion toward the house in which the Fraser family lived. There was a variety of other displacements too. Upon visiting her aging grandmother, for instance, there would always arise that 'unspeakable moment' when the children would line up to kiss her goodbye, their lips being 'swallowed in the decaying pulpiness of her cheek'. None of the children probably enjoyed this very much, but this little girl was nothing short of revolted, being forced to 'struggle against the heaving of my stomach, the yammering of my heart'. But why? 'Why this revulsion for an old woman's kiss? I do not know. I cannot say' (19). Only later was she to realize that the skin of her grandmother's cheek was not unlike the skin of her father's scrotum.

There was also a tendency on Sylvia's part to become drawn toward those other little girls who were themselves victims of some form or other of abuse, and this despite the protests of her more 'normal' friends, who were more exclusive with regard to who they would and would not play with. No one wanted to play with Magda, for instance; everyone knew that her father beat her up. They would be that much more 'scandalized', therefore, when she and the other 'rejects' would be invited to join the group. In short, Sylvia began to inhabit a world that was symbolically animated by her secret, with her own aversions and attractions alike being fueled, at least in part, by the knowledge that was locked away in the dark corridors of her unconscious.

The most telling sign that something was awry was in activities associated with that awful house. When her mother asked Sylvia why she never brought friends home to play, she couldn't come up with any answer. Was she becoming a snob, as her mother suggested? That was possible, but would hardly account for her growing as 'woozy' as she did when the prospect of having visitors arose. As an aside, we might note in this context that her mothers's – and indeed her own – hypothetical explanations for why she behaved as she did were probably integrated into her own self-image; and to the degree this was so, she probably went on to become, in part, the imaginary figure that was constructed in order to account for her deeds and misdeeds. By all (manifest) accounts, she could very well have been a snob, just like some of her friends, and would thus have come to live precisely that mythical life that common sense told her she was living: 'I guess I'm just ashamed of my family and my house', she might have said to herself. Though again, there was something going on here that common sense simply couldn't contain.[1]

When it finally came time for Sylvia to have a birthday party, she went outside in sub-zero weather, with the hope of dying of pneumonia before party-time came. If in fact she was a snob, she was certainly a strange one at that; to think of the lengths to which she went to prevent that party from happening. It was a good thing that the most massive blizzard of her life found its way to the Fraser house. The party would undoubtedly have gotten rather ugly.

'Who was my other self?' Fraser asks. 'Though we had split one personality between us, I was the majority shareholder. I went to school, made friends, gained experience, developing my part of the personality, while she remained morally and emotionally a child, functioning on instinct rather than intelligence. She began as my creature, forced to do what I refused to do, yet because I blotted out her existence, she passed out of my control as completely as a figure in a dream.' Fraser nevertheless had to ask: 'Like a dog that sometimes slips its tether, did she ever run free?' (24). It was difficult to say. Yet at least one incident suggests that this other within her had occasionally made herself known. For another memory that surged into consciousness many years later was of Mr Brown, a sleazy neighbor who had lived with his pregnant wife in a portion of her own house, and who, with his wife in the hospital having their baby, had ushered this seemingly precocious child into his kitchen, grabbed her wrist, and said, '*Don't try to fool me, kid. I know what goes on in this house*'. Should she decide to tell, it wasn't just her cat that would die. '*You tell anyone, kid, and I'll kill you!*' (33) Bad dreams followed, in which her 'reject' friend Magda was sometimes the protagonist. As for the brown stockings that she wore that day when she encountered Mr Brown, she would wear them no more. Why?, asked her mother. Simple: 'Brown stockings make my legs look like poop!' (35). But this didn't quite account for the fact of her lying on the floor, kicking furiously, in a manner not unlike what had occurred earlier during those fits when she would turn blue.

Meanwhile, as summer drew near, Sylvia's grade-school teacher was becoming more and more puzzled about why she had become so mean and irritable throughout the course of the year, why she had such a chip on her shoulder, why it seemed as if she had decided not to trust anyone anymore. 'Why do you hate me so?' her teacher had asked. 'I feel sorry for you', she went on to say. 'If you lock yourself away from everyone who cares about you, you're going to have a hard life' (37). The little girl was 'flabbergasted'. She didn't hate her teacher; she loved her, more than any other teacher she had ever had. So what on earth was this woman talking about? It was almost as if her description pertained to someone else, someone other than the loving and devoted student she believed herself to be. Curiously enough, she was quite right about this.

LINGERING DESPAIR, APPEARANCES NOTWITHSTANDING

Just when it might have seemed that some of the mysterious happenings in her life were getting out of hand, Fraser was fortunate enough to have won something of a reprieve from her father, who, upon her reaching the age of around 10, decided to leave her alone for a couple of years. Whatever the reason may have been for this, Fraser writes, 'this hiatus gave me a chance to stabilize, to imitate normalcy, to begin to close the gap in sexual awareness between me and my other self, to escape with relief into my peer group and to absorb its moral values'. By no means did this stifle her anger, however: 'If anything, tenuous safety made me more openly rebellious, more disdainful of all authority, more outwardly raging, the way a small dog yaps loudest when a glass door seems to protect it.' What was most important, though, was the fact that after several years of utter confusion and turmoil, Sylvia was finally growing more confortable with herself. Due especially to the care provided by her friends, a group of whom had decided to call themselves the Golden Amazons, she suddenly felt 'safe, legitimate, full of power' (41). When, before, she gazed at herself in the mirror, she would see her own face transformed into that of Magda, her fellow victim. Eventually she would see the Amazons instead.

Some of this security came crashing to a close when she came home one night, after being with the Amazons, only to find her father all alone, eager to return to his evil ways. The other resurges once more: '*She feels as if she were being repeatedly punched in the belly, forcing all air from her lungs. She feels used, not as one person exploited by another, but as a condom is used then discarded in the gutter . . . She is old enough, now, to know about blood and babies*'. She is also old enough '*to understand how completely she has been betrayed*' (43). The past of her other, therefore, was itself being rewritten; infused with the knowledge she (it?) had come to acquire as she had grown older, it had become clear enough just how wrong this situation was. No longer 'the seven-year old baby who had struck the dirty deal' with her father years ago, there was a new, somewhat more sophisticated other in her place: 'Just as the emotions of my other self often leaked up into my life, now my moral values began seeping down into hers' (39). It wouldn't be quite so easy, therefore, for this divided self to adhere to her imposture.

Things became particularly difficult when Sylvia was in the company of boys who expressed interest in her. After one of them asked her innocently whether she would like to come to his house, for instance, she contemplated it for a while and then, for no apparent reason, stopped dead in her tracks and then sprinted away. 'Again', she writes, 'I find myself overcome by an emotion for which I must find a reason.' What could possibly have sent her into such a sudden frenzy? Maybe it was the skates she had been wearing, which were old and hurt her feet. This was what her voice said. But there was also weeping, and rage, pouring out of her 'like lava, devastating everything in its path', her body becoming 'seized with convulsions' (46). When another boy got a bit too fresh during a movie, leaving her 'passing in and out of consciousness', dizzily alone in the dark, she bit him hard enough to draw blood and hear him cry out in pain, after which time she fled out of the theater into the harsh light of day.

If Sylvia was to maintain her credentials as an Amazon in good standing, she would have to devise some sort of way in which she would appear to be a bit more like the other girls, most of whom were more than willing to encourage, if not quite accept, the advances of the local boys. She thus created a 'glamor-puppet', nicknamed Appearances, which had been 'glued together out of tinselly bits cut from movie magazines'; she was an 'alter ego', whose function was to hide her 'shadow-twin', who was starting to cause trouble. 'I invented her', Fraser writes, 'to fool myself as well as the world', to show that everything was wonderful when it was quite the opposite. There is again the language of the other in this context: 'I ran her in school elections, entered her in popularity contests, placed her on athletic teams, bought her a cheerleading outfit' (65). Her only flaw was that she acted more like a computer, programmed for popularity, than she did a human being. She was akin to a 'billboard', as Fraser puts it, 'that increasingly advertised the wrong things' (66). As psychologically important as it was for this confused adolescent to immerse herself in the world of her peers, if only as a means of avoiding spending time at home – she had come openly to hate her father, though 'without knowing why' – the image she had devised brought forth dangers that proved to be no less threatening than the earlier ones. Filling her datebook like a 'junkie' was fun in some ways and reassuring, but failed to nourish her in the way that was needed. She was merely keeping up Appearances, as it were, while her own inner self starved. Her friends, in fact, began to wonder why it was she dated so feverishly, why she wound up 'ditching' every boy she saw, why she 'used' them like so many playthings. All she could say, in response, was that they all bored her, which they did: it would be no small feat to break through the defensive armor of someone as emotionally numb as she was.

Even her invitation to the Fall Frolic by one Daniel Hobson, heart-throb of many, left her cold and weary, as if she were preparing 'for the hundredth performance of a play that wasn't very good in the first place' (79). He seemed different and special, a cut above the others, and Sylvia herself had been delighted that she had been the one he had chosen to accompany him to the dance. There was nonetheless little point in assuming that this outing would be any more enjoyable, any more real, than the others: 'I pined for Daniel until the moment after he asked me' (80). After that it was business as usual, the foremost task being to pass the evening without too much pain. For once, however, this couldn't quite be accomplished, for as her attraction for this special boy grew during the course of the night, so too did her feeling of claustrophobia, his arms 'like clamps', taking her breath away, for better and for worse. 'Don't get serious', she had said to him. 'I play the field' (86). Just in case he didn't believe her, she would dye her hair – which she well knew to be an 'advertisement for moral turpitude' – to prove it.

By the close of her senior year of high school, things had become more tenuous and weird still. She was down to ninety-eight pounds, she could burn her arm with a cigarette without feeling any pain, and an endless stream of boys, mocking her one minute and asking her out the next, were coming her way. 'I see myself dancing across a stage like a stringless marionette', Fraser recalls, 'nodding, smiling, joking, laughing with red lips. Once this puppet was my slave, made up of shiny bits and pieces of what other people admired. She performed in my name. I held the strings. She protected me. Now', however, 'she is a caricature of what I want her to be. Appearances is my enemy, mocking me, serving me up. She is destroying me by destroying herself' (101). She didn't need to go this route, Daniel told her; she didn't have to be 'loose' to be accepted. 'It's not true!' she cried. 'They're liars!' (105). Well, they were and they weren't. Whatever the verdict, the sheer force of Daniel's accusation shattered her, 'like a reflection shot through with a bullet' (106).

Things would be different henceforth. Daniel would see to that: 'He holds me, binding the pieces of myself together, allowing me to heal. He strokes my hair. He kisses me. His lips are warm. He believes me. He believes in me' (109). Armed now with the power of love, which is the only power able to give her a sense of worth and value, there is finally some hope that the Fraser duo will be reduced to one. 'So this is how other girls feel', she could finally say, when he touched her. 'Against all possibilities, I am real after all. I am human' (109–10). Her despair was over, even if temporarily, and it would be time now to construct a strong and secure enough self to be able to deal with the hardships of the past. For the time being, the simple thought that she had been lucky enough to have met someone who could see beyond Appearances was enough to send her into swoons of redemptive rapture.

THE DEAD END OF RATIONALITY

Fraser's incestuous relationship with her father having finally come to a close by the end of high school, she found herself left with a 'sooty aftershadow of self-hate', which, sensibly enough, she had assumed derived from the shameless way she had betrayed herself in recent years, living as she did under the shadow of what she consciously knew to be a cheap and phony image. The primary task upon her arrival at college, therefore, was to do what she could to leave this part of herself behind. 'Philosophy was my high-minded defense against this legacy', she writes. 'Through rational knowledge I would put together a functional and successful person I could respect.' As for feelings, they would be put 'on hold. They were irrational, hence dangerous' (120). The only problem here – detectable, of course, only in retrospect – was that in some sense, only her head went to college: her 'severed head', as she puts it. She would wear a bun and horn-rimmed glasses. There would be no more lipstick. In place of Appearances, there emerged a 'brain', quite unlike most of the other girls, who were ultimately searching for husbands. Perhaps there would emerge a body later, when it was less tainted by the ravages of the past.

Some good unquestionably came from her immersion into the rational world. 'Man is the product of heredity and environment', she came to believe; 'scratch soul. He is a selfish animal who seeks pleasure and avoids pain . . . with no divine sense of morality.' These sorts of ideas 'exhilarated' her, particularly insofar as she felt 'freed at last from the burden of inherent sin – of being the bad child born into a nest of saints' (126). To the extent that her own actions were but the endpoints of forces, whether internal or external, she could be exonerated from the claim that she had plainly been the very incarnation of evil. As for the issue of deities, she would be skeptical at best, 'an agnostic-leaning-toward-atheism' (126). It was only sensible. There would be some changes in these beliefs over the course of her four years at college, with free will, for instance, gradually coming to appear to be a more suitable philosophical perspective than determinism, and Kant gaining the upper hand over Hume, but the basic thrust of her existence remained much the same: she was intellectualizing the conflicts through which she had been living.

It wasn't until the very end of college that, gazing in the mirror one more time, she could see that, 'The disembodied creature staring back isn't me any more than the gaudy marionette with movie-star pretensions I banished four years back' (134–5). Fortunately for her, Daniel, despite having gone off to another school, was still in the picture during those rather abstract years. For it was he, above all else, who served to remind her that she did indeed have a body and that she could let her hair down every now and then from that tightly-pulled bun and be herself – however difficult it might have been to define who exactly this was. They would eventually marry, elaborate ceremony and all. Much of this is hearsay, however, for when it came to trying to recall the details of that fateful day, especially the stroll down the aisle – on the arm of her father – she would inevitably come up blank. She found this strange. She also found strange the tenacity with which she had refused to wear the traditional white to the wedding; she had been nothing short of 'fanatical' about it. Except for these occasional bursts of irrationality, however, the next dozen or so years with the man who had rescued her from the abyss of her living death were as good as she could have dreamed.

But then, and for no discernible reason, Fraser's life seemed to change: 'Depression begins seeping like poisonous fog through the cracks in my life. In the past when I was down', she notes, 'I was able to look to specific causes. Now', however, 'the sun is shining' – rationally speaking, all was well – 'but I am slipping into the shadows. Increasingly, all I want to do is weep' (146). Depression became despair. There was some history of mental disturbance in her family. Did she have 'depressive genes'? She also began to want to return to some of her childhood haunts. But why? Why, upon rummaging through her own dusty trunk, did she discover pictures, that she herself had obviously drawn, filled with violent and terrible images? And why, finally, did she decide to sit at the typewriter, day in and day out, trying to relive her earliest years? She had wanted to write a novel that would chart the course of a woman's life from childhood on up through adulthood, but found, inexplicably, that she had written reams before even getting past the age of 8. There had been mysteries before, plenty of them in fact, but this one was full time. More questions: 'Why did I give my fictional father a hooked arm? Such an obvious phallic symbol now seems melodramatic. Why did I stud our family history with suicide? Why did I portray my father as threatening the life of my cat, and why does the thought of old Smoky, even today, reduce me to tears?' (152). However mysterious its origin and meaning, this book, which had been entitled *Pandora*, seemed to serve Fraser well. There was a kind of solidity to the project, a kind of realness, that suggested that something important was being said. 'Through Pandora', she eventually realized, 'my other self had acquired a voice' (153).

What happened subsequently, as Fraser tells it, is that, unable to follow the protagonist's story into her teenage years, owing to the volatility of the period, her other self devised a kind of 'secret agenda', whereby she would continue to speak, but in a muted enough voice for the horrors of memory to be able to issue gradually. As for the nature of this agenda, it would appear to have had something to do with a desire to reunite with her father. 'I had already lived out one fairytale in which a prince rescued me from a daddy-monster', she explains. 'Now my other self wanted to rescue her daddy-king from mommy so they could live happily ever after' (153). Now what does one do in such a situation? She certainly couldn't go to daddy himself. Not only was that immoral, but she hated his guts. 'My other self', then, 'required a daddy substitute, attractive to me as well as to her'. A married man would do particularly well, for just as she would be loving him, she could hate his wife, who would serve as 'a projection of the jealous fury she felt for the mother-rival who failed to protect her' (153). Whew!

What does this mean anyway? 'Does this mean my other self had secretly enjoyed her incestuous affair with Daddy?' She answers forthrightly: 'I don't know. I do believe the relationship began in tenderness and even innocence, and that those feelings had powerfully imprinted.' In terms of the later years, when things had become decidedly less tender and innocent, it was anybody's guess. 'Perhaps, in retrospect', Fraser ventures, 'the undercurrents of secrecy, of power, of naughtiness and of danger became enticing. Perhaps, like old veterans sitting around the Legion Hall, she grew to romanticize trench warfare.' Perhaps. But it was hard to say. Meanwhile, Fraser continues, she 'watched askance while someone who looked like me cast aside everything I valued to recreate an infantile world in which no will or desire existed outside of the illicit affair' (154). Infantile or not, she was hell bent for destruction.

ON NARRATIVE PLAUSIBILITY

It is difficult to know what to make of all of this. Unlike Fraser, Roth was interested in letting 'the facts' of his life speak for themselves, his operative 'theory' remaining largely implicit. Here, however, we have an especially clear instance of someone who is offering an explicit theoretically-based account of why her life came to take the strange twists and turns it did. I do not question in this context the recourse to theory per se. Although it could certainly be the case, I suppose, that this concatenation of events simply 'happened', in more or less random fashion, there would seem to be enough here in the way of structure — as well as mystery — to suggest otherwise: a basically content woman falls into a grave depression, commences to write extensively about things even she can't quite make sense of, and eventually goes on to have an affair with an older man, who, as it turns out, happens to be the father of one of her old friends. And since she cannot comprehend this sequence of events through ordinary discourse (e.g. her husband was a loser who hardly made any money, so she decided she wanted to find someone who could give her a more comfortable style of life), her presumption is that another sort of account altogether is called for.

In some sense, of course, this strategy has been used throughout the entire book. That is, Fraser, having finally discovered the secret of her incestuous affair with her father (the details of which we will learn about shortly), has gone on to reconstruct what had heretofore been largely inexplicable – her fits and rages, her strange aversions, her awkward relationships, and so on – and has thus made rational the formerly irrational. What is it then that distinguishes the present account from the broader narrative strategy she has used throughout the rest of the work? The difference, essentially, is that the present account remains distant – as perhaps it must[2] – from Fraser's own subjective experience. Whereas with most of the previous experiences she has discussed the task was to explain why she experienced the strange emotions she did, the task now is to supply, via hypothesis, the emotions themselves. Since 'it wasn't so much passion that tempted me but compulsion that drove me' (154), Fraser notes, she is forced to speculate again about what *must* have been the case, psychodynamically, for her life to become so radically transformed, the result being an archeology of her secret passion.

Now the main reason why I remain somewhat uncomfortable with this account is not so much Fraser's recourse to this archeology itself. Judging from what she has had to say thus far, my own sense is that there is ample – if not definitive – reason for her to move in this direction: by all indications, something must indeed have been going on. Once again, of course, I realize that this is not *necessarily* so; and I also realize that by assuming it is, I commit myself still more strenuously to invoking that particular notion of the unconscious that many seem to want to do without, namely, a secretive dimension of psyche that may be seen – in retrospect – to have exercised a certain measure of 'force' in effecting the trajectory of a life. What I am uncomfortable with instead is the specific account Fraser has elected to offer, the reason simply being that I, as a reader, haven't really been told why it is more plausible than numerous others. Why should this other self want to 'reunite with daddy'? I am not making a plea for common sense here, I want to emphasize. For reasons adduced earlier, common sense may well be inappropriate. But how exactly has Fraser arrived at this specific form of *un*common sense?

Two further issues need to be articulated before we move on. The first has to do with the idea that even though narration frequently involves rewriting the past by conferring new meanings upon it, it is nonetheless important, conceptually at least, to differentiate between meanings that seem *justifiably* conferred and those that do not – and this despite the fact that there may be no *definitive* way of doing so. If, in rewriting my past, I simply *project* new meanings on to it or give it the status of a kind of teleological push toward the future, as if the trajectory of my life were foreseeable, as if it *had* to become transformed as it did, then I may well be guilty of putting meanings where they do not rightfully belong. We don't have to be ardent positivists to make this sort of claim either. As most of us know, it is easy enough to to do this sort of thing every now and then, and there is no reason why our pasts ought to be considered exempt.

In Fraser's case, it could be argued (which is not to say it should), for instance, that her admittedly curious affair with her friend's father had little to do with reuniting with her father, and that she was merely transferring some of the fruits of her subsequent discoveries on to anything and everything that led up to them. The problem here is simply that without having provided a comprehensive enough narrative context within which the hypothesized account is to be fitted, we cannot know what is being done. Lest this problem seem simpler than it is, it should be emphasized that interpretations of the sort with which we are presently concerned can never be decided by recourse to the 'facts' alone; there could never be some discrete bit of evidence adduced that could lead to our proclaiming that, yes, this is unquestionably how it must have been. Furthermore, and relatedly, in speaking about which meanings may or may not 'rightfully belong', as I put it above, by no means am I equating 'rightfully belong' with 'as it happened then' – as if the only way to determine justifiably conferred meanings are their degree of correspondence with the past (i.e. the past present) as lived. Rather, I am talking about what might simply be called the *narrative order* of experience, by which I mean the plausibility of the story being told as such.

This brings us to the second issue we need to discuss, namely, this notion of plausibility itself. What is it that we mean when we claim that a narrative ought to be plausible? For one, we mean that it ought to be coherent; it ought to be able to make sense of the available information. This does not mean that all narratives ought to be able to resolve all of the events and experiences of the past into an unambiguous, interconnected, seamless whole. Nor does it mean that things aren't occasionally quite senseless. All it means is that with some particular body of historical data at hand, the resultant narrative scheme ought to be able to encompass these data in a way that isn't fraught with obvious contradictions, stupidity, and so forth.

In addition to coherence, however, plausibility also entails the idea that the narrative being told is a particularly *fitting* one. But what does 'fitting' mean? Here again the answer is relatively straightforward: all things considered, the narrative ought to be able to make better sense than other possible narratives, whether actual or hypothetical. Ricoeur (1981) refers in this context to a 'logic of subjective probability'. The text, he writes, is a 'limited field of possible constructions', and as such, demands both the inclusion and exclusion of certain modes of making sense of it. By way of clarifying this point further, he notes that, 'To show that an interpretation is more probable in the light of what is known is something other than showing that a conclusion is true. In this sense, validation is not verification'; it is 'an argumentative discipline comparable to the juridical procedures of legal interpretation' (212). This perspective is acceptable, I think, save in one respect; and that is that the idea of 'subjective probability', as Ricoeur puts it, is not an especially easy idea to get hold of. I am not convinced there are many lawyers who would like it much either. It is either probable that such and such a crime happened this way or it is not; there is nothing subjective about it – unless we consider those pursuits for which 'verification' is impossible (which, of course, would include any and all disciplines that make use of interpretation) subjective.

My hunch here is that Ricoeur is facing a fundamental and enduring dilemma, for which he hasn't quite found an appropriate solution. On the one hand, being as sophisticatedly hermeneutically-minded as he is, he knows better than to want to get too objectivistic in his perspective. To the extent that one recognizes the primacy of interpretation when it comes to reading texts, one also recognizes the impossibility of arriving at a neutral discourse of 'verification' and 'truth'. At the same time, common sense (not to mention a good deal of time actually spent *reading* texts) suggests to Ricoeur that some interpretations are plainly more plausible – he, again, prefers the word 'probable' – than others. Given the overtly objectivistic overtones of the very idea of probability, however,[3] 'subjective' is an apparent qualifier. It seems as if he is saying, 'We're kind of talking about probability, but not really.' In any event, my own interpretations of Ricoeur aside (plausible though they may be), I would like to suggest in bringing this excursus to a close that not only is it problematic to speak about subjective probability, whatever it might be; it is problematic to speak in the present context about probability in any case. This is simply because the idea of probability, as it is ordinarily conceived, is inseparable from the idea – and indeed the ideal – of *predictability*; and there are many interpretations that deserve to be called plausible without having anything at all to do with predictability.

Does it really matter, though, whether we speak of plausibility, probability, predictability? The issue at hand is more important than it may appear. To refer to Hempel (1966), some of whose ideas were discussed briefly in the previous chapter, the operative claim behind his inclusion of inductive or probabilistic hypotheses under the aegis of the 'covering law' model of scientific explanation is essentially that much of the empirical world, being as complicated and multifaceted as it is, does not readily lend itself to the formulation of strict laws of the 'if–then' variety. This is particularly so, he notes, in the case of historical inquiry, where there are usually so many variables at work that it is patently impossible to establish the sort of lawful regularities that the natural sciences occasionally seem able to obtain. As a result, about the best we can hope for, he argues, is to be able to say 'if A, then probably B'. With regard to historical inquiry, therefore, any given interpretation must be demonstrably probable, which for him means it must follow from a given set of initial conditions. But isn't it the case that even the most unpredictable, improbable historical outcomes can often be explained, *plausibly*, after the fact?

Now in order to show why a particular interpretation is to be deemed plausible, it is not only necessary to point to its coherence; it is necessary in addition to show why, among equally coherent interpretations, one is to be preferred over another. Is it always possible to find *the* interpretation that is to be preferred over all others? Certainly not. As difficult as it may be for us to accept, it is often the case that several interpretations appear not only equally coherent, but equally plausible. Is there a way out of such an impasse? The answer is plainly 'No', and I'm afraid we will just have to live with this.

One final problem, also reminiscent of some of those addressed in the previous chapter, remains to be addressed. As important as it is, as a general rule, for an interpretation to be plausible in the sense of being 'fitting', 'appropriate', 'sensible', and so on, it is no less important that we, as readers, have an expansive enough idea of what constitutes plausibility as to be willing to stretch our minds beyond the reach of the obvious. Stated another way, we must be receptive and respectful enough of the texts we encounter to remain open to the possibility of entirely new forms of interpretation: if the old plots don't do, then it might be time to explore something different. Even this something different, of course, will remain within the scope of our own idioms and habits of thought; a wholesale escape is out of the question. But stretching the boundaries of what is to be considered plausible is not. Do not confuse plausibility, then, with the superficial or the obvious, for it may be anything but that. Fraser was to learn this little rule of thumb firsthand. Let us continue and see how.

RECONSTRUCTION, RESTORATION, AND THE DIALECTIC OF DEVELOPMENT

It was on the last leg of Fraser's book promotion tour that she encountered her future partner, who owned the television station where the interview was held, along with an old friend from high school, who would conduct it. Apparently playing the journalistic provocateur, he discussed his puzzlement over certain scenarios related in the book, mainly those that concerned sexual assault. Although she had attempted to tell a story about an innocent child who became a victim, he saw things quite differently, or at least claimed to, perhaps for the sake of carrying out a spicy interview. 'For such a sexual assault to take place', he said, 'we must look to the conduct of the child . . . Some little girls can be seductive at an early age.' He went on to say, 'I think your book is typical of the kind of hysterical imaginings we're seeing too much of these days. According to you feminists, we men are always the enemy.' Not surprisingly, part of Fraser was angry and wanted to protest against this vicious nonsense. But another part of her, which she identifies as her other self resurfacing again, was too hysterical to move. 'I pace the lobby, struggling against tears, startled both at the depth of my fury and of my vulnerability' (158).

Then up walked a gray-haired man, her good friend Lulu's father, who had a slight limp, not unlike her own father had. He told her what a fine job she had done in the interview and how surprised he was that the interviewer, who was usually rather unctuous, had been so cruel. 'These reassurances, so unexpected, so wholehearted and from such an impeccable source, spawn my instantaneous and overwhelming gratitude' (159). He was handsome too. He had a big white Cadillac convertible. He was one of her biggest fans. Her other self 'telephones' from her 'underground prison', jolting her awake: '*I'm coming up*', she said. I could go on, but you get the idea. The rest can be guessed.

For all of its good times, the affair proved to be extremely painful for Fraser. 'Nothing matters to me any more but seeing Paul, touching Paul, being touched by Paul.' What's more, Fraser adds, 'I am so consumed by venomous jealousy of his wife and of his family, of his sailboat and his motor launch, of his television stations, of everything that keeps him from me, of everything that he enjoys without me. It's a feeling so murderous and so bottomless and so pointless and so disgusting that all I can do is despise myself more' (179–80). She would wait for the phone to ring like a crazed schoolgirl, so obsessively eager she was to plan the next rendezvous. Finally, her husband, having remained quiet for some time about the obvious dissolution of their once strong marriage, reached the breaking point. Should he leave? Her answer was a swift 'Yes'. It was only then that she realized just how bad things had gotten; she was 'a rocket set in a trajectory' (184), and there was no prospect of turning back. The only saving grace at this time, Fraser writes, was 'knowing that whatever lies ahead is better than the festering untruths, the screaming hurts, the split inside me' (185).

In her own estimation, therefore, this affair was clearly a necessary moment in the dialectical movement of her own psychological resurrection. Even then, it seemed, there was beginning to appear a strange logic – a 'trajectory' – to everything that was happening, as if these ever more sordid events had acquired a life and momentum of their own. Referring back to the developmental scheme outlined in the very first chapter of this book, there had arisen the moment of recognition: something here was radically wrong. The next moment, which we referred to as distanciation, and which involves a kind of divestment of oneself from present modes of experience so as to pave the way for newer ones, would soon follow. While Daniel seemed to assume, in fact, that the situation was temporary and that he would be reunited with his estranged wife soon enough, Fraser could tell right then and there that this was more of a watershed than he would ever know. 'One moment', she writes, their marriage was 'the centerpiece for which the rest of our lives existed. The next it was not. Someone – myself? – had turned out the lights' (186). In some sense, then, the process of distanciation had already begun. Although she was as yet unable to see where exactly the aforementioned trajectory would lead, she knew that what presently existed, whatever its worth, would have to be left behind for her to get there. Daniel had virtually saved her life, she admitted, by giving her 'unconditional love, the way a good parent does'. For this she would be eternally grateful. But now, she had said to her sister, trying to explain what had happened, 'I sense that I have to leave the nest and get on with my journey' (187).

Things changed. Fraser's new apartment was more 'authentic' in her eyes than the old one, as was her secondhand furniture. Whereas she used to like her environment 'lean and sleek', in the manner of the modern urban couple, she suddenly found herself putting ruffles on things, and frills. She ate and slept when she wanted. And she cried whenever the desire arose, which was often. But why did she leave him? Her affair was actually on the back burner by this time, so that really wasn't it. 'It makes no sense', she had said to herself; she was simply 'compelled'. In due time, though, she would have to learn. That is, she would have to follow through on her path of development toward what was earlier identified as the third moment of development, namely, articulation. 'The stage has been cleared', Fraser writes, 'but for what?' (189). How would she find out? Certainly not through her writing; that was every bit as blocked as her own self-understanding. Perhaps she would die instead. After attending a Halloween party, dressed as a cat no less (recall the earlier threats against Smoky), in which Paul (from the back burner) had finally made it clear that his wife still came first, this seemed like an especially sound option. The fact that she had punched him in the chest at the party, her hand bloodied from her broken champagne glass, didn't help much either. He too would be out of the picture, for good. But when push came to shove, death didn't seem quite right. There was still too much unfinished business to take care of.

It wasn't long after that Fraser would receive a call from her mother, asking her to please come home; her father, who had been in the hospital ailing for some time, was on the brink of death. As it turned out, she wouldn't make it home in time. When she finally did make it home, something curious had happened: for the first time in many, many years, she was able to cross the threshold into the house without immediately becoming consumed by fear and dread. 'My father's house', all of a sudden, 'is just a house' (204). But there was something downright 'uncanny' about it too, made more so when she looked through a cardboard box filled with pictures of herself, which her father had kept under his bed.

'When my father died, he came alive for me. A door had opened, like a hole cut in air. It yawned before me, offering release – from what to where?' Fraser's other self would finally 'have to give up her secrets'. As for herself, 'How would I feel to discover that the prize, after four decades of tracing clues and solving riddles, was knowledge that my father had sexually abused me? Could I reconcile myself without bitterness to the amount of my life's energy that had gone into the cover-up of a crime?' (211). It would be some ten years before the secret would be revealed.

In the interim, there would be lots of writing, still filled with sexual violence, and still substandard. She was learning things about herself, to be sure, but there remained something missing: 'like the thirsty Tantalus floating in water he couldn't drink, I was compelled by an inner vision I couldn't see'. She began to experiment with a variety of psychologies as well, ranging from psychoanalysis all the way to bioenergetics. These in turn led to questions that would have to be answered: 'Why had I been such an angry child? Why did I hate my father? What was the source of the icy terror I now sensed under that anger and hatred?' (211). She didn't know it then, but this moment of articulation, of her different passions and fears, would soon yield up memories, lots of them, bubbling to the surface of her existence like molten lava out of the secret strata of her unconscious. Owing especially to a prolonged hospital stay, in which, through the haze of operations and painkillers, she was to dream and hallucinate ceaselessly, as if she had been plunged into the land of unreality itself, she began to suspect that she had forgotten a whole lot about her earliest years. 'I also suspected', Fraser writes, 'something terribly wrong might have taken place, but I couldn't leap from suspicion to accusation, even in my own mind. I was never going to believe anything I dreamed to have literal truth, no matter how persuasive' (216). But she was unquestionably on to something.

Whether knowingly or not, Fraser's reflections at this point are very much reminiscent of certain of Freud's seminal ideas: 'The memories of my other self', she admits, 'are difficult to recapture because they are so fragmentary . . . For more than forty years the memories of my other self lay deeply buried in jagged pieces inside me – smashed hieroglyphic tablets from another time and another place.' There was, in addition, the dig itself: 'When I finally began excavation, I brought these pieces to the surface in random order, to be fitted into patterns and dated.' A narrative, quite unlike that which had been written previously, was beginning to take shape. But it wasn't until that 'blaze of discovery' – a discrete moment during what Fraser had thought was just another day – that those smashed tablets of the past resolved themselves, with her assistance of course, into an integrated, whole pattern.

The revelation began with a bit of gossip. There was an old friend, Fraser learned – who happened to be the same fellow who had interviewed her years ago – who had apparently tried to molest a little girl. His earlier statement to the effect that little girls can sometimes be too seductive for their own good was thus cast into a new light: 'Feeling a snub-nosed bullet explode in my chest, I pick up a dinner knife with my left hand and stab the table. "I want to kill that bastard!" ' (219). It was only a few minutes later that she herself, who, to the alarm of her friends, had begun to look rather sick, suddenly proclaimed, 'I think my father raped me.' After insisting upon walking home alone, 'in a state of heightened consciousness', she lay on her bed, as spasms – reminiscent of a child being raped – passed through her involuntarily: 'I recapture that moment precisely when my helplessness is so bottomless that anything is preferable.' It was nothing short of 'time travel', as Fraser describes it. By this time, 'I think' had turned into 'I *know*'. Her brain was suddenly 'alive with new memories, with shocking insights. In seconds, my history as I have known it undergoes a drastic shift' (220–1).

The task now was to appropriate this knowledge into her self, to integrate it in such a way that she could get on with her life. There still remained two selves after her discovery, Fraser explained: 'my adult self and my child self, whom I name the Child Who Knows. Though my restored memories come wrapped in terror', she continues, 'it is a child's terror I realize I must feel in order to expel. Thus, the adult me comforts the child, holds her hand, pities her suffering, forgives her for her complicity, assuages her guilt. She has carried the burden until I was prepared to remember our joint history without bitterness.' In any event, 'The mysteries of a lifetime, shadowy deeds dimly suspected, have been clarified' (223), and she could therefore feel, after all these years, 'that the past has been placed in decent perspective and that it's time to get on with the present' (224). Reminiscent of Freud once again, Fraser, freed from the tyranny of repetition by making the unconscious conscious, can finally exist *now*. The past had become past.

There was still one thing that had to be done, however, for her fully to move on: she had to speak to her mother. She had ignored this impulse for as long as possible; 'logic and humanity demanded it' (231). But she couldn't help herself. This was another piece of unfinished business, and with her mother now getting on in years, it would be imperative that the topic be broached. There might have been some hostility involved in this gesture as well, of course; after all, whether wittingly or not, her mother was the one who had let this crime continue. Why hadn't she protected her? The walls of the house were thin. 'How could you not know?' (231). Had she resented the attention that her husband lavished upon this little girl, and in her own lonely resentment decided to keep mum? 'It was safer to be a bad child with a perfect mother whom I failed to please, than to be a frightened child with a flawed mother who failed to protect me. And yet', Fraser writes, 'now that I have rescinded the legend of your saintliness, you too are released to become more human, to be worthy of understanding and love' (232).

There was so much that her mother had obviously refused to see; even when life was at its very worst, she had been obstinately cheerful, her primary goal being to keep up appearances in the eyes of friends and neighbors. Her father had hanged himself, two sisters had died young, and her husband was an angry and frustrated man; and she simply looked the other way through it all. But was she really at fault? 'So it comes to this: can I blame you for choosing selective sight, the same method of survival that I, your daughter would choose?' (233). 'Who knows?', Fraser had mused. Perhaps her mother also had an inner voice, a shadow-self, that yearned to be free from the burden of the past, to 'scream for release' and redemption. Perhaps by confronting her, therefore, she would be performing a service; she would be the midwife of her mother's own catharsis. Again, though, and somewhat less charitably, perhaps it was time for Fraser herself to do some punishing. Despite her insistence that the discoveries she had made had left her less angry than might have been expected, it could very well be that, for all she had finally brought into consciousness, the transformation was not quite as complete as she might have thought.

An interesting and important question nonetheless arises in this context. Why should remembering have a 'curative' effect? More specifically, why should rewriting the self, particularly along the lines Fraser has done it, be of any psychological value at all? Freud certainly gives us a partial answer to these questions by speaking about the 'economics' of psychic processes: to the extent that 'dammed up' psychic energy, which is thought to somehow be 'stored' in one's buried memories, is 'released' and is thus free to 'circulate' through quarters it had never been before, a new dimension of well-being may ensue; it is almost as if one is unclogging one's psychic arteries. But it would be unfair to claim that this redistribution of psychic energy was all that was going on for Freud. How else might we understand this phenomenon? Why is it that the two most fundamental aims of psychoanalysis – to remove symptoms and restore memory – are 'coincident'? 'When one is reached', Freud (1901–5a) writes, 'so is the other; and the same path leads to them both' (18). Why?

Perhaps our questions have not been formulated correctly. According to Freud, remembering is not the *cause* of cure; it is correlative with it. This is why remembering, if it happens prematurely during the course of analysis, may either result in nothing, therapeutically speaking, or be injurious. If one is not *ready* to remember – consider, for instance, what might have happened if Fraser had suddenly decided to go to a hypnotherapist when she was an adolescent – then psychic healing will probably not be forthcoming. There still remains a problem, however. Even if one is indeed ready to remember, as Fraser apparently was, it is surely not necessarily the case that the results will be immediately salutary. Freud knew this as well: one could just as easily be thrown for a serious psychic loop upon dredging up an ugly incident from the past as feel liberated or redeemed. Remembering per se, therefore, doesn't quite get us to the core of the issue.

What we can say, I will suggest, is this: only when memories are *appropriated* into the fabric of the self – which is to say, only when one commences to rewrite the self by incorporating one's memories within the context of a plausible narrative order – can they be coincident with a measure of psychic healing. Let us at least assume that this is so. The question with which we began nevertheless remains: Why? Why should life historical narration as we are considering it here be of psychological value? The answer is that implicit in the very idea of rewriting the self – and in the correlative idea of *development* as well – is the notion that one has progressed from what can now be seen as a less desirable mode of knowing and being to a more desirable mode; one has come to understand one's self and one's world in a way that is arguably or demonstrably preferable to what had existed earlier (see again Freeman and Robinson 1990).

'Now I understand', Fraser might finally have said. 'Now the mysteries of my life, which had existed through the years like a dead weight, are in the midst of being resolved.' By no means am I suggesting that rewriting the self always entails the resolution of these kinds of mysteries; as noted at the beginning of this chapter, in conjunction with our discussion of Kermode, the excavation of secrets, à la Fraser, may not be the most appropriate model for trying to comprehend most of our lives. The idea that rewriting the self may be of psychological value nonetheless stands. For whether the interpretive process involved in rewriting is one of *demystification*, in the sense of coming to see that which has been hidden, or *explication*, in the broader sense of developing a better understanding of a particular domain of experience, the dialectical movement through which it occurs is at one and the same time an exposure of the inadequacy of what was and a revelation of the greater adequacy of what is, now.

Fortunately for Fraser, her mother believed her when she learned what had happened. She herself had often found her husband a strange and difficult man, she admitted, and had been tempted to leave him many times. Judging by her response, it was almost as if this secret, as awful as it was, was in keeping with his character. At the same time, however, he would often go and do nice things as well, which is why she never did take the initiative to leave. If he was alive, she said, it would be difficult to forgive him. Now, however, with him dead and gone, there was little point in basking in bitterness and pain.

Fraser seemed to feel the same in the end. She knew that he had probably suffered a great deal anyway. 'I suspect', she writes, 'he paid as dearly as I for the amnesia that was once his salvation. As in the child's game of statues, we remained frozen at our darkest hour, with no possibility of forgiveness or compassion or redemption while he lived. I know that now' (240). What she also knew was that her father was not a monster. He was just another pitiful and tragic human being, shortchanged in his own way by the life he had come to live. He had often been tender to her when she was a child and had made her feel special, and even though this tenderness had become perverted as time wore on, it had conferred upon at least a part of her the conviction that she was worthy of love. There could be some rationalization at work here, I would venture; Fraser's father may well have acted more out of rage and violence than she may have wanted to believe. But ultimately, she suggests, he was not different from the rest of us: 'All of us are born into the second act of a tragedy-in-progress, then spend the rest of our lives trying to figure out what went wrong in the first act' (241).

Rationalization or not, Fraser's own way of processing and emplotting what had happened involves recognizing the foibles and weaknesses of human beings, of which her father was one. Even if he was less tender than she wanted to believe, then, he would have been no less tragic a character in her eyes and no less human. As much as we might loathe the sight of hardened criminals, she might have said, there may still be something to be said for regarding them with a modicum of charity.

To foreshadow an issue we will explore in greater detail in the chapter to follow, notice here how one's moral and, in some cases perhaps, religious commitments enter into both rewriting the self and, by extension, the process of development. The narrative Fraser elects to tell, of one human being affected by another, both of whom are engaged in the timelessly tragic pursuit of living their lives as best they can, is a function of the very beliefs she holds about what human beings ultimately are. Someone else, having undergone similar events, might have told a quite different story: of a man, for instance, who was the very incarnation of evil, and who, having ruined at least one person's life for good, could never be forgiven; he would be the albatross who remained around her neck until the end of time. The very way one understands the past, therefore, is the product of a narrative choice which, in turn, may issue from the most fundamental beliefs, values, and ideals one holds. As an aside, and as has we have already discussed in conjunction with Hayden White's (1973, 1978) work, it does not necessarily follow that one can understand and emplot the past *any* way; narrative choices are inevitably circumscribed by language, by the facts, as they are believed to have existed, by the availability of culturally-sanctioned storylines, and so on. But this moral dimension of both historical understanding and historical narration is nonetheless important to acknowledge, if only as a reminder of the fact that the histories we tell are inextricably intertwined with both our own understanding and our own narrative choices.

A similar thing may be said about the process of development. Although it might be argued that understanding, as we have been considering it, is itself developmental in some sense, in that it involves the expansion of one's grasp of a particular domain of experience, the process of development is often assumed to entail some sort of praxis as well, some sort of attempt to incorporate or appropriate this understanding into the fabric of the self. In Fraser's case, then, once she acquired the understanding that had been denied her so long, it was imperative that she *do* something with it, that she integrate it into a vision of life that she deemed to be morally viable and sound. Hence her decision to effect a kind of rapprochement with her father, to recognize, even despite the horror of his actions, his profound humanness, and to see herself and her family more generally as tragic players on the stage of life.

For another person, again, the telos at hand might have been quite different. To the extent that his or her moral code was other than Fraser's, it might have meant that some form or other of retribution was the appropriate end: there would be no room for rapprochement in responding to deeds as dastardly as these had been. And although we ourselves may find this hypothetical response to be less than adequate, given our own possible moral convictions concerning the value of retribution, it may still deserve to be subsumed under the rubric of development.[4] Charity, for some, may be decidedly inappropriate in this context; it would serve to exonerate not only the perpetrator in question but all of those others who have elected to victimize innocent people on account of their own perversity or hate. Human beings are ultimately free, it might be argued here; they have the capacity to transcend their own pathetic problems by simply refusing to indulge themselves in patently immoral acts. There would thus be little reason, from this perspective, to say that this man was but another tragic player. He was a criminal, plain and simple, and in the interest of being responsible both to oneself and to other potential victims, the only appropriate decision would be to wage war. Notice that this sort of decision, however much it may conflict with some of our convictions about how best to understand and work through a crisis of the kind that Fraser faced, is no less principled than her own; it involves mindful rather than mindless retribution and, as such, may be considered part of a developmental project.

The point of this brief discussion, in any case, is to highlight the moral dimension of the processes we are considering. For all that we might wish to speak about the objectivity of historical facts, the possibility of learning something akin to the truth about one's past, there is, in the end, no way wholly to cordon off the rewriting of the self, along with the process of development, from the moral visions with which we operate. Indeed, might we not say, further, that we will emplot the past in common ways precisely to the extent that we share a moral vision concerning its meaning and significance?

Whether we choose to applaud Fraser for her charity or condemn her for failing to fight back against that brand of male oppression that all too often culminates in violence of the kind she suffered, there is no way to make this choice on the basis of the events alone. Would knowing her father's intentions help settle the matter? Would knowing that he was a despicable misogynist, who perpetrated acts of violence whenever he could, help to objectify things a bit more? In some ways, yes: the more despicable he was, the less willing we might be to forgive him by considering the sorry hand he had been dealt; the sheer heinousness of his acts would outstrip any possibility of charity, just as it did for many in the case of Hitler. In other ways, however, no: in the eyes of some people, even the most despicable character may deserve to be seen as a child of God, who, in some other time or place, might have been able to do some good in the world. Knowing his intentions, therefore, would not settle definitively questions pertaining to the *meaning* of his actions. Wasn't Hitler himself, some might ask, another human being, who, like Fraser's father, had been corrupted by the myriad of forces that had shaped his sorry life?

I do not mean to suggest that intentions are wholly irrelevant; they can obviously be of use in helping the process of interpretation along. We must not, however, conflate them with the issue of meaning by positing a strict identity between the two. The same holds true, of course, for Fraser's text as well as any other text we might read: even if we found ourselves in the position of knowing comprehensively the intentions of their authors, the meaning of these texts would remain open. 'Though I don't understand him', Fraser admits, 'I can pity him and forgive him'. She can also love him, she insists, and live with that love rather than hate, which would only serve unnecessarily to darken her future. Loving him isn't merely a functional decision, however. 'I love my daddy, I know that now' (241). Does she? Could she? Aren't there other possible meanings to be derived than the ones Fraser herself has supplied?

Looking back on her life from one vantage point, 'I see nothing but devastation. A blasted childhood, an even worse adolescence, betrayal, divorce, craziness, professional stalemate, financial uncertainty and always, always a secret eating like dry rot at my psyche. That is the dark side, the story I have told in this book. Yet, like the moon, my life has another side, one with some luminosity' (251). There are many stories one can tell. One thing is certain, though: 'My life', Fraser writes, 'was structured on the uncovering of a mystery. As a child, I survived by forgetting. Later, the amnesia became a problem as large as the one it was meant to conceal. However, I did not remember my past until the homemade bomb was defused, until the evil was contained, until I was stable enough and happy enough that sorrow or anger or regret or pain was overwhelmed by joy at my release' (252). Just so; the ground must be well-paved for secrets like these to have their say.

In line with Fraser's stance concerning her father, 'Mine', she writes, 'turns out to be a story without villains'. Note the moral convictions fueling this story: 'Children who were in some way abused, abuse others; victims become villains. Thus, not to forgive only perpetuates the crime, creates more victims.' This is not to say that no crime was committed or that what happened is acceptable. 'That some people do survive, that emotional health often requires the abused to forgive the abuser does not make the crime more acceptable' (252). She had heard a story recently of a 9-month old girl who had been raped, by her mother's alcoholic live-in boyfriend. Given the situation into which the baby was born, there would be little prospect of recovery, little prospect of her someday telling a story with something like a happy ending. Fraser's 'is a middle-class story with built-in loopholes and rescue stations and options and timelocks and safeguards' (253). All this needs to be taken into account in the telling, and the reading.

'In retrospect', Fraser concludes, 'I feel about my life the way some people feel about war'. If you survive, then it becomes a good one. 'Always', she can now see, 'I was traveling from darkness into the light. In such journeys, time is our ally, not our enemy. We can grow wise', she insists. 'As the arteries harden, our spirits can lighten. As the legs fail, the soul can take wing. Things do add up. Life does have a shape and maybe even a purpose. Or so it seems to me' (253). There is a lot here in these few simple words – more indeed than Fraser may have intended.

The first point we already know about; it is about endings and beginnings, and their reciprocal determination. Since she has survived, the past *seems* to have been good and worthwhile as she looks backward. In reality, though, she also implies, it *was* good; it *had* to have been good, precisely in virtue of its having culminated in the outcome it has.

The second point, very much related to the first, is a bit more complicated. She moved from darkness to light. But what does this mean? Is it a statement about retrospection or about the forward pulse of coming to consciousness, about the upward drive of the desire to know and to be whole? It is, I would suggest, about both of these. While on the one hand it is exactly her having seen the light, as it were, that allows her to see the movement toward it, her very text itself serves as testimony to the notion that mysteries of the sort through which she lived sometimes place a serious demand on the self; the irrationality and opacity of life's meaning cannot easily be endured. So it is that interpretation, which may itself be seen as a movement of revelation, from dark to light, is incited.

The third point, though simpler in some ways than the first two, is no less important. It is that the process of development knows no age. This idea runs contrary, not so much to popular belief, but to much of developmental psychological 'wisdom', which often posits a kind of ceiling to the process, some stage beyond which, structurally speaking, there *is* no development.[5] Even Piaget, arch-structuralist though he was, surely knew that people could become cleverer and wiser as they passed through adulthood. In so far as there were no discernible, normatively-based structural revolutions taking place, however, the idea of calling these things development seemed inappropriate. But as Fraser's story suggests, it may be that those of us who are involved in taking up developmental issues need to become more alert to the possibility of detecting development — broadly conceived — where we assumed there was none. It is true; we would be hard-pressed to call the changes Fraser has undergone 'development' if the standard is that sort of structural revolution that is thought to occur between, say, the sensorimotor stage and the preoperational stage. But why should this standard be employed? In fact, why should *any* standard of this sort be employed? Perhaps we need to move beyond these normatively-based models, so that we can better see what there is to see.

As concerns the fourth point, which has to do with Fraser's conviction that 'things do add up', this is surely the most complicated issue of all. On one level, this may be seen as an epistemological issue. If life does indeed have a 'shape', as she puts it, where does this shape come from? Is it immanent in the events themselves? In the mind of the historian–author? In the mind of the reader? In language? I raise these questions here mainly to reacquaint you with some of the issues we have already considered in previous chapters. Let us now turn to another level of inquiry. In addition to Fraser raising an important epistemological issue, she has also raised a profound and enduring *theological* issue: Is life meaningful? Is there a purpose to it? If so, is this purpose conferred upon it by God? Does it emerge, as a matter of course, in the dialectic of development? If not, is it utter delusion to suppose that there is such a purpose? I will not be so audacious as to try to answer these questions. They would only be my answers, not yours. Do realize, however, that in taking up comprehensively the idea of rewriting the self, we are inevitably brought to raise questions pertaining not only to the domain of the moral but of the divine.

PRIMAL SCENES

We have spoken repeatedly about Fraser's process of understanding. Upon discovering this secret that she had harbored for some forty years, the scales fell from her eyes, her entire life assuming a measure of continuity and coherence that had never existed before. This new understanding, therefore, is deemed to be vastly superior to her previous understandings by virtue of its transparency alone; where before there was darkness, now there is light. Now I don't happen to think this is so, but what if there never *was* an incestuous relationship with her father? What if that bit of 'information', however functional it might be in supplying what would appear to be the missing piece of her life's puzzle, is simply untrue, deriving from a faulty hypothesis? More to the point still, does it matter, psychologically, whether events of this sort did or did not happen?

Freud faced this problem in an especially acute manner in his discussion of the Wolf-Man (1918).[6] A brief review of the Wolf-Man case is therefore in order; it will help us to see what some of our interpretive options are. Judging by his analysis, the first years of the Wolf-Man's life seemed to be unexceptional. His mother and father had both been ill throughout much of his childhood, leaving him to the care of nurses and the like, but by all indications he had been 'a very good-natured, tractable, and even quiet child' (14). Suddenly, however, things changed. 'He had become discontented, irritable and violent, took offence on every possible occasion, and then flew into a rage and screamed like a savage' (15). As with Fraser, there was good reason to believe that something, something very powerful, had happened.

Perhaps this discontentment was the effect of the new governess who had been hired, a woman who was judged to be 'eccentric and quarrelsome'. This, at least, was his mother's reasoning. His grandmother, on the other hand, felt that the cause of the Wolf-Man's problems lay in the dissension that had existed between the governess and the nurse. The problem, however, was that when the governess was sent away, apparent culprit that she was, everthing remained the same.

We also learn about an intense fear the Wolf-Man had come to have, upon which his older sister had capitalized. It seems there was a picture book, in which a wolf, standing upright, had a prominent role, the result being that 'whenever he caught sight of this picture he began to scream like a lunatic that he was afraid of the wolf coming and eating him up' (16). Other animals – butterflies, beetles, caterpillars, and horses, among them – became frightful as well. Curiously enough, though, he would often torment these very same animals, complementing his intense fear with violence.

Then there were his elaborate sleep rituals, where he would pray fervently, make an 'endless series' of signs of the cross, and kiss all of the holy pictures that hung about the house. He had apparently become a very pious little boy. There were also some curious accompaniments to this piety, however, including 'blasphemous thoughts which used to come into his head like an inspiration from the devil' (16–17).

'What', then, Freud asks, 'was the origin of the sudden change in the boy's character? What was the significance of his phobia and his perversities? How did he arrive at his obsessive piety? And how are all of these phenomena interrelated?' (17). The analysis begins like a detective story: 'It is easy to understand', Freud writes, 'that the first suspicion fell upon the English governess, for the change in the boy made its appearance while she was there.' In point of fact, she had apparently done her share to make things difficult for him. As such, Freud early on offered an interpretive construction to the effect that perhaps she had threatened him at some point. An interesting aside follows. Lest his readers be concerned with this technique, he notes: 'There is no danger at all in communicating constructions of this kind to the person under analysis', for 'they never do any damage to the analysis if they are mistaken' (19). As against those who claim that analysts simply supply functional explanations, which, whatever their truth value, may be appropriated by the analysand, Freud claims that false explanations do not customarily work therapeutically; they fail to yield further serviceable material. What this means, therefore – and this is precisely how he answers the familiar complaint that he is merely providing people with new and better fictions to live by – is that only the truth will succeed in setting them free. More on this is to come.

In any case, not much followed from Freud's initial attempts at interpretation; the scenario was too easy, too pat. Yet it wasn't too long into the analysis that an extremely important piece of information emerged. The Wolf-Man's sister had seduced him, and in the process had relegated him to a position of psychological passivity which, it appeared, had become transformed into aggression and rage; he had needed somehow to show, to himself and to others, that he was a little man, fierce and dominating – even if the objects of his ferocity had to be butterflies and beetles. You do what you can.

There were further difficulties, however. One of them was that although he had had his little appetite whetted to some extent by this naughty event, he didn't find his sister terribly appealing; he was all dressed up, so to speak, with no place to go. So he wound up pursuing others who were more desirable, including his beloved nurse, who immediately rebuffed his advances, and, later on, his father. Now the problem here, yet again, was that in order to love his father, so big and strong, he would again have to be relegated to a condition of passivity. This, in turn, Freud ventures, fueled his aggressiveness still further: 'By bringing his naughtiness forward', it would appear, 'he was trying to force beatings and punishments out of his father' (28), thus gaining a measure of satisfaction in lieu of what it was he really wanted. He also satisfied his burgeoning sense of guilt in the process, for it had become painfully clear that he had begun to enter some rather dangerous territory.

Sometime before his fourth birthday, there was yet another abrupt change in the boy's behavior, his rage suddenly being replaced by profound anxiety. The inciting event, it was learned, was a dream, a terribly frightening dream, with six or seven white wolves sitting on a big walnut tree, gazing silently. This was clearly a 'founding' event, Freud believed, and both he and the Wolf-Man became convinced that 'the causes of his infantile neurosis lay concealed behind it'. They thus spent several years, off and on, trying to unpack its meaning. There were two features that stood out above the rest: 'first, the perfect stillness and immobility of the wolves, and secondly, the strained attention with which they all looked at him' (33). There was also a 'lasting sense of reality', the Wolf-Man felt, which struck him as being significant in some way.

The following fragments emerged in the course of analysis: '*A real occurrence – dating from a very early period – looking – immobility – sexual problems – castration – his father – something terrible*' (italics in original, 34). Who or what did these wolves represent? Who, really, was doing the looking? Could it be that the stillness and immobility was a kind of cover for violent motion? You may not believe it, Freud warns us, but 'what sprang into activity that night out of the chaos of the dreamer's unconscious memory-traces was the picture of copulation between his parents, copulation in circumstances which were not entirely unusual and were especially favorable for observation' (36). There proved to be a good amount of evidence in support of this interpretation. The content of the scene surely wasn't out of the question; his parents had probably been a bit careless during a late afternoon romp. What made this interpretation a bit more questionable, though, was that all this was thought to have taken place very early in the Wolf-Man's childhood, at approximately the age of one and a half. Nevertheless, Freud asks us to join him for now 'in adopting a *provisional* belief in the reality of the scene' (39).[7]

Freud's comments in a footnote may be instructive here. 'We must not forget the actual situation which lies behind the abbreviated description given in the text: the patient under analysis, at an age of over twenty-five years, was putting impressions and impulses of his fourth year into words which he would never have found at the time.' Fraser, of course, has done something like this as well. 'If we fail to notice this', Freud continues, 'it may easily seem comic and incredible that a child of four should be capable of such technical judgments and learned notions' (45).

Now it could very well be, Freud admits – and Fraser was well aware of this problem too – that scenes of the sort we are considering 'are not reproductions of real occurrences, to which it is possible to ascribe an influence over the course of the patient's later life and over the formation of his symptoms', but are instead 'products of the imagination, which find their instigation in mature life, which are intended to serve as some kind of symbolic representation of real wishes and interests, and which owe their origin to a regressive tendency, to a turning-away from the tasks of the present'. If this is so, it would of course be possible 'to spare ourselves the necessity of attributing such a surprising amount to the mental life and intellectual capacity of children of the tenderest age'. What does Freud think about this? The first thing he says is that even if it were true, 'the carrying out of analysis would not in the first instance be altered in any respect' (49).

Is he saying what he seems to be saying? Perhaps he is: if what we are observing are not realities, but products of the imagination, all that can be done is 'to follow upon their tracks and bring these unconscious productions into consciousness; for, leaving on one side their lack of value from the point of view of reality, they are of the utmost value from our point of view, since they are for the moment the bearers and possessors of the interest which we want to set free so as to be able to direct it on to the tasks of the present.' In short, 'The analysis would have to run precisely the same course as one which had a *naif* faith in the truth of the phantasies' (50).

What we have here, suggests Peter Brooks (1985), is 'one of the most daring moments of Freud's thought, and one of his most heroic gestures as a writer' (277). He could have simply let the issue rest and claim that reality had been uncovered; this is more than likely what he believed anyway. Instead, though, he was bold enough not only to question his own account of this particular case but the issue of origins more generally: whether reality or fiction lay at the beginning of these narratives may not matter as much as we might suppose. But let us be clear about what he is and is not saying. He is *not* claiming that it makes no difference at all whether the scene was real or imagined, for it does – but only 'at the end of analysis, after the phantasies had been laid bare'. After this time, he continues, 'it would be possible to begin a second portion of the treatment, which would be concerned with the patient's real life' (50).

Freud does go on to admit that there is good reason to assume that these sorts of scenes are indeed frequently imaginary, including the fact that rather than emerging as recollections, they have to be constructed, hypothesized. (This is what happened in Fraser's case: she *thought*, she had said initially, that she had been raped.) But this in itself, Freud argues, does not mean that these scenes are necessarily imaginary, only that they can be. There is also the recurrent problem of 'suggestion'. Perhaps the analyst – or, in Fraser's case, her own observing 'I', which had assumed a kind of analytic role – simply supplies an event, either real or fictional, to believe in, an event that will be functional enough, in its missing-piece-of-the-puzzle role, to bring the desired measure of fit. How does he respond to this criticism? There is little for Freud to say in this context except that those who have experienced analysis tend to know better.

In the Wolf-Man's case the problem remains a thorny one, for he never did remember the scene that had been hypothesized to exist; it was thus incorporated into the narrative of his life in 'as if' fashion. In Fraser's case, however, her initial conjectures did indeed yield further serviceable material, in the form of recollections. By her own account, therefore (and she claims to have corroborative evidence as well), there was no doubting the reality of those earlier scenes. The skeptic, of course, may not be any more comfortable with the emergence of these (alleged) memories, for these too might be fantasies. Corroborative evidence aside, would it or would it not matter psychologically if this were so? My own inclination is to say that, practically speaking, it may *not* matter. In other words, it could be that fitting fictions serve just as well as realities in making sense of one's past. If, however, we are to place any credence in Freud, particularly as concerns the idea of the unconscious, there is surely good reason to suppose that it *may* matter. For in the end, he would no doubt argue, fitting fictions would be unlikely to have the same practical effects on the economy of the psyche as reality; there would still remain material in need of being worked through; there would still remain conflicts, perhaps self-generated rather than other-generated, that would strive to break through into consciousness. Along these lines, then, if indeed Fraser's father was innocent, the very praxis of her interpretations *might* reveal the error and the duplicity of her ways. At this point, of course, she would have to return to self-analysis and try to determine what it was that had led her to foist blame upon an innocent man.

Whether or not we have suffered the sort of discrete traumas that both the Wolf-Man and Sylvia Fraser are thought to have suffered, there somehow exists a call for many of us to consider what Lukacher (1986), borrowing from Freud, has referred to as the 'primal scenes' of our own formation of self. For the most part, we cannot say how we have originated; our past is indeed enshrouded in an inexorable secrecy and obscurity, such that try as we might to discover that which might succeed in making sense of it all, we are left with the interminability of interpretation. Lukacher puts the matter well:

> The primal scene is the figure of an interpretive dilemma; it is a constellation of forgotten intertextual events offered in lieu of a demonstrable, unquestionable origin. Thus conceived, the primal scene is a strategic answer to the dilemma of a critical discourse that on the one hand maintains the impossibility of moving beyond interpretation to a

discourse of truth but on the other hand has not forgotten that the burden of the truth continues to makes itself felt. [It is thus] an effort to answer the unanswerable call of the Real, a call that emerges from the undisclosed essence of language itself.

(24–5)

There is a sense in which we have arrived at a kind of check in regard to the overarching issue of rewriting the self. We have tended to emphasize looking backward in time rather than forward. We have shown how the meaning of the past becomes transformed in light of the present. None of this is to be denied. What we need to do at this point, however, is to reaffirm, cautiously, the idea that the notion of causation as such – this seemed to lead to that – must be reckoned with if we are to have a suitable grasp of the phenomena at hand. Fraser has indeed rewritten her self in light of the knowledge she has acquired; that much goes without saying. In this respect, it is precisely on account of the secret she has discovered that the determination of what seemed to lead to what has become possible. But is it not necessary to say as well that this secret that she harbored for so many years served to structure the very life she came to lead? And is it not necessary more generally to assume that even if we ourselves do not harbor discrete secrets such as Fraser's, our own lives are structured in much the same way, by a constellation of events that inheres – however unnameably – in the beginning of things?

Now the idea of causation, it might be suggested, is particularly appropriate in cases like Fraser's. Her very character had been determined, in significant part at least, by events of which she had been (consciously) unaware, and it was only through her own repetition – her life having been structured by an obstacle beyond which she could not move – that she began to see that something had to lie at the root of it all. We thus see a correlation of some general import: we become 'determined' as a function of the degree of our own self-alienation; the more we have repressed, the more we fall prey to the psychological deep freeze of repetition, which in turn can give our lives the appearance that there are secret forces responsible for their very shape. 'What happened?', we might ask. 'How did I get this way? Why can't I *move*?'

With other people, people who are less frozen in their respective primal conflicts, it may well seem as if they are more free and self-determining. Instead of being enmeshed within some ancient drama from which they cannot escape, they can move through life in more or less unhampered fashion: they are able to move *forward*, we can say, into the phenomena of the future rather than the epiphenomena of the past. When all was said and done, Fraser herself seemed able to do something like this. Some people were imprisoned for life, she said at one point; they were in effect 'caused'; their futures were foregone conclusions, wrought out of the inexorability of their own repetition. She, however, was lucky enough to have gotten a reprieve, which is exactly what allowed her to both rewrite her self and, with this self, step into the world knowing she no longer need be the hapless victim of its forces.

There will be no moments of revelation for most of us, at least not of the sort Fraser experienced; there will be no secrets, but only secrecy, never to be brought to the status of definitive conclusions. Our lives, then, rather than appearing as mysteries to be unravelled or nagging problems to be solved, will appear more like richly ambiguous texts to be interpreted and understood: texts like the ones Kermode was considering, whose meanings are inexhaustible, whose mysterious existence ceaselessly calls forth the desire to know, whose readings cannot ever yield a final closure. And far from merely being a function of practical limitations – too many 'variables', as we put it earlier – this absence of closure is the nature of the beast. Indeterminacy here is essential, fundamental. But so too is that lingering metaphysical conviction that the world, our world, can somehow be made known. To be made/known, to be constructed/discovered, to be created/revealed, this is the dilemma we face. Although it cannot be resolved, it is important that we endure it. For even as we must be vigilant enough to avow our own interpretive participation in rewriting the self, we must also be humble enough to see that the very past which has culminated in this rewriting is excluded from a total grasp, working its mysterious ways like a distant call in the night.

Chapter 7
Who to become

IN THE WILDERNESS OF THE SELF

In the previous chapter, we considered how, on the plane of intrapsychic events, one might succeed in breaking the spell of determinism. Indeed, the very process of identifying the manner in which Fraser had been determined simultaneously broke this spell; she was freed from the tyranny of her secrets even as she named them. In this sense, we might note, causation in the human realm would seem to be quite different in yet another respect from causation in the physical realm: the very 'causal' (or perhaps 'quasi-causal') relationship that had obtained between Fraser's earlier (repressed) experiences and the outcomes to which they led was on some level *dissolved* upon her bringing them to consciousness; they were robbed of their determining power (see Habermas 1971), which is precisely what allowed her to get on with her life in a less mystified and psychically frozen way than had previously been possible.

In the present chapter, we will be taking up a related issue, our primary concern being with the way in which one may become aware of being determined and, at the same time, liberated from the very forces responsible. Rather than remaining essentially within the domain of the intrapsychic, however, we will be moving outside, into the world. In this respect, we will seek to become more attuned to the social construction of narrative; we will see how certain stories become sanctioned and others disallowed, how the very world in which one lives becomes crossed with boundaries which all but dictate what can and cannot be said or done. In line with much of what has been said thus far in this book, however, we will also see how these same boundaries can be exploded and how, more generally, the self may be transformed from an object, prey to the potentially constrictive power of culture, to a willful agent: a creator, able to cast into question those stories thought to be 'given' and write new ones, thereby transforming in turn precisely that social landscape which is often deemed responsible for who we become.

I am not suggesting that one may, through a sovereign act of will, become exempt from the determinative power of culture or that one may simply step out of his or her particular world and behold it from afar. This would be too 'unhermeneutical', we might say; it would presume that one could extricate oneself from history, from all that is anterior to the birth of the self and that serves as the very ground of its existence. But don't some people manage somehow to acquire a consciousness *of* history? Don't they become aware – more aware than others, at any rate – of the ways in which they have been determined, indeed of the very words they have been permitted to speak? Even if we cannot extricate ourselves from history, we can surely aspire to have some consciousness of it. It is true enough: many of us move through our lives rather blindly, operating under the assumption that the status quo, being fundamentally 'in the nature of things', must be maintained and upheld, perhaps at all costs. But it is no less true that we, human beings, have also been endowed with the rather remarkable capacity to name the status quo, to see what is given as such, to have some awareness of the situations in which we find ourselves. Isn't it this awareness which often incites us to change these situations and, by extension, our selves? More to the point still, doesn't the very possibililty of rewriting the self entail human freedom?

We have come full circle in a sense. With Helen Keller, we were concerned with issues of authorship and identity, particularly in relation to language. We were brought to ask what it might mean to originate or create, in so far as the materials we use to do so are inevitably 'hand-me-downs', vestiges of what has come before. As it turns out, the issues we are about to take up are actually quite similar in many ways. For we are once again considering the possibility of creation, broadly taken: creation of new social realities, new stories to tell, and new selves to tell about them. What does it mean for human beings to be able to create all these new things? It means that in addition to being subjects in the sense of being subjected-to the determinative power of culture, we are subjects who have the power – in principle, if not always in practice – to recreate both culture itself and our place within it. Here, then, is yet another meaning of rewriting the self: in becoming aware of the ways in which we are determined and in considering alternate modes of living our lives than the ones bequeathed us, we denature and demystify the established order of selfhood itself, thus paving the way for different stories to be told.

What follows is a discussion of Jill Ker Conway's *The Road From Coorain* (1989), which is an especially compelling illustration of some of the principles we have been considering. Her story is a heroic one in some ways, as perhaps it was intended to be. From a remote sheep-farm in the grasslands of Australia to Smith College, where she became president (the details of which are not however discussed in the book at all), Conway's story shows that possibilities exist for radically transforming one's life even in the most unlikely settings; she called her life into question and decided there was a better way. More important for the present purposes, however, are Conway's reflections on how one might move from being a subject who is subjected-to, as we called it, to one who is able to chart, within certain limits of course, her own destiny.

Why, though, does this sort of story deserve a place here, in a book the primary focus of which has been on memory and related issues? The reason is that Conway, like most others in comparable transitional situations, had been subjected to the conditions of her life unconsciously (though in a different sense from Fraser's case); she was living through them without understanding their mode of operation and without seeing that there were quite different ways of interpreting her life than the ones she had been using. The way Conway ultimately came to interpret her life was not only different from her earlier ways but vastly enlarged, the reason being that she could finally see certain dimensions of her own history in a patently less obfuscated, mystified, and naive light than she ever had before. But let us begin at the beginning.

Conway's father had been fortunate enough, back in 1929, to get a sizeable piece of land out in the country, where he would raise sheep and build a house for his family. He had been 'elated', she writes, 'as he surveyed the realization of his dream.' As for her mother, on the other hand, it was a 'nightmare of desolation' (18); she had hardly hoped that this would be her lot in life, particularly given her urban background. Her decision, nevertheless, made mainly in the name of love, was that she was willing to give this new way of life a try: 'They would go together, run the risks, and reap the benefits' (19). By no means was this decision to be understood as an act of acquiescence to male desires, as if she would have done whatever her husband wanted. In point of fact, she had always 'reveled in blessed independence' (22); she had been a 'modern feminist', as Conway calls her, very much aware of male domination and its effects. But the purchase of this land was not an act of domination at all; it was only an act of hope and faith, that they would be able to forge a good, comfortable life. As it turned out, it was a bit more uneven than they would have wished.

Conway herself had faced a difficult situation from the very beginning of her life. 'My parents', she writes, 'had wanted a daughter in the vague way people think about the gender of a child. Neither stopped to ponder what possible role a female child could play in the setting in which they lived. The out-of-doors was exclusively male. The domestic world was exclusively under my mother's control' (28). Perhaps they ought to have pondered things a bit more. Yet for all of their vagueness and ill-preparedness concerning the future of their little girl, Conroy's parents had still given her a solid and strong beginning. She would learn, in particular, how to fend for herself, to be self-reliant, and to make up her own mind about things. She would read voraciously, from children's books to current affairs. She would also become her father's station hand out on the land, where despite her occasional inability to cope with 'the space, the silence, and the brooding sky' (42), she would learn the ways of the wild.

'All in all', Conway writes in summary, 'what might on the surface appear like a lonely childhood . . . was one filled with interest, stimulation, and friends. It lacked other children', she notes, 'and I was seven before I even laid eyes on another female child. Yet this world gave me most of what we need in life, and gave it generously. I had the total attention of both my parents, and was secure in the knowledge of being loved. Better still, I knew that my capacity for work was valued and that my contributions to the work of the property really mattered. It was a comprehensible world', where one saw 'visible results from one's labors' and received 'permanent instruction about the way human beings can transform their environment' (50). What Conway learned, in short, was an invaluable lesson about selfhood. Whether the environment in question was the physical world or the social world, one could have an effect on it; one could take what was and make something new. Right away, then, we see that there will probably be considerable resistance on her part to being a subjected-to kind of subject: the environment, whatever force it could exert on those who inhabited it, could still be acted upon and changed.

With this idea in mind, we might note that Conway's 'permanent instruction' was not only about human effectiveness and creativity; it was about power as well, the power one could exercise over the world, the power to make the other submit. Conway herself may not have seen her instruction quite in these terms; the idea of making another submit remains anathema to most of those inclined toward an ethics of personal liberation. But once it is said that my way is preferable to yours, and once measures are taken to convert you to this better way, I have begun to exercise my power. Now as Foucault (1980) has suggested, the idea of power itself has gotten something of a bad name. To the extent that it connotes the unwarranted, self-serving subjugation of another, we can see why this is so. But every religious or moral or political sentiment we hold, Foucault tells us, every truth we speak, is nonetheless contingent upon the exercise of power. 'Truth', he writes, 'is a thing of this world: it is produced only by virtue of multiple forms of constraint' (131). Isn't the desire to speak the truth laced with the desire to render ignorance or falsehood silent and defeated?

Conway had learned her lesson well. When a lingering drought had begun to render her father irritable and afraid of what the future would or would not bring, she would try to revive his sunken spirits by playing 'the child I no longer was' (55). When he took sick, she would volunteer for jobs 'I was not quite sure I could do'. So it was, she writes, that 'I fell early into a role it took me many years to escape, the person in the family who would rise to the occasion, no matter the size of the task' (58). This, at any rate, was how Conway elected to see herself in retrospect. She would even wake her father from his terrible nightmares, sparing him the pain of the unspeakable terror that came to fill his life. If there was any check at all on the rapture of her fierce independence and willingness to take on any task that came her way, it was the death of a friend of the family, who, apparently overcome by his own private anguish, had hanged himself right in the post office where he worked. 'He came to be one of my symbols', Conway writes, 'for our need for society, and of the folly of believing that we can manage our fate alone' (61).

Here, then, was a lesson in humility and in the fragility of the self, to complement what she had already learned about the power to transform the world. It was a double lesson, in fact: the environment itself, be it a terrible drought or the kinds of woes that make people want to die, had its own share of power; and one must not be so bold and arrogant as to assume that it could simply be dominated and overtaken at will. Secondly, perhaps sociality was as fundamental a concern as the autonomy she had come to cherish. It was all too easy out in the bush to become swept up into the essentially male ethos of the rugged individual, alone against a hostile world, refusing to burden others with just those fears and anxieties that would lead to nightmares, so silent did they have to be by day. But there was no good reason to live one's life this way. It was destructive and unnecessary, and it made the social world out to be a collection of monads rather than a community of persons, who could care for, and be cared for by, others.

She should leave after he died, her father had said; rather than continuing to fight the seasons and the elements, she should go out and get a 'real education . . . away from this damn country'. Go where there exists the opportunity for self-creation: '*Make something of yourself*' (64). This became a virtual demand. The only troubling thing about this demand, Conway notes, is that a bit too much had been vested in her own future success; she 'became the focus of all the aspiration for achievement that had fueled both parents' prodigious energies' (65). She also became 'an unnaturally good child', who would serve as the bright light in what often seemed a sea of darkness, and who 'accepted uncritically that goodness was required of me if my parents' disappointments in life were ever to be compensated for' (66). This sounds as if it would take some time to work out, which indeed it did.

She would be left in the wilderness of her own self for some time, trying as best she could to arbitrate between her own desires and those that were created for her by two frustrated people who yearned, even if vicariously, for a measure of solace from the hardships they had been forced to endure. On the one hand, she was independent and self-reliant, qualities that had been developed as a matter of necessity given the demands that were made upon her. On the other hand, though, it was almost as if this independence, along with the great achievements that would follow from it, was demanded to such an extent that it had made her problematically dependent at one and the same time; to spare them their pain, she would have to bend to their desires, living out their visions, a 'remarkable child' hell-bent on their redemption. She didn't quite know who to become.

Her confusion was only compounded by her father's death not too long after he had spoken to her about leaving. Their life 'seemed lived in an inferno', Conway writes, the drought having continued far too long for her father's response to be anything but the most severe and ceaseless depression. He had drowned, the story went. Whether or not it was an accident would remain unknown. Her mother would often sleep with her afterward, clinging 'like a drowning person' herself, afraid, once again, of the silence and wildness of their home in the bush. They would find a manager to take care of the property and get away quickly to some place where life was easier and the ghosts of their recent past would be kept at bay. 'I knew that in most important ways my childhood was over' (81). For although she could not know what the future would bring, it was eminently clear that she would serve as her father's 'agent' from that time on, dealing with whatever further blows fate would bring. There had thus been something of a philosophical and psychological turnabout in Conway's life. For one who had been so enchanted with her own effect on the world, her own power to transform it, it was no doubt difficult to see life shaped as much by accident as will.

THE SEEDS OF NEW LIFE

Despite the string of catastrophes that had befallen her family, including, subsequent to her father's death, the death of her dearly-loved brother, Conway and her mother seemed to make the most of their situation. While many of her more 'common' peers were being educated at the local state school – Conway herself had given it a try for a day, only to return home thoroughly drained of spirit – she would move on to private school, acquiring the best education possible. There were some regrets about this, she notes; had she remained in the state school, she surely would have had to confront the way the Australian working class thought about the world. 'It was to take me another fifteen years', she writes, 'to see the world from my own Australian perspective, rather than from the British definition taught to my kind of colonial' (95). At the same time, though, had she gone the route of the 'earthy irreverence' of the working class, she would no doubt have missed out on appreciating 'high culture'. Indeed, it may very well have led to an entirely different life from the one she lived.

Instrumental in furthering Conway's education at private school was a Miss Everett, the first 'free spirit' she had ever met, who was 'impatient with Australian bourgeois culture' and 'concerned about ideas'. She 'loved learning for itself', which made her 'a most unusual schoolteacher', particularly since the prevailing tendency was to treat knowledge more as a 'credential' than anything else. The only problem – and it really wasn't one at the time – was that however cultured her education was, and however excellent, it might as well have been taking place in Britain itself: 'We might have been in Sussex for all the attention we paid to Australian poetry and prose', for instance; 'it did not count'. Conway and her classmates would memorize Keats and Shelley, with their vivid depictions of the natural world, without ever having seen this world, thus giving them 'the impression that great poetry and fiction were written by and about people and places far distant from Australia' (99). There was a further implication as well, namely that their own land, since it deviated so much from that about which these great poets waxed rhapsodic, was ugly and inferior.

Unbeknownst to her back then, Conway was being instructed not only in so-called high culture but in the way it came to be constituted as such: through exclusion and the suppression of difference. Moreover, there was much about her education that was more in the service of 'knowing-about' than knowing. She was never really taught what art and music were, as forms of expression and creativity; it was enough that she learn how to carry a tune, read music, and so on. Her 'appreciation' of high culture, therefore, had to do with the inculcation of that which had been deemed, by the bearers of tradition, worth knowing. Conway ought not to have become too critical of this education, of course; for all of its one-sidedness and superficiality, it still culminated in the insights she was to have about it. But there was something stuffy and stultifying about the whole thing. Or so it appeared in retrospect.

When some of the more rebellious students asked why they had to be so prim and proper, both inside the classroom and out, the response was straightforward: 'We were an elite. We were privileged girls and young women who had an obligation to represent the best standards of behavior to the world at large. The best standards were derived from Great Britain, and should be emulated unquestioningly'. It really was a rather strange situation in some ways. 'No one paused to think that gloves and blazers [worn daily] had a function in damp English springs which they lacked entirely in our blazing summers' (102). Much of what she learned was, in a word, mystifying.

She was lucky to have been raised in the bush, Conway suggests at one point, for whereas many of her classmates would follow orders without giving them a second thought – they were there to become 'ladies' and were doing what was in their own best interest – she continued to seek the satisfaction of going about her own business, even managing 'some feat of wickedness' now and then, to remind herself, perhaps, that underneath those gloves and blazers she was still her own person. She was also lucky to not have her parents around when these misdeeds arose. This was her first opportunity, she writes, 'to rebel without the danger of doing psychological damage to adults of whom I was prematurely the care giver' (105). She was finally 'perversely carefree', even 'irresponsible', and it seemed to relieve her of some of the guilt she had suffered when she had made those magical associations between her own misdeeds and her parents' misfortunes. The school's regimentation, then, had served an important, albeit unintended, role in Conway's life; by and large, it was a safe haven for carrying out those shenanigans that earlier on would have reeked with infectious poison. Gender stereotypes had worked on her behalf as well, for while her brothers, who, refusing to depend on their mother financially, had gone off and gotten jobs with woolbrokers, she would not have a career based on the land; it simply was not a woman's place, particularly not a woman who was in the midst of becoming as well-bred as she was. Instead, she would attend university, to become a doctor perhaps, exempted from the fate of spending her life in the company of sheep. She would probably do well too. Except for something of a blind spot in mathematics, she was learning to move beyond the stiltedness and superficiality of some of her instruction and becoming an intellectual force, highly motivated and extremely intelligent.

Even though it would take her some time to regain the vividness of emotional life after her brother's death, Conway was nonetheless on the way to what appeared to be a solid future. This is not to say that the road there would be easy; in the aftermath of her brother's death, her mother had sought to control her remaining children's lives to an almost obsessive degree. They had to be within reach at every moment, lest she think that there would be yet another knock at her door, another knock of death. They had to capitulate to her desires, irrational though they often were, lest she saddle them with guilt over forsaking a mother as grieved and needy as she. Conway's brother Barry had even been banished at one point, sent back to the bush, where he might order his life in a way their mother deemed suitable; at 20 years of age, he shouldn't have been frittering away his life, as she believed he was doing. All told, 'she thought little about the consequences for others of the plans which would serve as her objective of the moment' (137). She had endured plenty already; it was time now that her own needs and desires be met, even if this meant riding roughshod over others. Conway's education proved to be her savior and guiding light. When she was entranced in the world of ideas, there was little that could stop her spirit from rising.

But what should she do with her life? Who should she become? In part, her education, along with her mother, pointed in the direction of intellectual life: 'We were privileged young women who owed it to society to develop our minds and talents to the limits of our ability' (142–3). Yet there were other messages too, about what was and was not sensible for girls to do. 'The things that were "nice for a woman" to study', she had learned, 'were unintellectual, like nursing, physiotherapy, or occupational therapy, or strictly decorative, like music or a foreign language, subjects which only the strangest parents thought their daughters might pursue professionally' (143). She should do something practical, her mother advised, the idea of becoming a doctor surfacing again; this would give her the economic independence that women needed if they were to carry on after catastrophes like the premature deaths of their husbands. The contradictions at hand began to weigh heavily: even as her education was preparing her for becoming her own person, Conway was being given advice, conflictual advice, from many different quarters about how she could best run her life. The only thing that rang true came from two of her teachers, who said that with her strengths, she should study history and literature – as unladylike as it might be. The prospect was exciting.

Her schooling had actually been quite good, Conway could eventually say: 'I forgave it its foolishly hot uniforms and its genteel rules of behavior; I even forgave some of its less admirable pretenses. It had given me a secure and orderly environment in which to grow, and adults to admire who took it for granted that women would achieve' (144). It would be difficult still to make her way in the world according to her own desires; even in a climate of potential and possibility there were walls to be broken down. Moreover, there was still the shadow of her mother hanging over her, and whether the issue in question was the viability of medical school or the shortcomings of her appearance – she wasn't quite so willowy and elegant as she ought to have been, apparently – it was clear that a good deal of psychological work would have to be done before she could move ahead freely and confidently. Finally, and most problematically, Conway seemed to be a bit too brainy for some people's liking. 'This was a bad thing to be in Australia. People distrusted intellectuals. Australians mocked anyone with "big ideas" and found them specially laughable in a woman.' Even her mother, as proud as she was of her daughter's academic achievements, had some serious reservations about a future in the world of ideas. 'One moment she would be congratulating me on my performance at school, and the next contradicting her approval by urging me not to become too interested in my studies. If I did', she had been warned, 'I would become a "bluestocking", a comically dull and unfeminine person' (146).

A rift, the dizziness of recognition that there was a serious problem to be dealt with, the initial moment in a cycle of development: what was going on here? Why the mixed messages? It was too early, it seemed, to work through the contradictions at hand. For now she would simply try to be like all her classmates, who found life less puzzling, whose humbler, more feminine yearnings kept everyone quiet and at ease. Her mother didn't like this much either. All she seemed to like, in fact, still, was her daughter's companionship, care, and sensibility; she wasn't flighty, like so many of these other girls. Others saw Conway in much the same light: 'I might not be pretty, and I was certainly dangerously bookish, but it was clear that I won lots of approval from the adult world' (147). Perhaps she would even follow in her father's footsteps and return to the bush one day, some thought; there was no one better qualified to run the show. But that was far away. Now, it was time to work out some things about the more immediate future. She would go off to university as planned and pursue her bookish career for a while.

But then what? 'What would I become after three years of higher education? Try as I might I couldn't conjure up a single image to fill in the blank prospect of the future' (147). If only there were 'pointers for life's journeys like the planets and constellations which could help pilot us along the surface of the earth.' Indeed, this was a matter of some urgency: 'I needed some pointers for the future', she realized, 'because I dreaded being stranded at home, the only companion of an increasingly dependent mother, even as I took my sense of self-worth from doing the job well' (148).

As much as her role as dutiful daughter had bolstered her ego, she knew she had to flee to save her soul. If she was going to do so, though, she had better know the destination. How would she decide where to go and what to do? What was the end, the telos, of this ill-defined project she was in the midst of forming? Distanciation, as we have called it, was troubling enough. In leaving her old self behind, she would not only give up her security and sense of self-worth, but she would annihilate her mother in the process. Here was a young lady, whom the adults loved, who cared with a maturity beyond her years, who would continue to give her life-blood to her emotionally ailing mother who, some said, could not live without her. And she's supposed to go ahead and try to fulfill herself? Yes, she said to herself, she was; she knew that dangers lay ahead, but she had to do what was right for her. But again, what *was* right for her? And should she really annihilate her mother just to go off and take some self-involved course that she couldn't even articulate yet? She had been urged at her graduation to help the less fortunate. 'Did helping the less fortunate mean that I was really meant to live my entire life caring for my mother, filling the emotional void left by my father and Bob?' (149).

There was some guilt over even asking this sort of question. How dare she neglect to pay perpetual heed to her mother's devotion and sacrifice. How dare she refuse to console her when her entreaties remained as loud and clear and pitiful as ever. Her mother had become an angry woman too, angry at the world, for having treated her so badly. Conway had no particular interest in incurring further wrath than already existed in the ordinary course of things. 'Thoughts of escape were unrealistic', she had decided. 'Daughters in Australia were supposed to be the prop and stay of their parents. Would I ever get away? Was I wrong to want to? How on earth could I set about doing it? How', she asked, 'could I tell this woman who lived for me that I did not want to live for her?' Far from merely being a matter of finding the right pointers, as Conway calls them, there was the need to make a decision 'about what would be the moral path to choose' (151). Could there be a definitive answer to this last and most basic question?

MEANING, MORALITY, AND THE SOCIAL CONSTRUCTION OF NARRATIVE

Let us consider in greater detail some of the dynamics of the dilemma Conway faced. To the extent that we are defenders of the faith of individuality and wish to abide by the demand that we be true to ourselves and follow our own inner lights, no matter what the cost, we may be inclined to say: Go! Flee! Run while you can! Hardly anyone likes to leave a mother in the lurch, but since you've only got one life to live and life is rather short, you ought to be able to do what you want. It wasn't *her* fault that her mother had become so dependent and needy, a fair amount of time had passed since the deaths of her father and brother, and in her mother's better, more other-directed moments she would probably want to see her daughter be the independent young woman she had raised her to be.

Or, taking a somewhat more developmentally-oriented approach, as exemplified in Gilligan's (1982) work, for instance, we could say that in addition to caring for others, as Conway had done amply through the years, perhaps it was time to care for herself; there would be little reason, from this perspective, to attend less to one's own needs and desires than anyone else's. Hadn't she paid her dues? Didn't she deserve more out of life than to be a nursemaid to someone who would be better off seeing if she could find some resources within herself? How is this for a solid rationalization: Wasn't Conway aiding and abetting her mother in a pathetic crime of parasitic dependence, and wasn't it therefore nothing short of a *responsibility* on her part to take whatever measures were necessary to ensure that her mother live her life to the fullest?

But then there is the proverbial other hand. Her mother *had* been devoted, she *had* sacrificed, and she *was*, understandably, needy. It would be crude, of course, to think of a mother's devotion and sacrifice as an investment to be repaid, but was it really stretching things to think that maybe Conway owed her something more than gratitude for all she had done? As for her neediness, who is to say when one should be beyond grief? How does one decide, on behalf of another, when it has been 'long enough'? There are still more serious and fundamental issues than these, though. In recent years, there have been some writers (see especially Bellah *et al.* 1985, Bellah 1987)[1] who have bemoaned the relentless individualism that has come to characterize much of contemporary life. They have spoken mainly about the United States, it should be noted, but the ideas are surely of broad enough significance to apply to Australia. A difficult marriage, which had once led to a desire to 'work it out', now leads to divorce. Therapists, adhering to the latest self-actualization dogma, tell their clients to do what's best for them. And a thirst for money, as we all know, often occludes whatever human concerns one might have had in a less greedy, 'me-first' society. Isn't it a perilously short step from these scenarios to the scenario of a young woman, eager to live out her own dreams, ambiguous though they may be, even if this means leaving one of the 'less fortunate', as they were called at graduation, to her own meager devices? We need to care more for others, many say. Autonomy needs the company of concern, agency of communion, individualism of community, freedom of responsibility, Self of Other. The individual is nothing to reject wholly; it has led to a good many good things. But, the story goes, perhaps it has gone too far. Little wonder that we have so much difficulty in establishing which moral concerns might conceivably cut across the lot of us; it's become an 'I do my thing, you do yours' world – provided, of course, there is no serious element of destruction involved.

Each of these perspectives has its positive features. Consequently, there is no simple-minded way to decide between them. But is there a *non*-simple-minded way of doing so? Is there, within the framework of some extant developmental model, for instance, a way to decide which of these hypothetical paths is the more 'advanced' one for Conway to take? The answer is plainly that there is not. And what this implies, I suggest, is that in charting one's own developmental project – and, by extension, in deciding how one's self will be rewritten – there is, inevitably, a moral component involved: one is making a determination about what sort of self one ought to be and, as a function of this determination, what sort of history to write.

Were Conway to take the first option, and flee, the ensuing story would no doubt be about subjugation and emancipation, about how a young woman, enchained in the prison of her mother's domination, escaped into freedom. She could of course tell another story – that she decided, for instance, to take the selfish, me-based way out since she was ultimately the top dog and didn't care as much about others as about herself – but this might not make for especially good autobiographical writing and reading, particularly for someone as notable as Conway came to be. Were she to take the second option, and stay, the story might be about the allure of individuation and the need, at times, to resist this allure, in the interest of doing what is good and right. The young woman here might almost have given in to her selfish desires, leaving her mother behind, but realized instead that one must sometimes make sacrifices in this world. Once again, there could be another story here too, of someone weak and dependent in her own right, for instance, who refused to flee the coop out of fears of reprisal or, more likely, unbearable guilt. But this too would be a questionable story to tell, both to others and to oneself.

The main point, in any case, is simply this: given the set of circumstances we are considering here, there are numerous ways Conway's history might be emplotted and, consequently, numerous stories that might be told. The story that ultimately *does* get told, therefore – and we might think back to some of the issues we took up in previous chapters, particularly the last – will inevitably derive from a moral commitment on the part of the narrator, a judgment about the meaning of the past that is 'underdetermined' by the constellation of events in question. Furthermore, and relatedly, the manner in which we, as readers, emplot what has gone on – which may, of course, be thoroughly different from the way the narrator does it – will also be a function of a moral commitment. If we are diehard individualists and Conway flees, we will likely applaud. If we are more communitarian types, we might condemn her, particularly in the light of all that her dear mother had done for her.

I do not mean to suggest that there is an infinity of different ways in which these events might be emplotted or that the way in which one does so is arbitrary. Quite the contrary; there are a limited number of ways, which is exactly why we see someone caught on the horns of a dilemma rather than babbling dumbfounded at the multifarious meaninglessness of everything that has happened. What is it, we might ask, that does the limiting? In the most obvious sense, it is the narrator; he or she is the one who decides, out of the possibilities that exist, what sort of story will be told. In a less obvious sense, however, it is the social world that does so, a world that is, as a matter of course, meaningful and morally charged in quite specific ways. If we wish to insist, therefore, that the stories we tell are a function of who is doing the telling, then we may do so; on some level it is surely so. But we also need to recognize that the narrator, rather than being the sovereign origin of what gets said, is instead a kind of passage through which those discourses presently in circulation speak.

As we noted in our discussion of Helen Keller, this does not mean that we can't say anything new or that we are merely the mouthpieces of others' words. It only means that the way we understand the world, and talk and write about it, is socially constructed. Without claiming that Conway and the rest of us speak and write words that are strictly derivative, therefore – which would itself imply a kind of master speaker or writer from whom we each descended – the point is that narratives of the sort we are considering here always and inevitably exist within a circumscribed discursive space: within a limited region of possible utterances and modes of representation, constituted by the social world. As I gaze back upon my life, even in the most private of moments, and try to make sense of its twists and turns, I organize it in ways that are dictated by the very order of things that inheres in my world, ways that are (more or less) consonant with how lives tend to be understood and represented in the place where I live. Depending on how severe these twists and turns are compared to those of my neighbors as well as on how imaginative a writer I am when I face the task of emplotting my history, I can *expand* the discursive space that presently obtains; I can say something new and different, thus creating a larger region of possible utterances and modes of representation for those who follow to draw upon. Yet even here, at my most imaginative, at the peaks of my creative frenzies, the discourse employed and the self who employs them are, again, socially constructed: they assume their very shape as a function of the social world in which they exist. Can I imagine beyond the limits set by the discursive space that presently obtains? Can I leap out of discourse and into the world – or, for that matter, into the stratosphere or the heavens? I don't know. It all depends, I suppose, on how much credence we place in the possibility of transcendence.

Now the idea of something being socially constructed is often taken as being synonymous with its being relative, to time and place, for instance. Thus social constructionists, are they are sometimes called, are often thought to be relativists as well, which on some level they usually are. But there is a way of understanding the idea of something being socially constructed, I will suggest, that might lead us to think of it a bit differently. How is it, we have asked, that we understand a life to mean roughly this or roughly that? We know that we cannot simply divine the thoughts of the person who lived it. Even if we are more empathic than most, there is no jumping into the other's skin; it is philosophically untenable and a bit rude too. No, we understand a life to mean this or that because as bearers of a tradition, in which certain ways of reading and writing – not to mention living – have achieved primacy, we arrive at the texts we encounter already prepared to understand them in certain specific ways; we bring our own stock of utterances, modes of representation and so on, which creates for us what Jauss (1982) has called an 'horizon of expectation' concerning what the text before us will bring. As we noted in our discussion of Gadamer's work, there is unquestionably a danger inherent in this situation: there is always the chance that our interpretations, contingent as they are on this horizon of expectation, will derive more from our own ('bad') prejudices as from the text. We must be cognizant of this fact, we said at the time, and keep a kind of vigilance over who we are and how we read (unless, of course, our aim in reading is something other than interpretation, as it is usually understood). It is nevertheless the case, we also noted, that the prejudices we bring to a text are precisely what make it possible for us to begin to understand it; without an horizon of expectation, there would be no inroad into meaning at all.

Let me bring these ideas together, then, by saying that just as narrators tell about their lives in ways that are circumscribed by the social world in which they live – hence the 'social construction of narrative' – so too do readers read, bringing their respective horizons of expectation with them to the texts they encounter. There is, I want to emphasize, an important qualification to all this, which I will frame as follows: if in fact writer and reader inhabit roughly the same discursive space (more simply referred to as a 'world'), then we are likely to have something of a happy coincidence. The writer writes in certain ways, the reader reads in certain ways, and because these ways happen to be similar, meaning can exist comfortably in the dialogic space between the two. But what about when writers' worlds and readers' worlds clash, as might even be happening now, as I read Conway? We share the English language and no doubt have some common understandings about how the world works, but here I am – an American man, hailing from suburban New York, living in 1992, etc. – trying to make sense of (Conway's rendition of) a young Australian woman, hailing from the bush, several years ago. Granted, she's not from some wholly alien culture, so I don't have to get *too* ethnographically self-reflexive about this situation, but I do have to do something. What?

Consider this: the pressure to stay by her mother's side, for instance, seems to have been especially severe for Conway owing to the fact that it was something of a norm in Australia; children were customarily expected to be dutiful, particularly when their parents were calling out to them in need. For others, however, who live in cultures where this expectation holds less weight, it may be difficult to comprehend all the hemming and hawing. Come on, we might want to say. Do what you have to do! All the more so, of course, to the degree that our own individual histories, within this culture, have been slanted in this way.

Now there is no means of extricating ourselves from our own culturally-based ways of understanding, as we have repeatedly seen, and consequently no means of neutrally grasping what she has to say apart from our own prejudices. The other doesn't coincide with me; she is different. Indeed, she might inhabit an entirely different world from mine. Is it audacious for me to even read this book and try to 'represent' it to you? More to the point still, how is understanding the other, particularly the significantly different other, even possible?

It is only possible, I suggest, through a kind of 'ethnography' of the other and her world. As readers, in other words, there is the need to become like cultural anthropologists in a sense, the aim being to attune ourselves, as best we can, to the 'native's point of view', in all of its potential otherness. And the way we do this, basically, is by creating interpretive contexts – plausible and appropriate interpretive contexts – within which what is said may be placed.

I say 'creating' here rather than 'finding' for a simple reason. If I could find an appropriate context by merely drawing on my own repertoire of interpretive possibilities, there wouldn't be any problem of understanding at all: the other would say something, I would have a context ready to hand to put it in, and that would be that. But if in fact I *don't* have that context ready to hand (as when I say, 'What are you talking about?'), then obviously I will have to create one. Simple enough: when I encounter an alien other, whether person or text, and try to understand what is being said, I will have to be interpretively sensitive and flexible and imaginative enough to make it work. Without this, no dialogue will be possible, only a rather mute monologue that I won't comprehend. But can't I be sensitive, flexible, and imaginative as can be – an empathic, open-minded, methodologically self-reflexive artful hermeneut of the highest order, a veritable paragon of right thinking – and still be unable to make sense of what the other has to say? Where does this context I am supposed to create come from anyway? It comes from learning enough about the world of the other – as Australian or American, as woman or man, as young or old, and so on – that I can slowly but surely begin to get a hold on what is being said. Can I grasp the other totally? Can my enhanced understanding of his or her world lead in the end to an all-encompassing, complete, no-holes picture? No. I can't do it with me and I can't do it with anyone else either; there can only be dialogue, evermore. But I can certainly try to understand these people better than I did initially, and I can sometimes succeed too.

Two corollaries follow from this brief digression, the first methodological, the second theoretical. In claiming that our understanding of others is in significant part contingent upon our understanding of the worlds they inhabit, the myth of observational neutrality and objectivity – traditionally defined – is exploded: the faceless observer, sans history, sans prejudice, blessedly open to the otherness of the text (would that this being could exist), could understand absolutely nothing. Our friends and lovers often seem to understand us better than other people, complete strangers for instance. Isn't it because they know our worlds well enough to hear what we say? Indeed, isn't the very possibility of establishing objectivity thoroughly contingent on our interpretive preparedness, on the knowledge and understanding that we are able to bring to bear upon the texts we encounter? If a desire to establish a measure of objectivity means that we ought to be hermeneutically sensitive enough to know where we stand as interpreters, in regard to our own sociohistorical location, then well and good; no argument there. If, on the other hand, it is taken to mean that we should somehow try to *forget* about who and what we are – as men and women, blacks and whites, young people and old, etc. – so that we can behold these texts in their pristine thingness, then this desire will have to be shaken. In sum, unless I have some idea of your and my interpretive context, there will be no understanding.

The theoretical corollary is not unrelated to the methodological one just considered. We have established that narratives are socially constructed; what a narrator says and the particular way he or she says it will be determined in part by the social world in which he or she lives. As such, we said, it was imperative to try to attune ourselves to this world so as to glean adequately the native's point of view and to ensure that we do not mistake it for our own: understanding the world of the other, therefore, is a precondition for understanding the other self. Can we not move in just the opposite direction as well, however, and say that in understanding the other him-or herself we learn about the world too? More generally, doesn't the very fact of narratives being socially constructed mean that we can study them not only in order to learn about individual selves but about the social realities in which these selves have lived – realities that have indeed become inscribed in their very being?[2]

In some ways, of course, Conway's dilemma was hers and hers alone; it was a function of her own unique history. In other ways, however, this dilemma was by no means hers alone, for its very existence *as* a dilemma was contingent upon there existing in her world a set of competing and contradictory demands, which, as above, had become inscribed in her very being. She had to arrive at an answer to the unanswerable, carving out that 'moral path', as she put it, that seemed most appropriate to take. We each would have our own feelings, no doubt, about what she ought to do. But how did she herself decide? How did she articulate a suitable resolution to this painful and confusing dilemma?

APOSTASY AND AUTHORITY

Conway's venture to university wasn't quite what she thought it would be. It was rather boring, for the most part, and she herself felt out of place. So taking care of her mother, while certainly not an exciting prospect, began to look substantially better than it had. It still wasn't easy, though, to give her all to her mother, who had become even more of a complainer than she had been.

High blood pressure and a hyperthyroid condition, she decided, required a totally predictable life with no distractions, no deviations from her schedule, and no emotional pressures of any kind. This meant that any attempt to oppose her will produced dramatic results. A disagreement raised her blood pressure, bothered her thyroid condition, or triggered a gallbladder attack.

(159)

Conway couldn't even be sassy at this point, for fear that she'd become a murderer! Maybe university wasn't so bad after all. What was looking even better, though, were those sheep, back in the bush. But upon her return there for shearing season, it became amply clear, yet again, that it was too 'heartbreakingly lonely' a place to be.

She decided to work for a while. Perhaps if she weren't financially dependent upon her mother, she had thought, some of the problems they faced would work themselves out better. The decision proved to be a good one. As an 'all-purpose medical records clerk, receptionist, appointments secretary, and occasional practical nurse', she witnessed firsthand the 'complexity of the human drama . . . It was like being thrust inside the mind of a gifted novelist'. The result was that she learned to look at people 'with more compassion and more distance' (161–2). In addition, her mother greatly respected the fact that she was earning her own living, such that even occasional 'patches of sunshine broke through our stormy domestic scene'. Finally, Conway herself seemed to be undergoing a transformation of sorts at this point, from a somewhat overweight 'brain' with a not-so-good complexion to a young woman whose appearance 'was beginning to approximate the glossy fashion magazines I studied so assiduously'. Big changes were happening. After all these years, 'I was painstakingly constructing an acceptable public self' (162). And for better or worse, this new self seemed to be one her mother got along with much better. A young man entered the picture too. At long last, Conway writes, 'I was traveling at a heady speed toward adulthood, dressed to kill and ready for adventure. My mother observed my comings and goings warily', she adds, 'but I was too elated to notice her watchful and guarded behavior'. The dilemma had seemed so big and unmanageable. Could it have been just a childish concern that had worked itself out, quietly and unobtrusively, as she turned into this glossier self? Her mother would even support her in her decision to return to university to receive a bit more stimulation than she had gotten at her job, its apparent merits aside. There would be a sizable allowance too, her mother having acknowledged that the previous one she had given was 'miserably small'. Was the battle over? 'I could scarcely believe this happy state of affairs'(163), she says. To think that there had been so much pain and suffering.

Not surprisingly, she was no longer the wallflower at university she had been earlier. She befriended some 'cheerful hedonists', cut classes occasionally, and in general became as interested in having a good time as in becoming the intellectual she had once desired to become. If only her mother knew! Well, before too long she did, and not surprisingly she was terribly disappointed at what her daughter's 'education' consisted of. Little did she know that when examinations came Conway would perform in superior fashion nevertheless, thus earning her vindication just when her mother was ready to swoop down on her to correct the errors of her ways. It was nothing short of a 'smashing psychological victory', Conway writes. 'It was hard to see how such results might have been improved on, and since success was what counted for my mother, the basis for future strictures about my conduct had suddenly been completely undermined.' Even more important, though, she continues, 'was my inner feeling that I could do something well, and my new awareness that university study was about learning and reflection, not the cramming of texts and information. Now', finally, after a painful dilemma and then a brief respite as a would-be cover girl, 'I had a purpose in life'. The dilemma, in fact, had acquired something of a tentative solution: 'If I were to become a success academically and choose a career that would take me away from Sydney', she had thought, 'it would finesse the whole question of leaving home. My mother would never stand in the way of success. Moreover, if it were public enough, its sweetness might cushion the blow of my departure' (168). Time would tell. For now, though, things were looking up. Not only had her mother apologized for her mistaken accusations, but she gave Conway a lovely gift besides. Were bygones bygones?

University life picked up as well. All of a sudden, by virtue of the honors that had been bestowed upon her, she acquired some notoriety as an up-and-coming intellectual light. More important, intellectual life itself had finally acquired some of the energy and excitement that she had hoped for: 'I found myself intoxicated by the pleasure of abstract ideas, by the company of others who shared my interests, and by the notion that one could get beneath the appearances of events to understand the property and class relationships which constituted the stuff of politics and culture.' Some of what she learned proved to be a bit disconcerting as well, particulary her encounter with Marx and Engels. Had her family monopolized the land, expropriating it to satisfy their own bourgeois desires? 'Who were the rightful owners and users of the land I had always thought to belong to us?' (170). She had come across aboriginal ovens and strange stones, which had been 'heedlessly trodden upon' in the course of her daily activities. Had she been so naive as to think that these things were merely abandoned, that the land hadn't been seized in the name of authority, that she herself had been an innocent recipient of the world's natural bounty?

Her eyes were in the midst of being opened to a new way of looking at all that had seemed so much a matter of course. The only irony – which she was unable to acknowledge until later, when the scales fell still further – was that even as she learned about the power of ideology, she was still an unwitting participant in it. These readings struck close to home, but they apparently did not quite apply to her – the lone woman in her history course, who appeared unusual to others for her academic drive, and who, most problematically, had 'unthinkingly taken on the identity of the male writer and intellect' in much of her work. It was not yet time to see herself as just the kind of subject of whom Marx, Engels, and others had written: a false consciousness reading about the same. Despite the fact that 'lightning' and 'thunderbolts' and other such things happened her way, then, deriving from the likes of Marx and Engels all the way to Jung (who seemed to have spied on her relationship with her mother only to write about it later on), Conway's journey toward self-consciousness had its share of ellipses and breaks, the strategic placement of which would become apparent in the future.

We might note here that not unlike Fraser, from the previous chapter, Conway has much to say about her own ignorance and unconsciousness; even as she tried to live her life, her life was living her. But again, Conway's brand of unconsciousness was radically different from Fraser's. Fraser's life had been structured by a secret, buried deep, within the recesses of her psyche. This is not to say that she hadn't been prey to many of the same ideological forces as Conway or that her problems had been strictly psychological in nature. Far from it; the very fact of her being subjugated as she was – not only in her father's bedroom, but even in places as bright and airy as the playing field where she had been a cheerleader (often, as she told it, for the private delectation of the hungry boys in the stands) – indicates otherwise. But Conway's story has a different inflection to it, being more about secrecy, using Kermode's (1979) terminology, than about secrets. What is it we mean by secrecy in this context? In line with what was said earlier, we are referring here to nothing less than the way in which, often unbeknownst to us, the social world becomes inscribed in our very being, in how we move, dress, speak, write, love, and live. Even the way we dance, however freely and frantically – we move in a spastic frenzy, in some corroded bar on the edge of civilization – has its own structure and locus of determination; and even the way we break rules is on some level rule-bound (see especially Winch 1958). Can this secrecy come to light? I would say yes, but not in the same fashion that a secret can. For as much as I might learn about the structures and designs by which I have lived my life, as self-conscious as I might become about the countless paths through which the discursive order of my world gets written on to my very being, 'I' am as inextricably bound to this order as the various 'me's' who are the objects of my emancipatory concerns. In other words, while I can discover a secret about my past and hold it before me, almost as if it were a thing, a piece of information, to be manipulated and appropriated, I can never see face-to-face the whole of my structuration as a self. This would necessitate that 'I' be at a remove from this structuration, looking down at myself and my world from some distant point on high. And this is exactly where 'I' cannot be. It is for this reason, of course, that coming to consciousness in the manner of Conway is so difficult: you've got to try to look *out* at the world from *in* the world; you've got to try to distanciate your self from yourself. No one said it would be easy. But if Conway's story is any indication, the process we are considering – which is at one and the same time psychological development and ideological critique – may nonetheless be worth the trouble.

Alongside her formal education, Conway benefited from many of her new friends, some of whom, on account of their different stations in life, helped to shed new light on her taken-for-granted world. Stated another way, these people served as vehicles for her own distanciation by giving her perspectives on the world she might otherwise not have had. Also important in her life at the time was a man who, to her 'astonishment and delight . . . liked clever women and didn't seem to think my reputation for learning detracted from my attractiveness. I was used to concealing how well I did academically when in male company', she explains, 'and to feigning interest in explications of subjects about which I knew a great deal more than the speaker.' This sort of posture was 'required conduct' for Australian women. 'It didn't do to question male superiority in anything' (178). Conway's new companion wouldn't stand for this, however, insisting on calling her bluff when she feigned ignorance for the sake of playing the part. 'In his company I enjoyed the experience an intellectual woman needs most if she has lived in a world set on undermining female intelligence: I was loved for what I was rather than the lesser mind I pretended to be' (179). In the midst of being exposed for her own socially-ratified duplicity – not to mention *com*plicity, with that monumental surveillant Other that insisted, however surreptitiously, that she behave this way rather than that – Conway was being affirmed for being herself.

There is an important message, I think, in this brief part of her narrative, namely that the notion of a 'true self', philosophical ambiguities (and perhaps, for some, liabilities) and all, is actually rather difficult, now, to cast aside. Even if we deconstruct the subject to pieces and argue over the duplicity of the self and the multiplicity of the self and the fictionality of the self and a thousand other things that the self isn't besides – whole, centered, integrated, unified, and what have you – don't most of us continue to posit in rather unabashedly romantic fashion that there are some things that are really 'us' and other things that are not? Indeed, even if one's life project is to call into question this very idea, isn't it still a project for all that? There is a need to be phenomenologically frank about these matters. Maybe some day in the future the self, as we know it now, will be a memory. Maybe it will become as dispersed and disunified as, in occasional moments of skeptical reverie, we imagine it to be: that 'face drawn in sand at the edge of the sea' that Foucault had spoken of. I have no qualms with this fantasy, and, in fact, I think it is important that this moment of suspicion *vis-à-vis* the unity and centeredness of the self, as exemplified by Foucault, Barthes, and others, has come about. There is much about humanism that is not only narcissistic and old-fashioned, but dangerous too: in neglecting our own possible *dis*unity and *de*centeredness, it might serve to obscure and perhaps even exonerate some of those forces responsible. But if there is a way of speaking about such important ideas as development, ideology critique, and so on without positing something akin to the integrity – if not the unity – of the human subject as such, I would like to see how it's done. Can we ever expose the dastardliness of the mantle of (unjustifiable) authority, in whatever forms it might assume, without invoking in some way a being who suffers, whose experience in the world is less than what it might be – less, indeed, than what it *should* be? I think not.

If the presence of Conway's new companion had presented her with just that possibility of legitimation that would give her comfort in her heart of hearts with who she was and who she was to become, her mother, now become 'a sardonic woman who mocked my emotional life as though it were the stupidest farce', was determined to keep things in check. 'I was startled and troubled by the destructiveness she revealed', says Conway, but 'tried to explain it away as the result of ill health' (180). Hadn't they taken care of business? Didn't that old dilemma fade away? Meanwhile, her companion had helped some of this turbulence along in some ways, for despite his manifestly enlightened attitudes toward women in some domains, he could still be somewhat backward in others, as shown, for instance, in his refusal to play second fiddle to his partner's studies, which were becoming more important to her all the time.

Further and still more disconcerting questions were sprouting forth, like wild shoots, in what had heretofore been a calm and graceful pasture. 'My schooling had been supposed to be training an elite for leadership', she eventually realized, 'but it had really been training me to imitate the ways and manners of the English upper class. To talk of Australian elites was to realize that the people I and my brothers had known in school were working not on Australia's social and political problems, but on gaining recognition from an external British world.' Even her leftist friends proved to be culpable: 'They were hostages to the worldview of the British working class, and the history of the nineteenth-century industrial revolution.' But wasn't this precisely at the cost of attending to Australia's history, which had its own unique circumstances and problems? It was as if nearly everyone she knew, whether on the right or on the left, had thoroughly negated the fact that they were Australians and were responsible for being so. Conway's own perspective, therefore, was that it was necessary 'to give up the pretenses of the old British empire, recognize that we were a Southern Pacific nation, and begin to study and understand the peoples and countries of our part of the globe' (182). This meant both greater respect for her homeland, in that she would attend to it more seriously than many others, but also more criticism and condemnation too, in that she was learning that there were many more different sides to her world, some of them rather ugly, than she had once been led to believe. Her mother didn't like this either.

Notice what is happening here. Her family, she had learned, had been a party to the accession of land that might not rightfully be theirs. Her boyfriend, for all of his help in affirming her as an individual, had gotten upset when she proved herself to be as serious about her studies as she appeared to be. Her friends, irrespective of their political persuasions, might as well have gone to British optometrists given the spectacles through which they saw the world. And the history texts she was reading were so selective (to put it kindly) in their rendition of Australia's heritage that there was hardly anything at all in them about forms of life, such as life in the bush, whose story deserved to be told as much as any other. People were thriving, it seemed, on all of these representations, the authority of which was going largely unquestioned. Or, put another way, they were so caught up in the discursive order in circulation at the time, whether manifested in a college friend's desire to run off to Oxford or Cambridge to lead the good life or a contemporary history text's portrayal of Australian society as fundamentally derivative from Great Britain, that they were blinded to the reality of their situations.

Maybe she could change some of this, Conway thought, by playing some role in the 'general reorientation' of Australian culture and its relation to other cultures. Along with two of her closest friends, men with whom she shared a good deal intellectually, she therefore applied for a job that not only seemed to fit the bill of uniting theory with practice, but might provide her the means of escape from the predicament with her mother, which, despite a few pauses in the action, was as intense as ever. Her boyfriend might not be too pleased with this latest development, given that Conway was once more showing what her primary commitments were, but she couldn't please everybody. What a renegade she had turned into! She was that much more dumbfounded when, despite her outstanding qualifications, she was rejected for the job for which she had applied. The problem, in a nutshell, was that she was a woman. Some of her friends, who had inquired into the specifics of the case, were told that she was anything from too good-looking to too intellectually aggressive. But she was no different, she felt, from her male counterparts, both of whom had gotten the jobs.

'I could not credit that merit could not win me a place in an endeavor I wanted to undertake, that decisions about my eligibility were made on the mere fact of my being female instead of on my talents.' The rejection was troubling enough in its own right, but its implications for the future were downright devastating. If she couldn't move in the desired direction through merit, was she condemned to lead a life of endless plateaus, compromised and unjust? 'It was all prejudice', she writes, 'blind prejudice. For the first time, I felt kinship with black people.' Moreover, 'I could never remember the image of my parents resting in the evening, sitting on the front veranda step at Coorain, quite the same again' (191). Indeed, she began to see double: on the one hand, 'a golden image from childhood' and, on the other, the oppression of those whose lives had once given way so that her own family could be happy and comfortable, the trampled relics of the past lying beneath their very feet. This past, both the distant and the recent, her ancestors' and her own, would never be the same again, and neither would she; they were being rewritten, in both anger and sorrow, at the moment of her awakening from the slumber of the years. Here was a lesson she hadn't bargained for during the course of her studies, however much insight and wisdom she had gained along the way. It 'chilled' her to realize 'that there was no way to earn my freedom through merit. It was an appalling prospect' (192). But it was just this chill, this blast of cold air that had been blowing her way from time immemorial, that would send her, reeling, into the future, knowing that there was a great deal to be done.

A TALE OF TWO WORLDS

How could she have been so 'blind' and 'stupid'? The signs of prejudice and discrimination had been strewn about everywhere, from the job vacancies in newspapers to the cheap jokes she would overhear. But somehow she had thought that none of this applied to her. And then, of course, she had to suffer the customary shame for being so angry with herself, for letting this one little incident anger her; in the general scheme of things, a job rejection was pretty trivial. 'Yet try as I might', Conway admits, 'I couldn't choke back a sense of grief for my lost self' (194).

There were, however, some benefits to this loss. For one, it was useful in some ways to receive a 'few hard knocks', if only to shake one loose from complacency and self-satisfaction. It was good especially to be forced to think, seriously, about what it meant to be a woman. All of the radical feminist tracts in the world might not amount to anything if the real life experience of oppression isn't there. It is one's own life activities and practices in the world that change consciousness, Marx tells us, not ideas alone. Perhaps she needn't chastise herself too much, then, for her ignorance and blindness. It is hermeneutically inappropriate, we might say: she is using an after-the-fact insight that accrued from the concrete fact of her oppression to reflect back on her before-the-fact world, thus bringing an interpretive context to bear on that world that did not exist at the time. In any case, she was gratified to have learned, even if the hard way, that one may occasionally be jolted out of the realm of appearance, only to realize, humbly, that one isn't so clever after all.

Conway also began to identify more with women and their various plights after this event, which gave her not only a strong intimation of what she might want to study in the future, but a healthy dose of empathy as well, even for her mother. The dilemma she had been dealing with was suddenly being thrust under a new light; her perceptions grew to be so troubling and painful they could hardly be endured. 'As I sat listening to her railing against her life', Conway writes, 'I would place beside her in my mind's eye the young competent woman, proud, courageous, and generous, I'd known as a child. I was living with a tragic deterioration', she realized, 'brought about because there was now no creative expression for this woman's talents.' The result was all too predictable: 'Lacking a power for good, she sought power through manipulating her children.' Her mother's life, therefore, was being rewritten too. It wasn't merely a pathetic decline, wrought by personal weakness or unending grief or poor health or some such thing; it was a tragedy, 'the outcome of many impersonal forces, which had combined to emphasize her vulnerabilities'.

So it was that a mind 'once engaged in reading every major writer of the day now settled for cheap romances, murder mysteries, and a comfortable fuzz of tranquilizers and brandy at the end of the day'. As for the source of this tragedy, a significant portion of the blame, Conway came to feel, could be levelled at the very world she had been inhabiting: 'Society encouraged a woman to think her life finished after her husband's death and encouraged a woman's emotional dependence on her children' (195).

It is true, of course, that someone else might have responded differently to the train of events that had come her mother's way. Perhaps, for instance, they would have used them as fuel for the future, as a means of provoking them into actions they might otherwise not have taken. As such, if we wish to speak of social determination or social construction, which seems thoroughly appropriate in a context like the present one – wittingly or not, Conway's mother had been operating under the ostensibly well-circulated idea that there were certain things widows like her could do with their lives, certain stories they could tell, while others were out of bounds – it is essential that we not do so in an overly mechanical fashion. As Durkheim (1951) told us, social facts undoubtedly exert something like causal force upon individuals, even to the extent of their sometimes electing to kill themselves; thus suicide, for some the pre-eminent example of the radicality of human choice and freedom, may itself be socially determined. None of this means that an individual's own unique existence is unimportant or beside the point; it only means that the social world, that realm of 'impersonal forces' of which Conway speaks, is nonetheless constitutive – in one way or another – of the shapes our lives assume. This, again, is why a life such as her mother's – and, of course, her own – may be seen as a sign, a double sign, signifying both an individual history and a social one.

I do not mean to separate these artificially, as if the 'purely individual' dimension of a life could wholly be teased apart from the 'purely social'; practically speaking, the twin histories we are discussing are collapsed into one, the life in question. More to the point still, there is good reason to believe that the notions of 'purely individual' and 'purely social' are idealizations, having no real referents in the world; there is nothing, in other words, that can be considered either of these in the strict sense, neither the most radical act of individuality nor the most conformist act of 'groupthink'. All I mean to say is that a life history, as the product of my own unique experiences within the social world, has a dual reference, to the unique experiences and to the world. This is why just as the psychoanalyst might have a field day with Conway's mother, so too might the sociologist or the anthropologist or the historian. Multivocal, these texts are. This, in fact, was precisely Conway's discovery as she began to see her mother's life in a different light from how she had. There were many ways to read, some of them quite sad.

Conway decided to accompany her mother on her 'long-dreamed-about' trip to England and Europe. Whether they would get along or not didn't matter much at this point; given all that her mother had done for her, it was the least she could do. It wasn't clear what else she could do now anyway. Academia still seemed the most sensible choice, but there also remained a nagging fear about doing something that was 'universally seen as unfeminine. I feared the only sensible choice for me', she writes, 'because I was too uncertain of my identity as a woman to risk the cultural dissonance the choice involved' (196). There were times when there was the urge to forget about becoming a scholar and adopt instead the 'expected pattern', settling down to a peaceful married life. But travel would do some good; it would serve as a kind of moratorium abroad, after which time perhaps her plans for the future might congeal.

It would also serve to correct certain of Conway's prejudices about both England and Australia. The landscape she encountered, for instance, proved to be disappointing. 'I could teach myself through literature and painting to enjoy this landscape', as she in fact had, 'but it would be the schooled response of the connoisseur, not the passionate response one has for the earth where one is born' (198). Further along these same lines, she writes, 'I realized that the English romanticism I had taken for a universal was a cultural category in which I did not participate . . . that I was from another world and would have to arrive at my cultural values for myself' (203). Once again, therefore, Conway, through her own concrete experience, was led to challenge and denature those modes of representation that conferred primacy upon a singular way of being in the world – as if those fortunate enough to live in a certain locale had somehow cornered the market on the sublime. This is not to detract from those who did indeed experience their worlds as sublime; for them, apparently, it was. But what becomes constituted as sublime, possessing a kind of transcendent value for those able to partake, she realized, does so in virtue of the cultural tradition – with its own circumscribed discursive space, as we called it earlier – of which one is a part.

Now as we noted in the third chapter, to speak of the centrality of tradition in this context is not to claim that we are merely taught cultural values or merely conditioned to have aesthetic experiences in some settings rather than others – which would imply that what gets designated as sublime and beautiful and what gets designated as vile and disgusting is essentially arbitrary. Rather, it means that belonging to a tradition, to a particular discursive space, with its own order, reality, and truth, is a necessary condition for the sort of experience we are considering. Whether or not there is any dimension of tradition that cuts across all cultures (we could, of course, speak of 'human nature' as well, as we are inclined), which would make for the possibility of universal (rather than local) aesthetic experience, I cannot say. I certainly wouldn't rule this out. But the relativity of what moves us, deeply and profoundly, is enough to suggest that at least some aesthetic experience depends on our own rootedness in culture itself.

This might strike the reader as a merely academic point, which, in certain respects, it is. But the more general problem – namely, the problem of representation, how it gets done, and who does it – is not. The perpetual battles that take place over curricular issues (of which the lingering 'great books' controversy is, again, an especially notable one) and the ideological blood that is spilled over them indicates otherwise. Conway herself, upon 'recharting the globe', as she puts it, would probably have much to say about this issue. For the very fact that she had witnessed firsthand a transmutation from (putative) nature into culture, thereby exposing the imperialistic presumptions of much of her previous education in the process, meant that significantly more than academic claptrap was at stake. Indeed, wasn't there a sense in which Conway's processes of both rewriting her self, subsequent to the job rejection, and recharting the globe, subsequent to her trip abroad, were each moments in a larger and more fundamental crisis of representation? Hadn't 'woman' been naturalized and made singular in its voice, with dissenters being regarded as deviants from the true path of femininity, in much the same way that cultural constructs, owing to repeated gestures of what Conway refers to as England's 'imperial complacency', had been reified into the status of things?

Despite the profound discoveries Conway made during the course of her travels, she eventually became bored, feeling that it was time to get on with her life. The moratorium had apparently worked, for it had become quite clear what she would do upon returning: 'I was going home to study history. It was no use pretending I wasn't a scholar.' This would have been an act of self-deception and, more perniciously, an act of acquiescence to that power structure that had sought to prevent her from joining the desired ranks; 'I could certainly make myself an idle life in London being another expatriate Australian enjoying the cultural riches of the city, but that was to live perpetually by the standards of a culture I now saw as alien' (209). There were better things to do. The flight home was a sign of what was to come, the accents of the Australian stewards and stewardesses, previously exemplars of 'deviation from standard English speech', being heard instead as one mode of speaking among others, 'an inheritance of history and dialect'. Conway would live in suspicion henceforth, and keep a vigilance over the issue of representation. She would be attuned to difference and plurality rather than hierarchy and deviation from socially constructed norms. A developmental project was in the making, and it would have at its foundation not the ironclad telos of some absolute idea, pulling her toward the future evermore with its inexorable force, but the open-endedness of life itself, which would be perpetually rewritten in line with the revelations to come.

THE VERTIGO OF DEVELOPMENT

If Conway were to go ahead and carry out her plans, she would have to make some sort of break with her mother by living apart from her. Only this, as simple a practical gesture as it was, could lead to the life she desired – more important, the life she felt she *ought* to be leading. Establishing an appropriate vocation, in other words, had been precisely the vehicle by which Conway had arrived at an authentic resolution to the dilemma she faced. Practically speaking, the job abroad would have done the trick; the separation would have been brought about. But no developmental work would have been done. She would simply have been seizing upon the immediate circumstances in order to flee from her responsibility to make the break clean. There was no avoiding this responsibility now, however. For the question was no longer one about self-interest versus filial devotion, as it had been years ago when she first felt the urge to flee. Indeed, in an important sense there was no longer a question at all; the project she had set before her had already acquired its natural contours from the course of her history, and the issue of its validity had come and gone.

In the language of the developmental framework I have been employing throughout this book, the moment of articulation was past. If there was any question at all, therefore, it was how to appropriate the decision that had been made, how to bring it into practice. Little wonder that Conway kept 'backsliding' about this matter. Meanwhile, by the time she returned to studying history and could see that the interests she was developing could well take her significantly farther beyond the confines of her mother's home than she had assumed, it was that much more clear that she would have to speak up, and soon. She would leave her mother and her motherland, in league all along, her desire to resist their authority outweighing the undying love she had for them. At one point there had been a pull to be responsible to her mother since it was the daughterly thing to do. Later on, there was the need to be responsible to her country, particularly in so far as it continued to suffer from an identity crisis. Now if we wanted to be simplistic about it, we could say that she had decided that her primary responsibility was to be to herself. But what had happened instead, I will offer, was that this project came to represent what – for her, for now – was a workable balance *between* self and other. I say 'for her, for now' in order to underscore the idea that just as there is no absolute end to the process of development, neither is there a definitive self–other balance. The balance tips, this way and that, throughout the course of our lives, in accordance – ideally – with the ends we deem most appropriate and most morally justifiable. Don't we rewrite the other and our relationship to the other at the very same time that we rewrite the self? Don't 'I' only exist in a kind of contrapuntal relation of difference to that which I am not? 'Your duty's to your talents', said a new companion of Conway's; 'no one else can develop your gifts' (228). The gift: that which is at once mine and yours, that which 'I' offer to the world.

Sad to say that Conway's break with her mother was being complicated by an 'increasingly stormy' relationship with her. She had been fortunate to gain the company of this new companion, she notes, who had confirmed her existence, including her commitment to her work, in every way; without him, she might not have dealt as well with the severe challenges she had to face. 'My mother was now an angry and vindictive woman, her rages out of all proportion to any real or imagined slight. She was most destructive toward her own children, especially where she had the power to damage their relationships with others' (231). Socially constructed venom or not, it was becoming more and more difficult for Conway to maintain that distance which would allow for empathy and sympathy to remain. There was a limit to the care and understanding she could give to a seriously disturbed and vindictive woman. Perhaps it was an admission of defeat to 'turn tail' and 'run for cover' at this point, but enough was enough.

Conway was anything but delighted on the day of her departure. 'I felt more like an early Christian convert who has died to the old ways and lives under a new law.' What was this new law under which this new self, having been rewritten, would live? 'Mine was going to be a law of affirming life, regardless of past training' (232). It would be a life, therefore, in which she would try, as best she could, to transcend the specific manner in which she had been constructed, to exercise her will in such a way that she would live this life differently from how her own history might have led one to expect.

There are two common ways to understand this sort of proclamation. From one perspective, perhaps Conway has uttered these words in an audaciously unhermeneutic way: to think that she believed it possible to leap out of her own history, to carry on 'regardless of past training'. How could she leave the past behind? From another perspective, however, we can understand her attempt to live under this new law as an act of unadulterated freedom, of the sort metaphysicians and the like are wont to think about. 'As a historian I knew how few free choices ever face us in life, but this choice of mine now was unquestionably one' (233). It does seem that way, on the surface. But does the idea of freedom imply, then, that we can in fact step out of our own history? Once more, I would say no, not necessarily. What it does mean is that the life we live prepares us for a multiplicity of possible projects, the one that is ultimately adopted being more or less expectable depending on both our will to do this rather than that along with the various twists of fate that happen our way. What it also means, more generally, is that we need to think beyond the freedom–determinism antinomy as it is usually posed and see if there isn't a better way – a way that abides by own our immersion in history and acknowledges the circumscribed discursive space in which we exist and at the same time allows for the possibility of our saying or doing something new and original.

One further point is in need of reiteration. This possibility of which I am speaking, whether manifested in the form of a new work of art or a radical decision to leave one's homeland, does not ordinarily emerge 'regardless of past training' – that is, *despite* our own immersion in history – but *because* of it. It is true that according to the odds, it might not have been predicted that Conway would turn out to be as life-affirming as she did. But all this means, as far as I can tell, is that predictability, in the domain of human affairs, and in the sciences that study them, may not be as important a goal as it is often assumed to be. It is hardly shocking or incomprehensible or bizarre that Conway elected to do something different in the world; certain strands of her history – as we can see in retrospect – prepared her for this too. Thus her own decision, indeed her own *freedom*, emerged in and through the soil of her history.

Herein lies one of the most fundamental reasons for studying human lives historically, through the narratives people tell: we can learn about trajectories of experience that even prophets, in their eagerness to foretell the future, might have missed. What this implies, of course, is that some of the texts we read will be tales of freedom, narratives of human beings who have managed to emancipate themselves, not from history but from the expected course of things, dictated by the powers that be. And these narratives, as was intimated earlier in this chapter, may be exemplary in at least two respects. First, they will serve to signify our capacity to become conscious of our worlds and to make something of them; they will serve as testimony to our own power to challenge power and our own will to create. Second, they will serve as vehicles of revelation, uncovering those rules and regulations of the social world – some of which are 'good', some not-so-good – that often take us unawares.

In sum, then, to speak of the social construction of the self and of the narratives used to represent the self is not to claim that we are prisoners of history, mechanically determined by our conditioning. This is indeed what must be concluded if we follow through on the claims of those for whom the social world is the pre-eminent reality, determining all that we do. My own inclination, however, is not to go this route. Nor is it to claim that we are endowed with the magical ability to stand wholly apart from history, gazing at what goes on as if we didn't always already know. I prefer to say that while what I think and feel and do and say is surely a function of the time and place in which I live, and while it would surely be audacious if I thought otherwise, I also have the power – contingent, of course, on the conditions present, whether they are stultifying or liberating – to become conscious enough of my world to shape my destiny. Needless to say perhaps, I am relying on a kind of faith when I make this claim; it could very well be, I suppose, that I have no power at all, that I am nothing but a product or an ideological effect, a marionette whose strings are being pulled – even in my most impassioned acts of apparent freedom – by forces I will never know. By and large, however, I just don't happen to believe this is so. Again, the very fact that I can, on occasion, move in the direction of becoming conscious of the ways I am determined, suggests that there exists a margin of freedom within which to think, act, and be.

I realize that this might sound humanistically old-fashioned to some readers. With the rise of social constructionism especially, there has emerged the tendency to think of human beings as effects of one sort or another; if indeed we exist in and through language, in and through discourse, it is often argued, then we cannot help but be hard-pressed to find a defensible place for such notions as freedom, origination, and, of course, development. As I suggested in the very first chapter of this book, however, what has happened in virtue of this very move, in the social sciences and elsewhere, is that empiricism has emerged in full bloom once more: rather than being the products of stimuli or contingencies of reinforcement or sensory information, we are now the products of discourse, or of history, or of culture. As I also suggested earlier, there is a distinct positivistic dimension to this line of argument – whether it comes from a behaviorist or a social constructionist – as well. We *know* that discourse and all the rest affect us; we can prove it through empirical study. But we can never know, with any certainty, whether freedom exists or whether the self can indeed be seen as an originator of meaning and action, whether it can take what is and do something different with it. Consequently, the prevailing tendency seems to be stay with what we know, positively, and relegate what remains, in all of its shadowiness and ambiguity, to the status of metaphysical anachronisms. The implication is an ironic one. There is not only empiricism and positivism lurking beneath the exterior of much of contemporary thought, radical though it may seem; there is also a kind of scientism, dressed up in new and fancier garb.

Did Conway – *could* Conway – break the stronghold of determination and thereby succeed in living 'her own' life? In an obvious sense, no; she was living in the world, in language, as a social subject, and it would be patently absurd to suggest that there existed the possibility of wholly divesting herself of the myriad of factors and forces that had influenced and 'constructed' her. In a less obvious sense, however, she did indeed seem to break free, which is precisely what allowed her to follow through on her own path of development. Now once again, if we wanted to be strict empiricists about all this, we could simply claim that her background made this 'freedom' all but inevitable, that it was not only *conducive to* but *determinative of* the 'choices' she was ultimately able to make. She would thus indeed deserve to be called a product, an effect, the end result of a chain of causes, every bit as out of her control as the movement of the heavens. Her narrative, therefore, would not only be fictional but, empirically speaking, false: she thought that she had exercised her freedom and decided to tell a story of how it came to be, but in fact she had done nothing of the sort; she had simply done what had to be done, given the determinative forces in question. But can't it be said that her own narrative reflection itself, her own attempt to think through her history – her family, her homeland, her very *world* – served, as I put it earlier, in some sense to dissolve the chain of causation? Indeed, isn't the process of rewriting the self, of conferring new meaning upon that which might at one time have appeared to be sealed in stone, an index of freedom in its own right?

When Conway finally told her mother that she would be off to the United States to continue her studies in history, she did it in such a way that they would have to 'act out these events by the script she followed in public, the one in which she was the strong woman urging her children to range far and wide' (234–5). Perhaps there was an element of trickery involved in this scheme, in that her mother was clearly no longer the same 'strong woman'. There was no small amount of fear involved as well, as indicated by Conway's reluctance to reveal that her departure was for good. In certain respects, in fact, I would suggest that this final moment of Conway's narrative, the moment of appropriation, may be deemed somewhat incomplete. Even if the stoicism and communicative reticence that was part of Australian life (not to mention her mother's weakness as a partner in dialogue) led her to suppose that things would be better left unsaid, it is simply not clear that Conway had worked through her departure sufficiently.

This could be a rhetorical device on her part. After having told something of an heroic story of her own emancipation from a whole slew of fetters, from mother to motherland, perhaps there was the need to show that she was a fragile human being after all, one who could still take the easy way out of a difficult situation. In her own eyes, however, she was more than just fragile, much more. Indeed, there really was no appropriate genre to represent what was happening. 'The journey I was about to take', Conway writes, 'didn't fit so neatly into any literary categories I knew'. She had come upon hard times and had sought a way out, 'because I didn't fit in, never had, and wasn't likely to'. Alongside the story of the hero was one about a lost soul, a woman who had found 'emotional exile' to be an appropriate option, a woman who, having found herself ill at ease in her own country, 'was going to another country, to begin all over again'. She had come a long way, and would no doubt go still farther along the path of development, but this was hardly the time for a triumphant ending. In some ways, says Conway, it was just the opposite: 'I searched my mind for narratives that dealt with such thorough and all-encompassing defeats, but could come up with none' (236).

Here was another rewriting. The truth was, there were many things she ought to have done. She should have tried to stop her mother from drinking and taking tranquilizers to cut her pain; she should have let her feel the rage that was rightfully hers, but she just hadn't risen to the occasion. 'I had certainly tried to rescue her, stimulate her interests, get her involved in charities', Conway could tell herself, 'anything to harness her energies creatively'. But there was still no getting around the fact that she had been a 'dismal failure'. Heroes often have high expectations, of course, and perhaps they fall that much harder when they meet with those events that can only be construed in terms of defeat. It could be that there was no way to help her mother as she wished, no matter what she had done. But for one who was used to shouldering the burden of responsibility for the course of events, this was inconceivable. The verdict was guilty as charged, and restitution would have to come later, through 'some sublimated expression' in her intellectual life. It was curious how things had turned out. 'It wasn't exactly the way I expected to find a vocation, out of guilt transmuted into an intellectual calling, but perhaps it was as good as any' (237).

The ending of Conway's story is bathed in self-punitiveness. Despite the care she had given her mother, it had been hopelessly inadequate. Despite the fact that her mother might have been beyond repair, she ought to have been able to perform a miracle. Despite the fact that she obviously had a thoroughly genuine interest in intellectual life, it was difficult now to understand it except as a pitiful sublimation, a transmutation from guilt, with little intrinsic validity of its own. Much of this has the ring of psychological truth. As she herself indicates, she was guilty. So what sort of story is this? Is it about a saint or a sinner?

Conway knew of no narratives, she told us, that could compare to the one she had been brought to tell. There simply weren't many people as interested in revealing such 'thorough and all-encompassing defeats' as she was. This was hardly a total loss, however. In the absence of these narratives, she would have to write a new one, which would be a strange fusion of pride and shame, ungraspable through any unitary theme or plot, irreducible to anything that had been before. There was freedom even in defeat. Indeed, Conway's ending could be read – by us, if not by her, not yet – as being about exactly this. Perhaps there *was* no final resolution to the dilemma she had experienced. Perhaps this story would never really end, but instead go on forever, haunting her by its steadfast refusal to be closed, shut tight, its refusal to become another dead script that someone lived. She was neither saint nor sinner, but herself, a human being, sometimes heroic, sometimes pathetic, who had sought to embrace the vertigo of development.

What is it that I mean here by the vertigo of development? The idea of vertigo – let us think of it simply as existential dizziness – is often used alongside the idea of freedom. We are thrown into a world, the existentialists were fond of saying, in which we are, for better and for worse, condemned to be free. Now some of these existentialists, Sartre especially (prior, at least, to his discovery of Marx), might have gone a bit too far in this line of thinking, as if our very destiny were wholly in our control, as if we could become whoever we willed to become. The more moderate version of this thesis, in any case, is that living in the world, as a human being, entails no small measure of ontological discomfort, uncertainty, and, as above, dizziness: we have before us a world of possibilities and, in part – precisely in virtue of our freedom – we are left with the responsibility of deciding to whom and to what we are to devote our lives.

Some people, many people in fact, tended to flee from both their freedom and their responsibility, perhaps by stepping into narratives that had already been written. In this way, they would fend off the anxiety and the vertigo that would be part and parcel of creating their own. Others, however – Conway seems to have been one – refused to do this. As

Conway herself tells it, the result of her living the life she did is a narrative that cannot easily be assimilated into those narratives she already knew. The path of her own development, as told in her story, had itself been vertiginous; it had been saccadic, it had been heroic and cowardly, beautiful and ugly, comic and tragic. Perhaps there were some who, in the interest of telling a more coherent tale with a more definite and happy ending, would have gone about the task of rewriting their selves in an entirely different way. Conway, however, knew better. Appropriation could never be brought to completion. There would always be leftover conflicts and contradictions, that would be grist for the mill of the future, occasions for further developmental work to be done. If all went well, the future would bring better days. The self would be rewritten again, and again. Is it not precisely this plenitude of meaning, as it exists in the dialogic space between the 'I' who interprets and the 'me' that is the text, that serves in the end to signal the free operation of the narrative imagination?

Epilogue
Toward a poetics of life history

Steiner (1989) speaks of 'the pivotal place of self-portrayal in poiesis'. Indeed, paradoxically enough, he suggests, 'It is the autobiographical motif, the self-portrait which is the least imitative, the least mirroring of aesthetic constructs.' In this respect, it expresses the 'compulsion to freedom', the 'agonistic attempt to repossess, to achieve mastery over the forms and meanings' (205) of one's own being. But what is meant here by 'poiesis'? What might it mean to move toward a poetics of life history?

We might turn to poets themselves for some clues. Poets, it can be said, do not customarily strive for a mimetic re-presentation of the world as such, but nor do they write fictions, taken in the usual sense. What they often do instead, I will suggest, is *rewrite* the world, and in such a way that we, the readers, may find ourselves in the position of learning or seeing or feeling something about it that might ordinarily have gone unnoticed or unexplicated. This conception of what poets do, I hasten to emphasize, is by no means an exclusive one. There are some poets, for instance, who see their creations as worlds unto themselves, as autonomous pieces of reality in their own right, bearing little or no relation to what exists outside the text. By and large, however, I think it is fair to say that poetry still retains a certain 'aboutness', a certain attempt to take our own understanding and appreciation of things – whether outer or inner – to a different, and indeed deeper, level than routine experience permits. In this sense, it might be said further, even if awkwardly, that poetry represents an effort to depict that which is somehow realer than real, at least as this latter term is usually understood: it is an effort to go beyond the exterior of things and thus to show, precisely through the revelatory power of language itself, that the world is always capable of being thought anew.

Notice what is being said here about language. The poet employs words that, optimally, will tell us something, will articulate, will reveal to us, that which may not otherwise have been revealed. Language, therefore, far from necessarily leading to the obfuscation of experience – in the sense of placing us one step removed from the world, as we put it earlier – may sometimes succeed in placing us in it, taking us a step deeper. Now it could still be said, of course, that the 'aboutness' poetry often holds within it pertains more to language, discourse, texts, than to the world 'in itself'. But to think of things in this way, I would argue, only serves to hypostatize and reify the world, by imagining it as that which exists outside of or beyond language. Can't we say, instead, that poetry is about that languaged world in which we dwell?

To confer primacy upon language need not result in breaking the covenant between word and world; it only breaks the spell of that conception of the relationship which supposes language to be a mere mirror of the world, a transparent vehicle for its disclosure. We have indeed moved beyond this conception. But this is hardly ample reason to leap to the conclusion that words cannot disclose or reveal. To leap to this conclusion is in fact to fall prey to a fallacy as well as to a particularly crude form of either–or thinking: either language is a mirror or it is a reality unto itself, autistically self-enclosed, a veritable prison, in which there exist no doors leading out. Poetry itself tends to defeat this conclusion; even while showing the possible tenuousness and ambiguity of the relationship between word and world, it utters an adamant refusal to succumb to a wholesale break. Narratives in turn, of the sort we have been considering here, tend to do much the same sort of thing.

I do not mean to suggest that these narratives are themselves extended poems. This would be to dilute both the meaning of poetry and the meaning of narrative. Nor do I mean to suggest that the process of rewriting the self, as we have been exploring it, is better understood from the vantage point of 'art' rather than 'science'. This would not only commit me to a kind of aestheticism, but would serve to reify the ideas of both art and science, which is done enough already. Indeed, what I do want to suggest in this context is that, in a distinct sense, this process – like poetry itself – explodes the boundaries between the two: the narrative imagination, engaged in the project of rewriting the self, seeks to disclose, articulate, and reveal that very world which, literally, *would not have existed* had the act of writing not taken place. In this sense, life histories are indeed artifacts of writing; they are the upsurge of the narrative imagination. This, however, is hardly reason to fault them or to relegate them to the status of mere fictions. We too, *as selves*, are artifacts of the narrative imagination. *We*, again literally, would not exist, save as bodies, without imagining who and what we have been and are: kill the imagination and you kill the self. Who, after all is said and done, would want to die such a death?

Let us briefly review the terrain we have covered with these ideas in mind. In the case of Augustine, we encountered what I regard to be the central feature of rewriting the self: the process of conferring new meanings on the past in light of the present. Now for some, we learned, this very process could not help but entail an illusion, in the form of a falsification of what was. It was but a short step from here to the idea that perhaps life historical narratives were to be regarded as fictions, in the sense of being untrue to the movement of life itself. What Augustine's story showed us, however, was that there was another way of understanding this state of affairs, for it was precisely through the wisdom of hindsight, which is to say through narrative itself, that he was able to see the error of his former ways. Life itself, therefore, rather than being the yardstick against which to measure the truth or falsity of narrative, could in a certain sense be untrue in its own right, such that only the passage of time could determine its meanings. Narratives, in turn, rather than being the mere fictions they are sometimes assumed to be, might instead be in the service of attaining exactly those forms of truth that are unavailable in the flux of the immediate.

What Augustine's story was also about, it was suggested, was the idea of development. Now the idea of development, as traditionally understood, is often seen to move, in parallel with life itself, essentially forward in time; that is, it is often seen as the steady, evolution-like emergence of a project, pointing irrevocably toward the future. In line with what Augustine told us, however, we learned that this too might be understood in a different way: development, rather than adhering strictly to the forward-looking arrow of linear time, was itself bound up with narrative and was thus thoroughly contingent on the backward gaze of recollection. Once more, of course, there may be some for whom this very fact signals the death knell to the idea of development itself: in exposing it for the narrative creation it patently is, it might be argued, the idea itself partakes of exactly those mythic tales of progress and growth we would do better without. My own perspective, however, is that this is not necessarily the case at all. Indeed, all that is implied in conceiving the idea of development through narrative is that the idea itself must be rethought in a more hermeneutically appropriate way.

In the case of Helen Keller, we inquired more fully into the relationship of word and world. Helen, having acquired much of her knowledge about both the outer and the inner world through what others told her along with what she read, had faced a painfully difficult and perplexing problem: she was ultimately unsure which of the words she uttered and indeed which of the thoughts she thought were her own, if any. Moreover, she was also unsure whether this 'self' she believed she was was anything more than a heterogeneous ensemble of texts. In true poststructuralist fashion, therefore, Helen herself had raised the possibility that both the outer and the inner world were in some sense artifacts of words, of language. What was suggested in response to this possibility, however, following Helen's very own reflections on the problem at hand (many of which seemed quite original), was that even while we are indeed bequeathed words that were on the scene well before we ourselves were, there nonetheless remained the prospect of breathing new life into them, thereby transforming their very meaning. What was also suggested, in turn, was that the self, despite its inability to be a sovereign origin of meaning, was significantly more than a merely imaginary artifact of words. The fact is, 'I' am often able to do something new with the words bequeathed me, thereby enlarging the scope of my self and my world.

After this time, we moved still further into the problems at hand by inquiring, through Sartre, into the relationship of living and telling. Living, Sartre's protagonist Roquentin seemed to believe, was in fact vastly different from telling about it, as it in fact is; while the former is a fundamentally open and indeterminate project, the latter, particularly in so far as it draws its very existence from endings, results in there being a kind of deceptive – and, once more, illusory – smoothness, consistency, and coherence to the stories told. Yet again, therefore, narrative was seen to be a far cry from life itself, perhaps even serving as a delusional defense against the cold realization that our lives are indeed without rhyme or reason. That the disjunction between living and telling about it exists, it was agreed, goes without saying; the experience of ongoing moments is not quite the same as reflection upon them. Be that as it may, it was suggested that these very moments, by occurring in time and by perpetually being imaginatively integrated in an interrelated fashion, were themselves a part of the narrative order of experience, serving to condition the more comprehensive stories we might come to tell. Living, in short, may not be quite so far from telling as Roquentin and company seemed to assume.

A question still remained, however, concerning the truth value of these stories. Philip Roth, having apparently grown tired of spinning fictional yarns about his life, had expressed his determination finally to tell the unadorned truth, which he referred to as the facts, about his life. In the process of doing so, however, there was a sense in which he undermined the very project he had set before him: the telling of the facts, he avowed, proved to be inseparable from his present concerns and desires, inseparable from the hypotheses he was interested in raising, inseparable, ultimately, from the story he wished to tell in the first place. In this respect, Roth's trio of texts served to demonstrate the impossibility of returning to what was, in itself, and thus the impossibility of ever disentangling the facts from the stories we tell about them. What he also demonstrated was the utter slipperiness of the project of arriving at the truth of one's history, particularly to the extent that one imagines this truth simply to be there, like a piece of crystal, hard and sharp, awaiting discovery. Far from implying that truth is out of the question, however, all that is implied, I offered, is that it is precisely this crystalline notion of truth, based as it is upon the apparent split between subject and object, that is being rendered suspect. The fact that there is no historical truth outside of the narrative imagination, I went on to say, hardly renders the idea of truth itself suspect. What it means instead, quite simply, is that the project of arriving at the truth of one's history must also be rethought in a more fully hermeneutical way.

The next chapter, which explored Sylvia Fraser's life, took us in a somewhat different direction. Many of the issues we had been led to discuss had seemed to place more importance on how present determines past than on how past determines present; given the centrality of the narrative imagination, as embodied in the process of rewriting the self, it was only sensible to proceed in this way. Since we might have lost sight of the fact that what actually happens during the course of one's life may indeed affect its very shape, however, it was deemed useful to consider a text that recounted how concrete early experiences, in this case having to do with incest, could indeed contribute to who and what one became. This text, therefore, served as a kind of counterbalance to what had been discussed earlier, showing that the idea of causation (in the very broad sense of past determining present), while unquestionably problematic when applied to the human realm, is in certain instances not easily left behind: even as the self is rewritten, through the eyes of the present, the 'past present' itself may be working its ways, powerfully determining what can and cannot be understood and known. As for the implication, ambiguous though it may be, it is that we cannot think of this state of affairs in either–or terms but must instead embrace what I called a 'both–and' perspective, in which we are willing to read the text of a life both backward and forward. Only then can we do justice to both the poetic figuration of the past and the humbling power of fate.

The final chapter, it was noted, was also about 'determination', broadly taken, but this time in a quite different way, dealing more with social than psychic reality. In Jill Ker Conway's work, we in fact observed how thoroughly pervasive social reality could be, how it could permeate and constitute the very life one led, the very self one came to be, and the very narrative one came to tell about this self. We also called attention to the moral dimension of narrative in this context, for the sake of illustrating that the way in which one understands the movement of one's life – and, by extension, the way in which one understands development – is unthinkable outside of who and what one ought to be. Most centrally, however, what we learned through Conway's story is that even while both narrative and development may indeed deserve to be called 'socially constructed', in that the very conditions in and through which they emerge are part and parcel of social reality, there nevertheless exists the need to maintain a space for the exercise of human freedom: in relation to both living in the world and telling about it. Not only had Conway managed to indict certain features of the social reality in which she had lived, her consciousess arising essentially out of her own praxis, but she had also transgressed the very boundaries of narrative itself: there simply were no available storylines, she told us, that could adequately contain the unique contours of her own life. So it was that she would have to write a new story, one that was faithful to the vertiginous ambiguity of the developmental path she had traversed. And so it is, we might add, that what Steiner referred to as the 'compulsion to freedom', as expressed in both the poetic in general and the life historical in particular, plays itself out in the process of rewriting the self.

Now I want to offer a few brief words that I hope will be of some practical import for those interested in studying the self – along, of course, with the world – through life historical texts. My task in the present book has been to take up a variety of issues pertinent to this notion of rewriting the self through exploring autobiographies and, in one case, a work of fiction. Given the kinds of readings I had been doing and given the profound hold some of these texts wound up having on me, this seemed like a good route to take; they would put some much-needed flesh on the issues with which I was dealing and thus allow me to concretize the overarching project at hand.

There is much more to be done along these lines, I believe. Despite calls throughout the history of the social sciences (psychology in particular) to take on the challenges posed by the kinds of works we have been considering, it has been done only rarely. Among the many reasons for this, there is but a single glaringly obvious one: inquiries of this sort have not been considered important enough and valid enough by traditional empiricist standards to warrant attention. Relatedly, there may also be the suspicion – and I must admit, this one is quite correct – that inquiries of this sort are simply not 'psychological', taken in the strict sense. It is true: what I have done here is part psychology, part philosophy, part literary criticism, and part several other things too. I also realize that for some, and precisely in virtue of these different 'parts', this book may reek of just that sort of liberal pluralistic eclecticism that defenders of the faith in the hermetically-sealed autonomy of the disciplines love to rip apart. There are many different ways to respond to these criticisms. Here are a choice few.

As concerns the putative failings of this sort of work by 'traditional empiricist standards' (As in, Where are the hypotheses? The methods? The findings?), my own feeling is that these standards – parochial, restrictive, and downright silly as they often are, particularly to the extent that they are assumed to be *the* way – need to be challenged, and challenged radically. No one has cornered the market on what does and does not constitute valid and important knowledge. As concerns the suspicion that works of this sort are not truly or strictly 'psychological', while this is undoubtedly so on some level, as I have avowed above, we might wish to question this very strictness as well. Despite what the 'authorities' may maintain, there is no reason to assume that psychology *is* this or *is* that simply because they say so; again, things can, and do, change. Finally, as concerns the notion that works of this sort signal the possible demise of discipline-based (and for some, perhaps, disciplined) thinking more generally, all I will say is that there is often good reason to move beyond the confines of singular methodological approaches, modes of analysis, and genres of writing. While 'blurred genres', as Geertz (1980) has called them, may occasionally lead to blurred vision, they can also lead to a greater fidelity to the proverbial 'things themselves' than might otherwise have been possible.

A couple of qualifications of these points are in order. If in fact there exists the desire not only to do interesting and innovative work but to transform the discipline of psychology itself, then it will be necessary to proceed in such a way that people will listen. As I have already suggested, one of the less salutary outcomes of the rise of interpretive approaches, particularly in psychology, is that rather than narrowing the split between the sciences and the humanities, some of the work presently being done serves, even if unintentionally, to deepen it, thereby leaving the 'two cultures' largely intact. More specifically, what often happens is that the notion of science gets hypostatized in order both to cast it aside and to pave the way for the latest (non-scientific) thing. Now as I also suggested earlier, science-bashing undoubtedly has its allure, particularly for those humanists eager to put forth a 'softer' vision of things. But the truth is, it gets us nowhere.

The second qualification is that there is the need, among interpretively oriented psychologists, to move beyond programmatic pronouncements about why the discipline ought to change and to begin to do the desired work itself.[1] Many of us have a certain fondness for the 'meta' level of analysis, i.e. that level from which we gaze upon the totality of our respective fields to see what's gone wrong. This moment of our inquiries must certainly remain. But to the extent that the methodological and the metatheoretical become ends in themselves, we run the risk once again of excluding ourselves from those very arenas of discourse with which we wish to become engaged.

Qualifications aside, my own conviction is that inquiring into human lives – whether through autobiographical texts, fictional texts, interviews, ethnographic fieldwork, whatever – holds rich opportunities for those who are interested both in keeping a foothold in the 'meta', as it were, and in generating ideas that will ideally be of value not only for furthering psychological understanding but for furthering our own practical impact on these lives themselves. I am neither talking here about social engineering nor claiming that we, academic researchers and theorists, ought to be in the business of telling others how to live. Our own lives are often troubling enough. But surely it is not outside the bounds of possibility to suppose that some of the work we do, even if its primary role is but an exemplary one – i.e. 'This is what a life can be like', 'This is how someone can be defeated or rendered unconscious', 'This is how someone can reclaim his or her history', and so on – might be of value to someone besides ourselves. As an aside, it should be noted that, whether we intend it so or not, the work we do does indeed have impact on people, even if only in what might appear to be relatively insignificant ways; for better or worse, it often steps outside the offices, labs, and so forth we inhabit. To the extent that this is so, we had better be cognizant both of what it is we are doing and what sort of impact we would like it to have.

I have entitled this epilogue 'Toward a poetics of life history', which might on the face of it have seemed strange and perhaps even contradictory, given my earlier comments regarding some of the pitfalls of aestheticism. Let me therefore explain a bit further, calling attention now to another dimension of this project. In considering life histories, and especially in considering the process of rewriting the self, as it has been discussed here, we are immediately confronted with the reality of not just one poetic act – that of the person who is pausing to reflect on the movement of his or her life – but two: we ourselves, to the extent that we aspire to do anything more than merely transcribe the texts of those we study, are involved in the task of making sense of what gets said, of creating an interpretive context within which the information before us may be placed. There is thus no effacing the poetic dimension of the processes at hand: historical interpretation, whether of self or other, far from simply finding what is already there, immanent in the data, relies through and through on the imaginative capacities of those doing the interpreting. I will be quick to add, however, that this same interpretive context, while underdetermined by the data themselves – in all of their potentially profound multiplicity and heterogeneity of meaning – must still take its primary call from them.

Without stretching the analogy too far, consider once more for a moment what it is that poets are customarily thought to do. I said above that what poets often try to do is say something meaningful about the world, something that somehow articulates what might heretofore have been inarticulate, that takes our appreciation or understanding beyond where it had previously been. Stated another way, they do not ordinarily rest content with merely transcribing the world, in purely 'documentary' fashion. Instead, and again, the desire is to seize upon what exists and imaginatively transform it, through language, such that we, the readers, find ourselves in the position of seeing it in a new light. Along these lines, then, it was said that poets seek to *rewrite* the world, the juxtaposition of the new against the old being embodied metaphorically in their resultant visions.

In a crudely empiricist sense, we also noted, the poet's work may be seen as a step removed from the world, and thus a kind of fiction in its own right; if indeed the work represents an imaginative transformation of the data, the argument may go, then it is, by definition, set irrevocably apart from what *is*: in the non-poeticized reality we are thought to inhabit. But just as most poets will insist that they take their cues from reality itself, so too will they insist that the works they create, fictional though they may be from an empiricist perspective, are designed to speak something very much like the truth. Very well, then, the critic may continue; we will assume that poets aspire to seek the truth. But isn't their truth, derived as it is from the workings of their imaginations, of an entirely different sort from the one social scientists and the like seek? Only, I would answer, to the extent that the imaginations of the latter have been thoroughly excised from their endeavors. The fact of the matter is, when I sit down with the text of a life history before me and try to make sense of what it is that's being said – in line, of course, with the specific questions I bring to it – I had better be willing to exercise *my own* imagination, and strenuously, if my aim is to say something meaningful and truthful about it. Where then do meaning and truth reside? In the texts themselves or in me? The answer is plainly that they reside in *both*, precisely in the dialogic space of interpretation itself. This is so, I would argue, for any inquiry – be it 'artistic' or 'scientific' – that seeks to understand the features of the world.

In speaking of a poetics of life history, therefore, there is the need to reiterate that I do not do so at the expense of some other, manifestly more scientific point of view; that would be to serve as an accomplice in maintaining just the sort of epistemological splits I have been trying in this work to move beyond. I do so instead in order both to highlight the hermeneutically imaginative dimension that life historical inquiry requires and, more specifically, to suggest that at least a portion of our attention, as students of the genre, be devoted to the project of what might be termed a literarily-informed psychological criticism. This is not quite the same, I should note, as a psychologically-informed literary criticism, which is already well in place in certain quarters and which tends more toward generating literary theory than psychological theory. What I am proposing instead is a mode of inquiry that precisely in virtue of its being attuned to the poetic figuration of life itself – both as lived and as told – opens the way toward an enlarged understanding of self and world.

Lest this seem too grand a project, I will hasten to add that this idea is by no means mine alone – witness Freud's earliest psychoanalytic work, for example. Freud himself, it seemed, was a bit uncomfortable with the direction in which some of this work was taking him. He wrote (1893–5)

> Like other neuropathologists I was trained to employ local diagnoses and electro-prognosis, and it still strikes me myself as strange that the case histories I write should read like short stories and that, as one might say, they lack the serious stamp of science.

Even as he was trying desperately to be scientific, in other words, the resultant works, oddly enough, were literary and artful, thus taking him away from what science was *supposed* to do and be. But why should this be so? Was it mainly Freud's own literary imagination that was responsible? Was it his own secret humanism, striving for expression? Not at all, he answers: 'I must console myself with the reflection that *the nature of the subject* [my emphasis] is evidently responsible for this, rather than any preference of my own.' The fact of the matter was, Freud goes on to explain, the usual methods led 'nowhere'; they simply didn't facilitate the acquisition of the understanding being sought. Despite their veneer of scientificity, therefore, they failed to do justice to the phenomena at hand. A 'detailed description of mental processes such as we are accustomed to find in the work of imaginative writers', on the other hand, resulted in 'at least some kind of insight' (160–1). Was Freud to be faulted if his own methods led him to see that the data at hand lent themselves to a more literary approach than he had initially assumed?

It was difficult for him to see what he was doing in terms other than of 'lack'; it simply didn't appear as rigorous and as 'serious' as what others were doing. The problem, however, was that if he was to stick with the usual methods – which, unlike his own, did indeed have the serious stamp of science – the results would ultimately be *less* faithful to 'the nature of the subject' than the more imaginative ones he himself was inclined to employ. Simply stated, then, what Freud realized was that if he wanted to be *truly* scientific rather than superficially so, if he wanted to abide by the phenomena themselves, he would have to include a measure of the poetic in his work.

He therefore decided to keep his own methods, toward the end not of surpassing science but of transforming it, provoked first and foremost by the call of the phenomena at hand. A science of human life shorn of the poetic, he had learned, would be incomplete; it would be rigorous, perhaps, but ultimately empty and false. In significant part, it was exactly this conviction that got Freud into so much hot water through the years. His creation was too much of a hybrid, many have complained, a strange amalgam of both science and art, which in certain important respects cast into question the very dividing line between the two. Little wonder that scientists and humanists alike have persistently taken him to task for refusing to play by the rules. We would nevertheless do well to follow his lead. Needless to say perhaps, skeptics beware: only if we are ready and willing to take a leap of the imagination – a leap, indeed, of faith – will we find inquiry into the elusive being we call the 'self' worthwhile.

Notes

1 REWRITING THE SELF

1. On the basic concepts and problems attendant to the idea of hermeneutics, see Gadamer (1975, 1976, 1979), Habermas (1971, 1983, 1984), Heidegger (1962), Hoy (1978), Ricoeur (1970, 1974, 1976, 1981); also, with more explicit reference to the social sciences, see edited volumes by Messer, Sass, and Woolfolk (1988), Packer and Addison (1989), and Rabinow and Sullivan (1979, 1987).
2. Much of what has come to be called deconstruction can be traced to the work of Derrida (e.g. 1976, 1978, 1982).
3. Although there are few thinkers who actually call themselves poststructuralists, Foucault (e.g. 1973, 1977, 1980) might be considered a suitable exemplar, as might Barthes (e.g., 1973, 1977, 1989). See also Megill (1985) for an extended discussion of those whom he considers to be 'prophets of extremity', including Derrida, Foucault, and Nietzsche.

2 THE STORY OF A LIFE

1. On the emergence of the modern self, see Bellah (1987), Bellah *et al.* (1985), Lasch (1984), MacIntyre (1981), and, for an especially comprehensive treatment, Taylor (1989).
2. For accounts discussing the relativity of concepts of self to time and place, see Baumeister (1987), Geertz (1979), Mauss (1979), Sampson (1989), Shweder and Bourne (1984), and Weintraub (1975). See also the volume edited by Carrithers *et al.* (1985).
3. For anthropological comments on the interrelationship of concepts of person and concepts of time, see Geertz (1973).
4. See Barthes (1973), Eakin (1985), Gunn (1982), MacIntyre (1981), Ricoeur (1981), and also the volumes edited by Mitchell (1981) and Sarbin (1986).
5. For the issue of 'plotting', see Brooks (1985), White (1973, 1978), and, once again, Ricoeur (1984, 1985, 1988).
6. The issue of memory is taken up in considerable detail by Bartlett (1967), Bergson (1959), Casey (1987), Crites (1986) Earle (1972), Husserl (1964),

Mandel (1980), Meacham (1972), Olney (1980), Schachtel (1959), Wollheim (1984), and a variety of others besides.
7   On the issue of metaphor, see Lakoff and Johnson (1980), Olney (1977), Ricoeur (1977), and also the volume edited by Johnson (1981).
8   For reflections on the notion of 'text' as a model for human action, see especially Ricoeur (1981), and also Bakhtin (1986), Freeman (1985a), Gergen (1988), and also the volume edited by Shotter and Gergen (1989).
9   On the problem of 'endings', see especially Brooks (1985) and Kermode (1967).
10 For a notable variant of this thesis in relation to psychoanalytic epistemology, see Spence (1982) and also Schafer (1983). For a critique, see Freeman (1985b).

3 IN THE NAME OF THE SELF

1   For important reflections on the 'borrowed' dimension of language, see especially Bakhtin (1981, 1986).
2   Particularly relevant here is the notion of 'intertextuality', which is discussed by Caws (1981), Culler (1981), and Riffaterre (1978).
3   One of the most compelling discussions of concepts and problems attendant to the idea of identity remains James (1950).
4   For further discussion, see Nietzsche (1980). For an interesting consideration of this problem in relation to Nietzsche's work, see Nehamas (1985).
5   In recent years, much of this debate owes existence to Bloom's provocative *The Closing of the American Mind* (1987). For a somewhat less philosophically informed treatment of related issues, see also Hirsch (1987).

4 LIVING TO TELL ABOUT IT

1   For further reflections by Sartre on the issues at hand, see his autobiography, *The Words* (1981) as well as useful comments by Charmé, whose *Meaning and Myth in the Study of Lives* (1984) offers an in-depth treatment of both Sartre and Freud.
2   See especially Weintraub (1975), who tries to distinguish between the memoir and autobiography 'proper', Lejeune (1989), and also the volume edited by Olney (1980b).
3   In addition to Freud's reflections on archeology already referred to (1901–5a, 1913, 1937), see also Freud (1901, 1910, 1914, 1918).
4   See Brooks (1985) for his interesting idea that the 'anticipation of of recollection' may be seen as 'our chief tool in making sense of narrative, the master trope of its strange logic' (23). See, in addition, Danto (1985).
5   On the idea of 'deferred action,' see Freud (1895, 1896, 1918).

5 FACT AND FICTION

1   Freud conveys a similar idea in his insistence that infantile mental formations, rather than being superseded, are better seen as 'overlaid', the result being that

'in spite of all later development that occurs in the adult, none of the infantile mental formations perish' 1913:184).
2 On the problem of defining autobiography, see Lejeune (1989).
3 Lacan (1981) conveys a similar idea that 'it is in relation to the real that the level of phantasy functions. The real supports the phantasy, the phantasy protects the real' (41).
4 See Schiff (1990) for comments related to Roth's largely mistaken assumption that he was indeed having a breakdown. As it turned out, part of Roth's problem was organically based; two prescribed drugs had interacted, apparently, in such a way as to culminate in something that appeared very much like 'madness'. In this respect, some of his own self-accounting may have been somewhat more fictional than he himself knew at the time. Strange that his book should be about precisely this issue.
5 See Martin's *Who Am I This Time?* (1988) for some interesting comments related to the 'fictionalization' of contemporary life.
6 See Gergen and Gergen (1986) for a variant of this basic thesis, as applied to developmental psychology.
7 See, for instance, Danto (1965, 1985), Dray (1957), Gallie (1964), Mandelbaum (1977), Mink (1965, 1968, 1981), Walsh (1951, 1974), and Wyatt (1964).
8 Von Wright's (1971) comments may be useful in this context.
9 See again Lejeune (1989) for his discussion of the 'autobiographical pact'.
10 This 'central motive' may be seen as tied to what Luckacher (1986) calls the 'primal scene,' which refers not only to the sorts of founding events Freud referred to, but to the unseen scenes, as it were, that are inevitably pointed to as we consider the problem of our own origins more generally.
11 Bakhtin's (1986) comments are once again useful in this context, as are those of Gadamer (1975, 1976) and Jauss (1982, 1989).
12 See especially Ricoeur (1970) for a masterful treatment of the symbol as a vehicle of both concealment and revelation.
13 In addition to this essay, see also Gadamer (1975, 1976) for comprehensive discussions of the interpretation of texts. On the relation of text and context, see Bakhtin (1986) and, also, for an interesting application to developmental psychology, Tappan (forthcoming).
14 See Ricoeur (1981) on the model of the text in relation to the idea of 'traces'.

6 THE PRIMAL SCENES OF SELFHOOD

1 For a treatment of the 'common sense' dimension of psychoanalysis, see Schafer (1976, 1978). For a critique of just this, see Barratt (1978).
2 On the question of why psychoanalysis can't help but be 'experience-distant' on some level, see Ricoeur's (1981) essay on the question of 'proof' in psychoanalysis.
3 See, for instance, Hempel's (1966) rationale for including 'inductive-probabilistic' hypotheses under the aegis of his 'covering law' model of scientific and historical explanation.
4 As I, along with Rick Robinson, argue in 'The development within' (1990), it may very well be the case that what is morally objectionable by most

consensually-established standards may still be in the service of development, taken broadly.
5 See again Freeman and Robinson (1990) for an attempt to question the notion that there may indeed be a 'ceiling' to the process of development.
6 In addition to Freud's own discussion of this case (1918), see especially Brooks (1985), Culler (1981), and Lukacher (1986).
7 For further comments on related issues, see Chapter 4, pp. 103–11.

7 WHO TO BECOME

1 For critical comments on Bellah *et al.*'s (1985) work, see Taylor (1989).
2 On the interrelationship of biography and society, see especially the volume edited by Bertaux (1981), in particular the pieces by Bertaux, Ferraroti, Hankiss, and Kohli. See, in addition, Bertaux and Kohli (1984).

EPILOGUE

1 For recent work on narrative, mainly from the perspective of psychology, see Bruner (1986), Cohler (1979, 1981), Freeman (1984), McAdams (1985), Polkinghorne (1988), Runyan (1982), Tappan (1989), as well as Sarbin's (1986) edited volume, Tappan and Packer's (1991) edited volume on narrative approaches to moral development, and the *Journal of Narrative and Life History* (Lawrence Erlbaum Associates Publishers).

References

Augustine, St (1980) *Confessions*, New York: Penguin Books (originally written 397).
Bakhtin, M. M. (1981) *The Dialogic Imagination*, Austin, Tex.: University of Texas Press.
—— (1986) *Speech Genres and Other Late Essays*, Austin, Tex.: University of Texas Press.
Barratt, B. (1978) 'Critical notes on Schafer's "action language" ', *Annual of Psychoanalysis*, 6: 287–303.
Barthes, R. (1973) 'An introduction to the structural analysis of narrative', *New Literary History*, 6: 237–72.
—— (1977) *Image, Music, Text*, New York: Hill & Wang.
—— (1989) *Roland Barthes*, New York: The Noonday Press.
Bartlett, F. C. (1967) *Remembering*, Cambridge: Cambridge University Press (originally published 1932).
Baumeister, R. F. (1987) 'How the self became a problem: a psychological review of historical research', *Journal of Personal and Social Psychology*, 52: 163–76.
Bellah, R. (1987) 'The quest for the self: individualism, morality, politics', in P. Rabinow and W. M. Sullivan (eds) *Interpretive Social Science: a Second Look*, Berkeley, Calif.: University of California Press.
Bellah, R., Madsen, R., Sullivan, W. M., Swidler, A., and Tipton, S. M. (1985) *Habits of the Heart: Individualism and Commitment in American Life*, New York: Perennial Library.
Bergson, H. (1959) *Matter and Memory*, Garden City, NY: Doubleday Anchor Books.
Bertaux, D. (1981) 'From the life-history approach to the transformation of sociological practice', in D. Bertaux (ed.) *Biography and Society*, Beverly Hills, Calif.: Sage.
Bertaux, D. and Kohli, M. (1984) 'The life story approach: a continental view', *American Review of Sociology*, 10: 215–37.
Bird, L. (1989) *Drive*, New York: Doubleday.
Bleich, D. (1978) *Subjective Criticism*, Baltimore, Md.: Johns Hopkins University Press.
Bloom, A. (1987) *The Closing of the American Mind*, New York: Simon and Schuster.
Brodski, B. and Schenck, C. (1988) 'Introduction', in B. Brodski and C. Schenck

(eds) *Life/Lines: Theorizing Women's Autobiography*, Ithaca, NY: Cornell University Press.
Brooks, P. (1985) *Reading for the Plot*, New York: Vintage.
Bruner, J. (1986) *Actual Minds, Possible Worlds*, Cambridge, Mass.: Harvard University Press.
Carrithers, M., Hollis, M., and Lukes, S. (eds) (1985) *The Category of the Person*, Cambridge: Cambridge University Press.
Casey, E. (1987) *Remembering: a Phenomenological Study*, Bloomington, Ind.: Indiana University Press.
Cassirer, E. (1944) *An Essay on Man*, Garden City, NY: Doubleday Anchor Books.
Caws, M. A. (1981) *The Eye in the Text: Essays on Perception, Mannerist to Modern*, Princeton, NJ: Princeton University Press.
Charmé, S. L. (1984) *Meaning and Myth in the Study of Lives*, Philadelphia, Pa.: University of Pennsylvania Press.
Cohler, B. J. (1979) 'Adult developmental psychology and reconstruction in psychoanalysis', in S. I. Greenspan and G. H. Pollock (eds) *The Course of Life*, Washington, DC: Government Printing Office.
Cohler, B. J. (1981) 'Personal narrative and life course', in O. G. Brim and J. Kagan (eds) *Life-span Development and Behavior*, vol. 4, Cambridge, Mass.: Harvard University Press.
Collingwood, R. G. (1946) *The Idea of History*, Oxford: Oxford University Press.
Conway, J. K. (1989) *The Road From Coorain*, New York: Alfred A. Knopf.
Costa-Lima, L. (1984) *Control of the Imaginary: Reason and Imagination in Modern Times*, Minneapolis, Minn.: University of Minnesota Press.
Crites, S. (1986) 'Storytime: recollecting the past and projecting the future', in T. R. Sarbin (Ed.) *Narrative Psychology: the Storied Nature of Human Conduct*, New York: Praeger.
Culler, J. (1981) *The Pursuit of Signs*, Ithaca, NY: Cornell University Press.
Danto, A. C. (1965) *Analytical Philosophy of History*, Cambridge: Cambridge University Press.
—— (1985) *Narration and Knowledge*, New York: Columbia University Press.
Derrida, J. (1976) *Of Grammatology*, Baltimore, Md.: Johns Hopkins University Press.
—— (1978) *Writing and Difference*, Chicago: University of Chicago Press.
—— (1982) *Margins of Philosophy*, Chicago: University of Chicago Press.
Dillard, A. (1987a) 'To fashion a text', in W. Zinsser (ed.) *Inventing the Truth: the Art and Craft of Memoir*, Boston, Mass.: Houghton Mifflin.
—— (1987b) *An American Childhood*, New York: Perennial Library.
Dilthey, W. (1976) 'The construction of the historical world in the human studies', in H. P. Rickman (ed.) *Dilthey: Selected Writings*, Cambridge: Cambridge University Press (originally published 1910).
Dray, W. (1957) *Laws and Explanation in History*, Oxford: Oxford University Press.
Durkheim, E. (1951) *Suicide*, New York: The Free Press (originally published 1897).
Eakin, P. J. (1985) *Fictions in Autobiography*, Princeton, NJ: Princeton University Press.
Earle, W. (1972) *The Autobiographical Consciousness*, Chicago, Ill.: Quadrangle Books.

Ferrarotti, F. (1981) 'On the autonomy of the biographical method', in D. Bertaux (ed.) *Biography and Society*, Beverly Hills, Calif.: Sage.
Foucault, M. (1973) *The Order of Things*, New York: Vintage.
—— (1977) *Language, Counter-Memory, Practice*, Ithaca, NY: Cornell University Press.
—— (1980) *Power/Knowledge: Selected Interviews and Other Writings, 1972–1977*, New York: Pantheon.
Fraser, S. (1987) *My Father's House: A Memoir of Incest and of Healing*, New York: Perennial Library.
Freeman, M. (1984) 'History, narrative, and life-span developmental knowledge', *Human Development*, 27: 1–19.
—— (1985a) 'Paul Ricoeur on interpretation: the model of the text and the idea of development', *Human Development*, 28: 295–312.
—— (1985b) 'Psychoanalytic narration and the problem of historical knowledge', *Psychoanalysis and Contemporary Thought*, 8: 133–82.
—— (1989) 'Between the "Science" and "Art" of interpretation: Freud's method of interpreting dreams', *Psychoanalytic Psychology*, 6: 293–308.
Freeman, M. and Robinson, R. (1990) 'The development within: an alternative approach to the study of lives', *New Ideas in Psychology*, 8: 53–72.
Freud, S. (1895) 'Project for a scientific psychology', in *Standard Edition* I, London: Hogarth.
—— (1893–5) 'Studies on hysteria', in *Standard Edition* II, London: Hogarth.
—— (1896) 'Further remarks on the neuro-psychoses of defence', in *Standard Edition* III, London: Hogarth.
—— (1899) 'Screen memories', in *Standard Edition* III, London: Hogarth.
—— (1901) 'Childhood memories and screen memories', in *Standard Edition* VI, London: Hogarth.
—— (1901–5a) 'Fragment of an analysis of a case of hysteria', in *Standard Edition* VII, London: Hogarth.
—— (1901–5b) 'Three essays on the theory of sexuality', in *Standard Edition* VII, London: Hogarth.
—— (1910) 'Leonardo Da Vinci and a memory of his childhood', in *Standard Edition* XI, London: Hogarth.
—— (1913) 'The claims of psychoanalysis to scientific interest', in *Standard Edition* XIII, London: Hogarth.
—— (1914) 'Remembering, repeating, and working through', in *Standard Edition* XII, London: Hogarth.
—— (1918) 'From the history of an infantile neurosis', in *Standard Edition* XVII, London: Hogarth.
—— (1927) 'The future of an illusion', in *Standard Edition* XXI, London: Hogarth.
—— (1937) 'Constructions in analysis', in *Standard Edition* XXIII, London: Hogarth.
Gadamer, H.-G. (1975) *Truth and Method*, New York: Crossroad.
—— (1976) *Philosophical Hermeneutics*, Berkeley, Calif.: University of California Press.
—— (1979) 'The problem of historical consciousness', in P. Rabinow and W. M. Sullivan (eds) *Interpretive Social Science: a Reader*, Berkeley, Calif.: University of California Press.

Gallie, W. B. (1964) *Philosophy and the Historical Understanding*, New York: Schocken.
Geertz, C. (1973) *The Interpretation of Cultures*, New York: Basic Books.
—— (1979) 'From the native's point of view: on the nature of anthropological understanding', in P. Rabinow and W. M. Sullivan (eds) *Interpretive Social Science: a Reader*, Berkeley, Calif.: University of California Press.
—— (1980) 'Blurred genres', *American Scholar*, 49: 165–79.
Gergen, K. J. (1977) 'Stability, change, and chance in understanding human development', in N. Datan and H. W. Reese (eds), *Life-span Developmental Psychology: Dialectical Perspectives in Experimental Research*, New York: Academic Press.
—— (1980) 'The emerging crisis in theory of life-span development', in P. Baltes and O. G. Brim (eds) *Life-span Development and Behavior*, vol. 3, New York: Academic Press.
—— (1988) 'If persons are texts', in S. B. Messer, L. A. Sass, and R. L. Woolfolk (eds) *Hermeneutics and Psychological Theory*, New Brunswick, NJ: Rutgers University Press.
—— (1991) *The Saturated Self*, New York: Basic Books.
Gergen, K. J. and Gergen, M. M. (1986) 'Narrative form and the construction of psychological science', in T. R. Sarbin (ed.) *Narrative Psychology: the Storied Nature of Human Conduct*, New York: Praeger.
Gilligan, C. (1982) *In a Different Voice*, Cambridge, Mass.: Harvard University Press.
Gunn, J. V. (1982) *Autobiography: Toward a Poetics of Experience*, Philadelphia, Pa.: University of Pennsylvania Press.
Gusdorf, G. (1980) 'Conditions and limits of autobiography', in J. Olney (ed.) *Autobiography: Essays Theoretical and Critical*, Princeton, NJ: Princeton University Press.
Habermas, J. (1971) *Knowledge and Human Interests*, Boston, Mass.: Beacon Press.
—— (1983) 'Interpretive social science vs. hermeneuticism', in N. Haan, R. N. Bellah, P. Rabinow and W. M. Sullivan (eds) *Social Science as Moral Inquiry*, New York: Columbia University Press.
—— (1984) *The Theory of Communicative Action: Reason and the Rationalization of Society*, Boston, Mass.: Beacon Press.
Hankiss, A. (1980) 'Ontologies of the self: on the mythological rearranging of one's life-history', in D. Bertaux (ed.) *Biography and Society*, Beverly Hills, Calif.: Sage.
Heidegger, M. (1962) *Being and Time*, New York: Harper & Row (originally published 1927).
Hempel, C. G. (1942) 'The function of general laws in history', *Journal of Philosophy*, 39: 35–48.
—— (1965) *Aspects of Scientific Explanation*, New York: New York University Press.
—— (1966) 'Explanation in science and in history', in W. Dray (ed.) *Philosophical Analysis and History*, New York: Harper & Row.
Hirsch, E. D. (1965) *Validity in Interpretation*, New Haven, Conn.: Yale University Press.
—— (1976) *The Aims of Interpretation*, Chicago, Ill: University of Chicago Press.
—— (1987) *Cultural Literary*, Boston, Mass.: Houghton Mifflin Co.
Hoy, D. (1978) *The Critical Circle: Literature, History, and Philosophical Hermeneutics*, Berkeley, Calif.: University of California Press.

Hume, D. (1874) *A Treatise on Human Nature*, London: Longmans, Green, & Co. (originally published 1739–40).
Husserl, E. (1964) *Lectures on the Phenomenology of Time Consciousness*, The Hague: Martinus Nijhoff (originally published 1905).
James, W. (1950) *The Principles of Psychology*, New York: Dover (originally published 1890).
Jauss, H. R. (1982) *Toward an Aesthetic of Reception*, Minneapolis, Minn.: University of Minnesota Press.
—— (1989) *Question and Answer: Forms of Dialogic Understanding*, Minneapolis, Minn.: University of Minnesota Press.
Johnson, M. (ed.) (1981) *Philosophical Perspectives on Metaphor*, Minneapolis, Minn.: University of Minnesota Press.
Keller, H. (1908) *The World I Live In*, New York: The Century Co.
—— (1974) *The Story of My Life*, New York: Dell Publishing Co. (originally published 1902).
—— (1988) *The Story of My Life*, New York: New American Library (originally published 1902).
Kermode, F. (1967) *The Sense of an Ending*, Oxford: Oxford University Press.
—— (1979) *The Genesis of Secrecy*, Cambridge, Mass.: Harvard University Press.
Kohli, M. (1980) 'Biography: account, text, method', in D. Bertaux (ed.) *Biography and Society*, Beverly Hills, Calif.: Sage.
Kundera, M. (1984) *The Unbearable Lightness of Being*, New York: Harper & Row.
Lacan, J. (1981) *The Four Fundamental Concepts of Psychoanalysis*, New York: W. W. Norton.
Lakoff, G. and Johnson, M. (1980) *Metaphors We Live By*, Chicago: University of Chicago Press.
Langer, S. (1942) *Philosophy in a New Key*, Cambridge, Mass.: Harvard University Press.
Lasch, C. (1984) *The Minimal Self*, New York: W. W. Norton.
Lee, D. (1959) *Freedom and Culture*, New York: Prentice-Hall.
Lejeune, P. (1989) *On Autobiography*, Minneapolis, Minn.: University of Minnesota Press.
Lukacher, N. (1986) *Primal Scenes*, Ithaca, NY: Cornell University Press.
MacIntyre, A. (1981) *After Virtue*, Notre Dame, Ind.: University of Notre Dame Press.
McAdams, D. P. (1985) *Power, Intimacy, and the Life Story: Personological Inquiries into Identity*, New York: Guilfor.
Mandel, B. (1980) 'Full of life now', in J. Olney (ed.) *Autobiography: Essays Theoretical and Critical*, Princeton, NJ: Princeton University Press.
Mandelbaum, M. (1977) *The Anatomy of Historical Knowledge*, Baltimore, Md.: Johns Hopkins University Press.
Martin, J. (1988) *Who Am I This Time? Uncovering the Fictive Personality*, New York: W. W. Norton.
Mauss, M. (1979) *Essays in Sociology and Psychology*, London: Routledge & Kegan Paul (originally published 1938).
Meacham, J. A. (1972) 'The development of memory abilities in the individual and society', *Human Development*, 15: 205–28.
Megill, A. (1985) *Prophets of Extremity*, Berkeley, Calif.: University of California Press.

Messer, S. B., Sass, L. A., and Woolfolk, R. L. (eds) (1988) *Hermeneutics and Psychological Theory*, New Brunswick, NJ: Rutgers University Press.

Mink, L. O. (1965) 'The autonomy of historical understanding', *History and Theory*, 5: 24–47.

—— (1968) 'Philosophical analysis and historical understanding', *Review of Metaphysics*, 21: 667–99.

—— (1981) 'Everyman his or her own annalist', in W. J. T. Mitchell (ed.) *On Narrative*, Chicago: University of Chicago Press.

Mitchell, W. J. T. (ed.) (1981) *On Narrative*, Chicago: University of Chicago Press.

Nehamas, A. (1985) *Nietzsche: Life as Literature*, Cambridge, Mass.: Harvard University Press.

Neugarten, B. L. (1969) 'Continuities and discontinuities of psychological issues into adult life', *Human Development*, 12: 121–30.

Nietzsche, F. (1968) *The Will to Power*, New York: Vintage (selections referred to originally published 1887, 1888).

—— (1980) *On the Advantage and Disadvantage of History for Life*, Indianapolis, Ind. Hackett Publishing Co. (originally published 1874).

Olney, J. (1972) *Metaphors of Self: the Meaning of Autobiography*, Princeton, NJ: Princeton University Press.

—— (1980a) 'Some versions of memory/Some versions of *Bios*: the ontology of autobiography', in J. Olney (ed.) *Autobiography: Essays Theoretical and Critical*, Princeton, NJ: Princeton University Press.

—— (ed.) (1980b) *Autobiography: Essays Theoretical and Critical*, Princeton, NJ: Princeton University Press.

Packer, M. J. and Addison, R. B. (eds) (1989) *Entering the Circle: Hermeneutic Investigation in Psychology*, Albany, NY: SUNY Press.

Polkinghorne, D. (1988) *Narrative Knowing and the Human Sciences*, Albany, NY: SUNY Press.

Rabinow, P. and Sullivan, W. M. (eds) (1979) *Interpretive Social Science: a Reader*, Berkeley, Calif.: University of California Press.

—— (eds) (1987) *Interpretive Social Science: a Second Look*, Berkeley, Calif.: University of California Press.

Ricoeur, P. (1970) *Freud and Philosophy: an Essay on Interpretation*, New Haven, Conn.: Yale University Press.

—— (1974) *The Conflict of Interpretations*, Evanston, Ill: Northwestern University Press.

—— (1976) *Interpretation Theory: Discourse and the Surplus of Meaning*, Fort Worth, Tex.: Texas Christian University Press.

—— (1977) *The Rule of Metaphor*, Toronto: University of Toronto Press.

—— (1980) 'Narrative time', in W. J. T. Mitchell (ed.) *On Narrative*, Chicago: University of Chicago Press.

—— (1981) *Hermeneutics and the Human Sciences*, Cambridge: Cambridge University Press.

—— (1983) 'Can fictional narratives be true?', *Analecta Husserliana*, 14: 3–19.

—— (1984) *Time and Narrative*, vol. 1, Chicago: University of Chicago Press.

—— (1985) *Time and Narrative*, vol. 2, Chicago: University of Chicago Press.

—— (1988) *Time and Narrative*, vol. 3, Chicago: University of Chicago Press.

Riffaterre, M. (1978) *Semiotics of Poetry*, Bloomington, Ind.: Indiana University Press.

Roth, P. (1988) *The Facts*, New York: Farrar, Straus & Giroux.
Runyan, W. M. (1982) *Life Histories and Psychobiography*, Oxford: Oxford University Press.
Sampson, E. E. (1989) 'The deconstruction of the self', in J. Shotter and K. J. Gergen (eds) *Texts of Identity*, London: Sage.
Sarbin, T. R. (ed.) (1986) *Narrative Psychology: the Storied Nature of Human Conduct*, New York: Praeger.
Sartre, J. – P. (1964) *Nausea*, Norfolk, Conn.: New Directions (originally published 1938).
—— (1981) *The Words*, New York: Vintage Books (originally published 1964).
Schachtel, E. (1959) 'On memory and childhood amnesia', in *Metamorphosis*, New York: Basic Books.
Schafer, R. (1976) *A New Language for Psychoanalysis*, New Haven, Conn.: Yale University Press.
—— (1978) *Language and Insight*, New Haven, Conn.: Yale University Press.
—— (1983) *The Analytic Attitude*, New York: Basic Books.
Scheibe, K. (1986) 'Self-narratives and adventure', in T. R. Sarbin (ed.) *Narrative Psychology: the Storied Nature of Human Conduct*, New York: Praeger.
Schiff, S. (1990) 'Rothballs', *Vanity Fair*, April: 71–8.
Shweder, R. A. and Bourne, E. J. (1984) 'Does the concept of the person vary cross-culturally?', in R. A. Shweder and R. A. LeVine (eds) *Culture Theory: Essays on Mind, Self, and Emotion*, Cambridge: Cambridge University Press.
Shotter, J. and Gergen, K. (eds) (1989) *Texts of Identity*, London: Sage.
Skinner, B. F. (1971) *Beyond Freedom and Dignity*, New York: Alfred A. Knopf.
—— (1974) *About Behaviorism*, New York: Vintage.
Smith, P. (1988) *Discerning the Subject*, Minneapolis, Minn.: University of Minnesota Press.
Spence, D. P. (1982) *Narrative Truth and Historical Truth*, New York: W. W. Norton.
—— (1988) 'Tough and tender-minded hermeneutics', in S. B. Messer, L. A. Sass, and R. L. Woolfolk (eds) *Hermeneutics and Psychological Theory*, New Brunswick, NJ: Rutgers University Press.
Steiner, G. (1989) *Real Presences*, Chicago: University of Chicago Press.
Tappan, M. (1989) 'Stories lived and stories told: the narrative structure of late adolescent moral development', *Human Development*, 32: 300–15.
—— (forthcoming) 'Texts and contexts: language, culture, and the development of moral functioning', to appear in T. Winegar and J. Valsiner (eds) *Children's Development Within Social Contexts: Metatheoretical, Theoretical, and Methodological Issues*, Hillsdale, NJ: Lawrence Erlbaum Associates.
Tappan, M. and Packer, M. J. (eds) (1991) *Narrative and Storytelling: Implications for Understanding Moral Development*, New Directions for Child Development, 54, San Francisco, Calif.: Jossey-Bass.
Taylor, C. (1989) *Sources of the Self: the Making of the Modern Identity*, Cambridge, Mass.: Harvard University Press.
Tomkins, J. P. (1980) *Reader-Response Criticism*, Baltimore, MD: Johns Hopkins University Press.
Updike, J. (1989) *Self-Consciousness*, New York: Alfred A. Knopf.
Von Wright, G. H. (1971) *Explanation and Understanding*, Ithaca, NY: Cornell University Press.

Walsh, W. H. (1951) *An Introduction to Philosophy of History*, London: Hutchison.
—— (1974) 'Colligatory concepts in history', in P. Gardiner (ed.) *The Philosophy of History*, Oxford: Oxford University Press.
Weintraub, K. (1975) 'Autobiography and historical consciousness', *Critical Inquiry*, 1: 821–48.
—— (1978) *The Value of the Individual: Self and Circumstance in Autobiography*, Chicago: University of Chicago Press.
Werner, H. and Kaplan, B. (1963) *Symbol Formation*, New York: Wiley.
White, H. (1973) *Metahistory: the Historical Imagination in Nineteenth-Century Europe*, Baltimore, Md.: Johns Hopkins University Press.
—— (1978) *Tropics of Discourse*, Baltimore, Md.: Johns Hopkins University Press.
Winch, P. (1958) *The Idea of a Social Science and its Relation to Philosophy*, London: Routledge & Kegan Paul.
Wollheim, R. (1984) *The Thread of Life*, Cambridge, Mass.: Harvard University Press.
Wyatt, F. (1964) 'The reconstruction of the individual and the collective past', in R. W. White (ed.) *The Study of Lives*, New York: Atherton Press.

Name index

Addison, R. B. 233n
Augustine *see* St Augustine

Bakhtin, M. M. 24, 146, 234n, 235n
Barratt, B. 235n
Barthes, R. 8, 12, 67–8, 146, 207, 233n
Bartlett, F. C. 233n
Baumeister, R. F. 233n
Bellah, R. 196, 233n, 236n
Bergson, H. 233n
Bertaux, D. 236n
Bird, L. v
Bleich, D. 57
Bloom, A. 234n
Bourne, E. J. 233n
Brodski, B. 17
Brooks, P. 108, 181, 233n, 234n, 236n
Bruner, J. 236n

Carrithers, M. 233n
Casey, E. 233n
Cassirer, E. 56–7
Caws, M. A. 234n
Charmé, S. L. 234n
Chomsky, A. N. 73
Cohler, B. J. 236n
Collingwood, R. G. 116, 140
Conway, J. K. 23, 186–98, 200, 202–16, 218–21, 226–7
Costa-Lima, L. 31
Crites, S. 233n
Culler, J. 234n, 236n

Danto, A. C. 234n, 235n
Derrida, J. 10–11, 13, 117, 121–2, 144, 233n
Descartes, R. 69
Dillard, A. 88–91
Dilthey, W. 116, 140
Dray, W. 235n
Durkheim, E. 211

Eakin, P. J. 233n
Earle, W. 233n
Engels, F. 204–5
Erikson, E. 134

Ferraroti, F. 236n
Foucault, M. 12, 47, 67–8, 94, 117, 188, 207, 233n
Fraser, S. 22–3, 150–63, 165–78, 180–5, 187, 205, 226
Freeman, M. 12, 20, 36, 100, 150, 171, 234n, 236n
Freud, S. v, 23, 41, 48, 50–2, 62, 87, 90–1, 99–102, 107–8, 115, 121, 130, 140, 146, 148, 149–50, 152, 169–71, 178–82, 231–2, 234n, 236n

Gadamer, H.-G. 16–17, 140–5, 199, 233n, 235n
Gallie, W. B. 235n
Geertz, C. 27–8, 228, 233n
Gergen, K. J. 47, 99–100, 102, 234n, 235n
Gergen, M. M. 235n
Gilligan, C. 196

Gunn, J. V. 233n
Gusdorf, G. 25–6, 29–31, 52, 54, 109

Habermas, J. 233n
Hankiss, A. 236n
Hegel, G. W. F. 117
Heidegger, M. 2, 33, 233n
Hempel, C. G. 118, 164, 235n
Hirsch, E. D. 139, 234n
Hollis, M. 233n
Hoy, D. 233n
Hume, D. 11, 68–70
Husserl, E. 2, 233n

James, W. 234n
Jauss, H. R. 199, 235n
Johnson, M. 74, 234n
Jung, C. G. 205

Kaplan, B. 57
Keller, H. 20–1, 23, 50, 52–68, 70–80, 90, 112, 124, 144, 186, 198, 224–5
Kermode, F. 144, 149, 172, 184, 205, 234n
Kohli, M. 236n
Kundera, M. 109–10

Lacan, J. 235n
Lakoff, G. 74, 234n
Langer, S. 57
Lasch, C. 233n
Lee, D. 28
Lejeune, P. 234n, 235n
Lukacher, N. 108, 182–3, 235n, 236n
Lukes, S. 233n

McAdams, D. P. 236n
MacIntyre, A. 21, 110–11, 233n
Mandel, B. 234n
Mandelbaum, M. 235n
Martin, J. 235n
Marx, K. 117, 204–5, 210, 220
Mauss, M. 233n
Meacham, J. A. 234n
Megill, A. 233n
Messer, S. B. 233n
Mink, L. O. 235n
Mitchell, W. J. T. 233n

Nehamas, A. 108, 234n
Neugarten, B. L. 47, 99
Nietzsche, F. 11, 69–70, 106, 233n, 234n

Olney, J. 234n

Packer, M. J. 233n, 236n
Piaget, J. 48, 176
Polkinghorne, D. 236n

Rabinow, P. 233n
Ranke, L. von 116
Ricoeur, P. 2, 7, 16–17, 19, 38, 43, 108, 113–14, 146, 163–5, 233n, 235n
Riffaterre, M. 234n
Robinson, R. 20, 36, 171, 235n, 236n
Roth, P. 22, 112–39, 144, 146–8, 161, 225–6
Runyan, W. M. 236n

St Augustine 18–20, 25–9, 33–49, 53, 90, 109, 137, 144, 151, 224
Sampson, E. E. 233n
Sarbin, T. R. 233n, 236n
Sartre, J.-P. 21, 81, 103, 220, 225, 234n
Sass, L. A. 233n
Schachtel, E. 51–2, 87, 234n
Schafer, R. 91, 234n, 235n
Schenck, C. 17
Schiebe, K. 92
Schiff, S. 235n
Shotter, J. 234n
Shweder, R. A. 233n
Skinner, B. F. 11, 69–70
Spence, D. P. 91, 100–3, 234n
Steiner, G. 7–8, 15, 222, 227
Sullivan, W. M. 233n

Tappan, M. 235n, 236n
Taylor, C. 233n, 236n
Tomkins, J. P. 145

Updike, J. 68

Von Wright, G. H. 235n

Walsh, W. H. 235n
Weintraub, K. 26, 233n, 234n
Werner, H. 57
White, H. 21, 95, 173, 233n

Winch, P. 206
Wollheim, R. 234n
Woolfolk, R. L. 233n
Wyatt, F. 235n

Subject index

archeology (in psychoanalysis) 23, 90–1, 100–1, 108, 149–50; *see also* psychoanalysis

author, authorship 60, 62, 67–70, 113, 115; *see also* originality; self, concept of

autobiography, autobiographical reflection 9, 12, 17, 21, 22, 26–7, 30, 31, 32, 50, 52–3, 79–80, 83, 110, 112–14, 120, 122, 130–7; *see also* memory; narrative

beginning(s) 20, 30, 33, 43–5, 92–6, 106, 107, 115, 132, 151, 176; *see also* origin(s)

cause, causation 22–3, 106, 108, 183–4, 185, 226

critical psychology 17–18

deconstruction 10–11, 70
development 9–10, 12–13, 20, 23, 28, 33, 35, 38, 40, 43–9, 79, 99–100, 165–77, 194, 197, 214–21, 224, 227
dialogue 26, 221

ending(s) 20, 30, 33, 43–5, 92–6, 106, 132, 151, 176, 225

fiction, fictionalization, fictive 8–9, 11, 12, 21, 22, 30–2, 47–8, 69–70, 81, 90, 102, 109–11, 112–19, 120, 128, 130–2, 136, 179, 182, 218, 223–4, 230

hermeneutics 2, 5, 6, 7, 13, 15–17, 44, 102, 119, 140, 144, 226, 231; *see also* interpretation

history, historical inquiry, historical understanding 5, 12, 20, 22–4, 26, 28, 29, 30, 32–3, 47–8, 84–5, 94–5, 112–19, 136, 165, 173–4, 215–16, 225–6, 229–31; *see also* narrative

individual, individuality 26, 66, 67–8, 196–7; *see also* self, concept of
interpretation 3–18, 22, 29, 30, 46–7, 48, 77, 101, 105, 119, 131, 139–48, 149–50, 161–5, 172, 182–4, 199–202, 229–32; *see also* hermeneutics

language 7–14, 21, 51, 53–67, 73–5, 77, 79–80, 82, 87–8, 143, 146, 217–18, 222–3
life history *see* history

materialism 18–19, 38–41, 47, 91
memory 6, 8, 9, 11, 29, 33, 43, 44, 46–54, 86–94, 105–9, 117–19, 126, 146, 170–2, 177–84
metaphor 30, 73–4

narrative 8, 9, 12, 14, 20, 21–2, 28–9, 32–3, 47–9, 54, 56, 81–4, 91–4, 100, 103–11, 117–19, 161–5, 173–7, 196–202, 216–21, 223–7

origin(s) 12, 33–6, 107–8, 114–15,

117, 122
originality 63–7, 68, 70, 80

poetry, poetic(s) 10, 20, 222–32
positivism 15, 16, 18–19, 217–18
poststructuralism 11–12, 16, 225
psychoanalysis 23, 50–2, 62, 87, 90–1, 100–2, 107–8, 140, 149–50, 169–71, 178–82, 213–32; *see also* archeology
psychology 1–6, 14–15, 17–18, 121, 227–9

recollection *see* memory

self, concept of 8–9, 11–12, 25–8, 67–70; self-understanding 145–8; 'true self' 206–7; *see also* author; individual; originality
social construction, social constructionism 11, 23, 185, 196–202, 211, 217, 218, 227
social criticism, social critique 23–4, 185–6, 206–7
story *see* beginning(s); ending(s); history; narrative

temporality *see* time
text, textuality 7, 8, 30, 66, 131, 133, 137–45, 146, 147, 184
time 9, 20, 21, 28, 32, 43–6, 49, 54, 85, 105, 106, 108, 183–4, 226
truth 11, 22, 31–2, 40, 85, 89, 111, 137, 142–3, 164, 179, 182–3, 225, 230